Sean Fewster is the senior court reporter with *The Advertiser* newspaper in Adelaide, South Australia, where he covers cases in the state's Supreme, District and Magistrates Courts — from serial killers to petty thieves, and every-thing in between. In 2004 he won the Law Society of South Australia's Des Colquhoun Award for best print journalist. In 2008 the Supreme Court dubbed him 'mischievous' for criticising its system of secret hearings while, in 2009, the State Government complained of his 'snide' attitude toward its policies. He also contributed to *Cold Blooded Murder: True crimes that rocked Australia*.

Sean, his wife and daughter divide their time between Adelaide and Vancouver, Canada.

http://www.facebook.com/seanfewster

Sean Rooster is the author court reporter with the Newswriter newspaper in Adelaide, South Australia, where he covers cases in a state's Supreme and District and Magistrates Courts – from serial affairs to petty thieves and every thing in between. In 2004 he won an award for South Australia's Description Award for best print journalist. In 2005 the Supreme Court clothed him unmasking a system of secret history as white. In 2009 the late 70-temptation compelled him his inside story towards royalties. He then contributed to Cold Blooded Murder.

That means that he has author.

Sean interviews and daughter dividing his time between Adelaide and Vancouver, Canada.

Stops was a flock of commentariacter

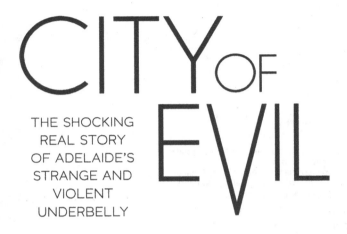

CITY OF EVIL

THE SHOCKING REAL STORY OF ADELAIDE'S STRANGE AND VIOLENT UNDERBELLY

SEAN FEWSTER

hachette
AUSTRALIA

AUSTRALIA

First published in Australia and New Zealand in 2010
by Hachette Australia
(an imprint of Hachette Australia Pty Limited)
Level 17, 207 Kent Street, Sydney NSW 2000
www.hachette.com.au

This edition published in 2018

10 9 8 7 6 5 4 3 2 1

NATIONAL
LIBRARY
OF AUSTRALIA

A catalogue record for this
book is available from the
National Library of Australia

ISBN:978 0 7336 2883 2 (pbk.)

Cover design by Luke Causby, Blue Cork Design
Cover photo courtesy of Adobe Stock
Author photograph by Sarah Reed
Text design by Bookhouse, Sydney
Digital production by Bookhouse, Sydney
Printed and bound in Australia by McPherson's Printing Group

MIX
Paper | Supporting
responsible forestry
FSC® C001695

The paper this book is printed on is certified against the
Forest Stewardship Council® Standards. McPherson's Printing
Group holds FSC® chain of custody certification SA-COC-005379
FSC® promotes environmentally responsible, socially beneficial
and economically viable management of the world's forests.

Contents

Adelaide is the perfect place to set a horror story. You know why all those films and books are always set in sleepy, conservative towns? Because sleepy, conservative towns are where those things happen. Exorcism, omens, shining, poltergeists. Adelaide is Amityville, or Salem, and things here go bump in the night.

Salman Rushdie
Adelaide Writers' Week, 1984

Introduction
Churches and Graveyards

The victim was in the Royal Adelaide Hospital fighting for his life. He'd been stabbed in the chest with a letter opener, puncturing his heart and collapsing one lung. The man, newly paroled from prison, was not expected to live. His alleged assailant had been arrested for attempted murder and conveyed to the Port Adelaide Magistrates Court. In a press release, South Australia Police made it clear the charge would be upgraded to murder if the man died.

Reporters from Adelaide's media outlets had taken over the front row of the court's public gallery. While they waited to see the accused – Robert Leaver, also a recent parolee – they passed the time with idle chatter. The journalists discussed the more obvious motives for the vicious attack: revenge for an incident in jail, drug debts or simple bad blood.

When two guards led Leaver into the dock half an hour later, he immediately commanded the room's attention. Not because of his crime or odd appearance – the completely shaved head, the blue star-shaped tattoos on his earlobes – not even because of his pungent body odour, inescapable in the hideous heat of January 2003. All eyes were fixed on

Robert Leaver because of his attire. The gnome-like man was dressed in a white plastic jumpsuit, the sort worn by crime scene examiners. The outfit could mean one of only two things. Either Leaver's clothes had been seized as evidence upon his arrest or – more tantalisingly – the 37-year-old had been apprehended while nude.

Blair Tremaine, Leaver's lawyer, asked the court to indefinitely delay his client's arraignment. 'Your Honour,' he said, 'I would like to ask that my client be released on bail. I can tell Your Honour the charges will be contested, and we have a strong case for self-defence.'

Magistrate Roseanne McInnes was incredulous. 'Mr Tremaine, a man is in hospital with significant, life-threatening wounds inflicted with a letter opener,' she said. 'He may yet die. Your client was allegedly found standing over the wounded man while naked, still clutching the weapon. How can you possibly say this is a case of self-defence?'

Before Mr Tremaine could answer, his client opened his mouth – displaying a gap where his four front teeth should have been – and spoke for himself.

'I knew [the man] in prison, Your Honour,' he lisped. 'We were cellmates, and he used to grab me by the ears and force me to perform oral sex. He turned up at my place last night and I thought he'd try it again, so I stabbed the fucker.'

Embarrassed, Mr Tremaine hid his face in his hands. The public gallery exploded with laughter. Ms McInnes, busy fighting to retain her composure, did not censure the mirth; Leaver, for his part, stared uncomprehendingly at the hilarity he had caused.

Though he was eventually acquitted, Leaver's story is the quintessential Adelaide case – odd, violent and disturbing. And, if you believe the myth, South Australia's capital city is the nation's home of murder. Scanning the internet or chatting in an east coast pub will provide you with reams of so-called evidence dubbing Adelaide 'murder town', the place with more serial killers per capita than anywhere else in the world. So deep runs the idea that it transcends borders. A 2008 commercial for the US television series *Dexter* shows the titular serial killer waiting to board a flight to the southern city. The message: Adelaide is Dexter's kind of town.

It is a good myth, an interesting myth, but one that is wrong and easily dispelled. Since 1989, South Australia's murder rate has remained stable at 1.7 deaths per 100,000 people. You have far more chance of being hit by a car – the road toll reached 119 in 2009 – than you do of meeting your end via a deranged predator. With an average of just 25 homicides per year, Adelaide's killers cannot compare with their peers in New South Wales and Queensland. Thanks to an incredibly dedicated and efficient police department, more than 95 per cent of those crimes are solved. And, while Adelaide murders are indisputably grotesque, they are no worse than the New South Wales woman who stabbed her boyfriend to death on Christmas Day 2009, then invited her friends around to feast on the body.

The truth is inescapable: Adelaide is not, and never has been, 'murder town'. The false legend, the erroneous myth, is no more than a convenient peg for naysayers to hang their hats upon. The worst thing about the 'murder town' fallacy is that it obscures the truth: *all* of Adelaide's crime is far worse – more twisted, more perverse, more sick – than you could possibly believe. From a simple petrol station robbery to the most Byzantine white-collar fraud, every South Australian crime is tinged with the hideously bizarre. Consequently, there is no shortage of examples.

In February 2008, Frederick Walkuski kidnapped his former lover, Donna Pridham, from her car. Leaving Ms Pridham's toddler son alone in the back seat, Walkuski forced the object of his affection into another vehicle and sped away. In any other city, Ms Pridham would have been taken to an abandoned warehouse or garden shed, blindfolded and chained to a chair. But in Adelaide, kidnappers do things differently. Walkuski drove his beloved to an isolated shack, miles from the nearest town, and led her gently inside. He had filled the tiny dwelling with Ms Pridham's favourite food and DVDs, as well as clothing he had bought in her size. He planned for them to spend the rest of their lives together, sequestered in his 'love shack'. It was a scene straight out of a James Patterson novel and yet there it was, in real life, on the plains of Adelaide.

Three months later, John Martin Cheney faced the District Court for collecting child pornography. His already abhorrent crime grew more twisted because it happened in Adelaide. As Cheney's lawyers explained, their client had 'accidentally fallen into' his interest in child pornography while searching for naked pictures of actress Angelina Jolie. Further, he had only begun his quest for digital flesh because he was depressed, had been drinking too much and had recently had an operation on his genitals, leaving him with 'too much time on his hands'.

Cheney's fellow deviant, Samuel Paul Healy, claimed to use his free time more constructively. As a teenager, he developed a sexual fascination for pre-pubescent girls – he believed they could not fall pregnant. He put his theory to the test by abducting a five-year-old girl from her suburban home, taking her to a nearby oval and sexually assaulting her. Healy would do the same again the following year – this time in Byron Bay, New South Wales – before he was caught. By the time he faced court, he said he had 'cured himself' of his paedophilia. In his spare time between rape and arrest, he had taken part-time work in a day care centre. By interacting with children, he believed he had learned to control his urges.

Uncontrolled lust was also Benjamin Ainsworth's problem. An aspiring actor and would-be rapper, Ainsworth was best known for a bit part on the television series *McLeod's Daughters*. Once off the set, Ainsworth grabbed women off the streets and dragged them to secluded areas for enforced, kinky sex. Because his victims survived their bondage nightmares, Ainsworth fled to the United States, hoping to escape arrest and land a recording contract. He was caught and returned home, and a psychological report concluded – unsurprisingly – he suffered from narcissism. Rape, according to the diagnosis, was Ainsworth's way of giving his self-esteem a little boost. 'Having consensual sex,' he had told his doctor, 'is like buying a new car. Both get boring over time.'

Celebrity was on the mind of another of Adelaide's twisted citizens. Depending on when you met him – and how much money you had – the concrete pumper would introduce himself as either Romeo Pacifico or Richard Sambora. The former was his real name, the latter an identity he stole from his idol, the guitarist for rock band Bon Jovi. In either identity, Pacifico was a consummate fraudster who swindled more than $25 million from banks and businesses. The money funded an extravagant lifestyle of luxury cars and top-of-the-line building equipment before his crimes were detected. In an absurd twist, the real Richard Sambora had to retain lawyers in Adelaide to represent him until the courts were satisfied he had no involvement in the scam.

Absurdity also surrounded the case of Andre Parenzee. He had unprotected sex with three women despite knowing he was HIV positive. Convicted of three counts of endangering life, Parenzee's case was the first of its kind in South Australia. It paved the way for changes to the law, leading to other reckless sex fiends facing jail for their conduct. Determined to overturn his conviction, Parenzee lodged an audacious appeal. In the face of decades of research, he claimed HIV could not be transmitted through sex and he was therefore innocent. Shockingly, he won the support of an actual scientific body. The Perth Group, a maverick think-tank, sent its top spokesperson to testify on Parenzee's behalf. Elini Papadopulos-Eleopulos told the Supreme Court that science had never conclusively linked HIV with AIDS. This galvanised the world's top immunity experts – they gathered in Adelaide to give evidence against Parenzee, fearful a successful appeal would set sex education back 20 years and put thousands of people at risk. Their efforts were successful, and Parenzee remained in jail. Only in Adelaide could a single crime pose such immense danger to humanity.

And while Adelaide does not corner the market on bizarre murder, its wholesale slaughters are among the most gruesome in the nation. John Justin Bunting and Robert Joe Wagner murdered almost a dozen people in the 'bodies in the barrels' case. Eight bodies were found in a disused bank vault in the country hamlet of Snowtown, two in a suburban backyard, one in a regional area and one in the Adelaide Hills. Styling themselves as paedophile-killing vigilantes, the duo tortured their victims using handcuffs, pliers, sparklers and an electric shock machine. They even played music – *Throwing Copper* by the band Live – as they experimented with cannibalism.

Along with the Truro Killings – the murders of eight young women in the 1970s – and the Family Murders – the sex killings of five young men in the 1980s – the 'bodies in the barrels' are the best known of all South Australian crimes. Yet for all the international attention it garnered, Bunting and Wagner's atrocities were just typical Adelaide crimes. More people fell victim to the same kind of repulsive, unforgivable impulses that sparked dozens of other murders in the city's history. Those cases did not grab interstate headlines like Bunting and Wagner, but were just as depraved.

June Busson, for example, grew murderously tired of her cancer-stricken husband, Dennis. In December 2003, her need for affection drove her into the arms of another man. Though happy with James Slade, she felt she would never be truly free until Dennis was dead. And so, one month after the affair began, Busson and her lover stood over the ill man and commenced what prosecutors called 'a vicious attack of the most dreadful kind'. That night, in the bedroom he'd shared with his wife, Dennis sustained 80 injuries – 56 of them stab wounds – at the hands of the new lovers. Just days later, as police investigated the crime, Busson and Slade moved into that same room together and continued their love tryst. Each is now serving a life sentence.

In jail, Busson has likely encountered Julie Michelle Dunn – a woman with whom she has much in common. Dunn had tired of her partner, too. Desperate for 'some time to herself', Dunn fixed Graham Wilks his favourite snack – a curried egg sandwich – laced with seven tablets of the sedative temazepam. Utterly fatigued, Wilks fell asleep and, mercifully, did not feel the torrent of blows Dunn rained down upon his head. Wilks died and Dunn was found guilty of murder.

The undisputed queen of Adelaide's killers, though, is Michelle Burgess. Her weapon was not a blade or a gun, but her body. She used it to cultivate multiple lovers, then played them off against each other to get what she wanted. In 2000, what she wanted was Kevin Matthews all to herself. He felt the same way – meaning his wife, Carolyn, had to go. Burgess arranged for her other paramour, David Key, to carry out the hit under her supervision. She watched as her puppet stabbed Carolyn in her own home, all the while shouting 'kill her, be a man, show me you love me'. The murder was a success but the cover-up was not. Burgess, Matthews and Key all went to jail for their hideous crime. Undaunted, Burgess seduced a male prison guard to ensure her time in custody was as comfortable and sexually charged as possible. The woman knows how to get what she wants.

The evidence is clear: Adelaide is far worse than a mere 'murder town' could ever be. In a murder town, you would only have to worry about being killed by a crazed deviant. In Adelaide, you have to worry about the crazed deviants not only killing you, but robbing you, raping you, kidnapping you, stealing your sons, sexually assaulting your daughters, murdering your wives and poisoning your curried egg sandwiches.

What is it about Adelaide that creates such monsters? When considering the history of the place, it becomes apparent South Australia has always been a fertile breeding ground for disordered minds. One of the driving forces behind the creation of Adelaide was British politician Edward Gibbon Wakefield. His revolutionary idea was to settle the colony not with convicts, but with free men. His much-publicised belief was that Britain's social problems had been caused by overcrowding, making emigration an essential 'safety valve' for Mother England. By 1831, Wakefield had fine-tuned his colonisation plan and was the toast of London. To this day, his influence is remembered in Adelaide through the streets, statues and institutions that bear his name.

Wakefield was a visionary – a man who had clearly given a great deal of thought to devising the best method of colonisation. What history forgets is that he was afforded this time not in smoking rooms, university lectures or libraries, but in the depths of London's prisons. Months before grabbing the headlines with his colonisation ideas, Wakefield finished a three-year sentence for kidnapping a 15-year-old girl. In 1826, he had conspired with his brother to abduct Ellen Turner, a rich manufacturer's daughter who caught his eye. Wakefield lured the girl into his trap by way of a false letter, warning Miss Turner her mother was gravely ill. Once the teenager was in his clutches, Wakefield took her to Scotland and demanded she marry him, saying it was the only way to spare her family financial ruin.

Obsessed with power and influence, an utterly shameless Wakefield wrote to his new father-in-law and demanded his financial support. He was sure the man would acquiesce to his demands rather than risk a public scandal. Imagine his surprise when constables caught up to the newlyweds at Calais and clapped him in irons. His trial – the biggest sensation of 1827 – ended with Wakefield and his brother jailed and the marriage annulled by a special act of Parliament.

A driving force behind the creation of Adelaide, then, was a duplicitous, power-hungry, greedy kidnapper. With a guiding hand like that, it's not hard to see from where the darker side of Adelaide sprung. Wakefield's choice of free settlers only worsened matters. He tirelessly hawked his new colony to two groups: religious dissenters and social progressives. The first, burned by their dealings with the Catholic and Protestant faiths, wanted a place to pursue their beliefs in privacy and without persecution. They brought with them a natural inclination toward secrecy, and the unwillingness to judge others. The progressives, meanwhile, believed the basic concepts of human nature and morality were not fixed and should be reviewed based on scientific advances. In other words, they carried a certain permissiveness and willingness to experiment with them to the new shores.

Once combined, these vastly disparate values did great good in South Australia. It became a land of tolerance, the first place in the world to grant women the right to vote, and a bastion of religious thought. But every light cast by the City of Churches created a shadow – within which darker, more perverse thoughts festered. In a land where experimentation was encouraged, where secrets were to be kept, where judgement was slow to pass, deviant mindsets developed unhindered and spread without condemnation. Over time, this underbelly became attractive to more people with monstrous thoughts, and a new group of émigrés arrived. It is no coincidence that John Justin Bunting – born in Queensland – and Jean Eric Gassy – from Sydney – found notoriety in Adelaide.

Secrecy is a defining aspect of South Australia. Those who resist the flow are smacked down harshly, as Harold Salisbury discovered. By 1972, he had served London's Metropolitan Police Division and other law enforcement divisions for 40 years. He was South Australian Premier Don Dunstan's top choice for police commissioner, a role Salisbury accepted after two weeks of closed-door negotiations.

It was an odd choice, given Dunstan's politics. The Labor leader fancied his state to be Australia's social laboratory.

He lowered the legal drinking age to 18 and removed public drunkenness from police blotters. Dunstan legalised homosexuality, sex shops and nude beaches. In keeping with Wakefield's ideals of social progressivism, the Premier sought to make Adelaide a more freethinking place. Why he chose Salisbury – a Freemason, a war veteran, a veritable figurehead of the old regime – to head up the police will forever be a mystery.

Salisbury was beloved by his charges. A reformist in his own right, he introduced the dog squad, Aboriginal language lessons for officers and air-conditioning in patrol cars. He was also very interested in keeping a close eye on the movers and shakers in his new patch. The extent of this became clear in 1977, when *The Australian* newspaper revealed the existence of the Police Special Branch.

A small, covert arm of Salisbury's forces, the branch had an open-ended remit to gather intelligence on the people of South Australia. That information was, in turn, passed on to ASIO and other national security institutions. *The Australian* wanted to know why Dunstan, the 'architect of the modern Athens', had allowed such cloak-and-dagger work to go on under his nose.

The Premier could not countenance such an embarrassment. Salisbury and his team had broken the rules of Adelaide by asking what went on behind all that progressivism. An inquiry concluded the Special Branch investigated people 'on the unreasoned assumption' that anyone who 'thought or acted less conservatively' than they posed 'potential danger to the security of the nation'. Further, held the authorities, the files contained information that was 'inaccurate, and sometimes scandalously inaccurate' about high-ranking members of Parliament and important members of the community.

Salisbury was asked to resign. He refused, saying his duty was to 'the crown, not any politically elected government, or to any politician, or to anyone else for that matter'. Dunstan arranged for him to be fired on 17 January 1977, telling no one but his staffers and *The Advertiser* newspaper. When the news was published on the morning of 18 January there was widespread public outcry – but a Royal Commission vindicated Dunstan's actions. The Special Branch was disbanded and its files burned, under heavy guard, in a cemetery crematorium.

The twisted incident wore heavily on both men. Dunstan stepped down in February 1979, blaming poor health. Salisbury stayed in Adelaide until May of that year and then retired to his homeland. Neither was eager to speak on the matter – as I learned, first-hand, in 1996.

I was 16 years old and had been watching a Supreme Court trial – my interest in the justice system started early. To my surprise, I found myself sharing an elevator with Dunstan and a dark-suited minder. It was fortuitous timing, for my Year 12 thesis was on the Salisbury affair. What better opportunity would there be to speak to a living, breathing primary source?

'Mr Dunstan,' I said, extending my hand, 'I'm an Australian history student writing a project on the dismissal of Commissioner Harold Salisbury. Would you mind me asking you a few questions?'

Dunstan's expression did not change. He made no move to take my hand. Instead, his minder reached out and pushed a button so the elevator would stop at the next floor. 'You're getting off here, kid,' he barked as the doors opened. Given his massive size, I didn't argue.

Almost 20 years on, and the former Premier of South Australia was more prepared to menace a teenager with a bad haircut than talk about his past. I was absolutely staggered. Over time, I've learned to be less surprised.

Once again: secrecy is a defining part of South Australia. The courts provide daily reminders in the form of suppression orders – media gags that inhibit the public's right to see justice done. Every judge, lawyer and journalist in the state knows the provisions of Section 69A of the *Evidence Act* (1938) by heart. The section permits judges to prevent the publication of any material that could 'prejudice the proper administration of justice' or 'cause undue hardship'. Such broad parameters make suppression applications difficult to resist. In the Snowtown case alone, the courts made 220 orders – some of which remain in force to this day. Gags were slapped on Robert Joe Wagner's adoration of Hitler, the name of his dog – Adolf – and the colour of the barrels used to store the victims. The large volume of orders was far from unusual. The courts made 204 suppressions in 2004, 211 in 2005 and 216 in 2006. Some of those orders were double-headers; the banned information was topped with a second one, preventing discussion of the reasons for the ban.

In 2007, the Labor Government re-wrote the *Evidence Act*. The amendments limited the scope of suppression orders and granted the media greater rights to oppose them. Judges are now required to consider 'the public interest, and the news media's subsequent right to publish' before pulling down the blinds. The change was dramatic – just 90 suppression orders were made in 2008 – but also catastrophic.

Robbed of their blindfolds, the more secrecy-minded litigators found other ways to obscure their work. They used other sections of the Act to clear courtrooms before 'dangerous' submissions were made – a judicial discretion the media has no right to oppose. Some would spontaneously declare open court sessions to be 'directions hearings', meaning they were confidential and could not be reported. And the few suppression orders that were made were of questionable value. In March 2010, a court banned publication of the identity of a man accused of killing his wife. It believed publication would prejudice police line-ups and other identification techniques. The gag was nonsense as – on the police version of events – the alleged murder occurred in front of 100 members of their local community, all of whom knew the man personally.

At times, the South Australian community breaks free of its mindset and questions the horrors that occur every day. As younger, fresher minds step into the public arena, they ask – in conversation, on talkback radio, over the internet – what the authorities are doing to protect them. They want to know why the hard work of police amounts to nothing in court; why a paedophile, a child pornographer, a killer receives so light a sentence. They call for harsher penalties, for those in power to cage the monsters.

Their pleas fall on deaf ears. According to the state's top judge, he and his peers are not personally accountable to the public. In 2007, Supreme Court Chief Justice John Doyle said those behind the bench are above such concerns. 'A lack of personal accountability is the price you pay for a fair and impartial judicial system,' he said. 'We must be independent of the community's view. If you want a system where judges are personally accountable, you might say: "go to China".'

Clichés persist because they contain some truth: evil will flourish whenever good men do nothing. When no one asks questions, or when those in power do not listen, shadows form in the City of Churches. Within those shadows breeds more perversion, more monstrous thought. Adelaide is stripped of its progressive, welcoming veneer and revealed for what it is — a City of Evil. The vicious cycle that started with Edward Gibbon Wakefield spins around again.

A Remorseless Betrayal
Casagrande and McGuinness

She was used to the pain of heroin withdrawal, that was nothing new. She'd grappled with the ravenous, gnawing drug hunger most of her life. This unfamiliar pain was unbearable. It was the sting of conscience, deep in her soul, and it refused to die down. It was Remembrance Day 2001, and Donna Lee Casagrande could no longer forget the sins she had committed.

Distressed and dishevelled, the junkie staggered into a police station in Redfern, New South Wales, and said she wanted to talk about a murder. Homicide detectives Robert Allison and Malcolm Lanyon led the blonde prostitute into an interview room and started its recorders. For more than an hour they listened as Casagrande spoke – alternately hysterical and chillingly calm – of slapping, torturing, smothering and stabbing a man to death.

The victim, Casagrande said, was a truck-driving pro-wrestler transvestite. Her accomplice was her lesbian lover and fellow prostitute. Remorse crept into her tone as she spoke of the victim's immense weight; his corpse was too heavy, she explained, to load into his own four-wheel drive for disposal. And so the women had hacked the cadaver to pieces, de-fleshed each segment and buried the body fat in the victim's beloved strawberry patch. Loading the torso pieces into a car, the lovers dumped them at several different locations, pausing only to drop the cross-dresser's head and arms in a rubbish bin and set them on fire. Having finished her sickening tale, Casagrande glared hungrily at the detectives. 'All I want is my methadone,' she said.

Though her confession had been made in New South Wales, the Detectives Allison and Lanyon were in no doubt Casagrande could only have committed such a heinous killing in Adelaide.

◆

The life and death of John 'Joanne' Lillecrapp was, on the surface, bizarre and surreal – perfect tabloid fodder. No newspaper editor alive could resist a headline like 'Lesbian Prostitutes Decapitate and Dismember Transvestite Pro-wrestling Truck Driver'. Beneath it all, however, the tale is even sadder than it is twisted. The undoubtedly horrific, inexcusable crime centred on one lonely man's desire for friendship and acceptance.

In 1993, Lillecrapp moved into a house on Norton St, Angle Park, a suburb west of Adelaide. Like the western suburbs of Melbourne, it is an area that has long been home to Asian families and refugees from African nations. Violence is common, as is the death of young people in high-speed car accidents. 'It's best to keep to yourself around here,' one resident said in 2001. 'You keep out of trouble that way.'

Initially the locals called him 'Tex' because he wore large cowboy hats. Soon they got to see the woman behind the man – Lillecrapp had taken up cross-dressing two years before his arrival. One would think that he would have experienced enormous difficulties with his neighbours, but nothing could be further from the truth. He felt most comfortable when surrounded by his peers at the Parks Community Centre, just a few kilometres from his home. He considered them part of his extended family and volunteered many hours of his time driving the centre's free bus service. The African, Vietnamese and Indian communities looked to him for advice, help and support. He entertained them by taking part in professional wrestling bouts, playing both the hero and villain for the crowd's benefit. Above all else, he insisted everyone call him Joanne.

'He wasn't your average bloke,' Lillecrapp's brother, Ron, conceded in 2003, 'but he helped the community and he was a worthwhile member of the community. If anyone needed help, he would be there . . . The people at the Parks Community Centre thought the world of him . . . he found a place to belong there, something that was missing from other areas and times in his life. And while I wasn't always close to John, if something were to happen I would have been there for him – that's what brothers are for.'

A photograph of Lillecrapp taken on the night of his brother's 1994 wedding sums the man up well. His dark wig and make-up are immaculately applied, his legs are swathed in stockings and his wrists and neck adorned with simple gold jewellery. In a plain white top, dark green miniskirt, stiletto heels and colourful jacket, Joanne Lillecrapp is the sort of 50-year-old woman one would pass in the street without a second glance.

But looking the part and being tacitly accepted by his neighbours was not enough. Lillecrapp felt his life was one of solitude, and he went further and further afield seeking what he felt would be true acceptance – the understanding of those like him, who shared his outlook and beliefs. During a trip to Sydney in 1996, he met Casagrande.

Born in Addington Hospital, New South Wales, in 1970, Casagrande was the youngest of nine children. Her father was a foreman at a sheet metal factory; her mother worked until she lost a hand in an industrial accident and moved to home duties full-time. In reports later tendered before the Supreme Court Casagrande claimed she was repeatedly abused – first by her father, then by the men for whom she worked as a prostitute. She came to the sex industry after leaving school in Year 9 and moving unsuccessfully through jobs as a waitress, process worker and factory hand. Two abusive marriages brought forth two children – son Joshua and daughter Talia – who remained with their fathers. One of those men, she often claimed, would beat her senseless with a baseball bat and kick her in the head. Drug addiction and abuse was the defining factor of her life, ruining any chance of stability and taking a vicious toll on her long-term health. In particular, Casagrande struggled with heart valve problems and seizures.

Big-hearted, generous and full of empathy for a fellow 'lost soul', Lillecrapp opened his home to Casagrande, vowing to aid her rehabilitation. It was a decision that did not sit well with his family – especially when, during a visit with Ron and his wife, Lindsay, Casagrande retired to their driveway to shoot up heroin. 'That was Joanne's downfall, after that,' Lindsay said in 2003. 'We were worried about him, but he wanted to live his life the way he did. We tried to advise him but he was a man of 50 – you can't tell anyone of that age how to live their life.'

Ron said his 'slightly naive' brother truly believed he could help Casagrande kick her habits. 'He was a cross-dresser, that was the lifestyle he chose and that was his prerogative,' he said. 'He was a big sort of a bloke but he was a sucker, he was gullible. He was lonely and eager to befriend just about anyone. He wanted to help Casagrande – that's what he was like. He probably went about it the wrong way but, if that's the case, I don't know what the right way is.'

Much later, Casagrande introduced her would-be benefactor to her lesbian lover – Nicole Therese Courcier McGuinness. The women had been in a relationship for three years – Casagrande would travel between McGuinness's various residences and Lillecrapp's home as her finances allowed. The couple had similarly unfortunate backgrounds. McGuinness's father left her family when she was three, exposing her to a stepfather who routinely abused her mother. McGuinness herself fell victim to rape at the age of 15. She spent her life, according to defence lawyers, 'either witnessing violence or being a victim of violence'. She turned to drugs, they explained, to 'blot out the past and the present'.

Lindsay said the duo took advantage of her brother-in-law. 'They seduced him into believing he had friends and that people accepted him and wanted to be around him. We thought it would end in theft, that they'd rip him off – but we never dreamed it would end like it did. We thought we could see what was coming and we knew it was going to be terrible, but not to the extent it was.'

For a time, the trio lived together in Lillecrapp's home. He set up a bank account for the women, keeping the PIN a secret. That way, he reasoned, Casagrande's and McGuinness's spending would be vetted by him, ensuring they could not get money for drugs. It was a simplistic, overly optimistic plan that was doomed to failure from the outset. Lillecrapp had no experience with addiction, no concept of how cunning a junkie could become to satisfy their need for drugs. His possessions and belongings began to go missing; McGuinness and Casagrande seemed to have drugs in their room more and more often. On their visits to his family, the women became threatening and began to demand money. For Ron and Lindsay, it was the final straw.

'He was vulnerable, and she poisoned his mind,' Ron said of Casagrande. 'She also stole a lot of things from him, including a video camera. They said they would trash our place if we didn't give them money. The history, from then on, I do not know about because we could not allow this to happen in our home, so we had to distance ourselves from him.'

Little is known of the final 18 months of Lillecrapp's life. He continued to drive trucks, volunteer for bus runs and wear dresses. He remained a regular sight around the Parks and checked in sporadically with his community-centre friends. Neighbours remember him working in his garden, and that his strawberry patch was a point of pride. Unless he was actively volunteering, however, Lillecrapp kept to himself and spent his time at home with Casagrande and McGuinness. Occasionally, rumours would surface that he was 'pimping out' his houseguests, forcing them back into prostitution to pay their way. Such claims always lacked the facts to support them. In truth, the women would travel between Adelaide and Sydney as they could afford, most often to see Casagrande's children.

In November 2001, South Australian police received word that Lillecrapp was missing. Days later, they became aware Casagrande and McGuinness were gone as well. Concerns began to mount, and came to a head on 9 November, when an anonymous caller told triple-zero operators that 'someone might be dead' at the Norton St house. Forensics investigators and Major Crime Investigations Branch detectives moved quickly. What they discovered was among the grisliest, most gruesome finds in the state's criminal history. Human remains had been buried in the strawberry patch but they were not whole. Officers found body fat, flesh and chunks of torso between and beneath the fruit. The deceased had been butchered, either before or after he was killed, and the offal left behind.

On 13 November, police confirmed the remains belonged to Lillecrapp. They continued the search for the rest of his body, and appealed for help finding Casagrande and McGuinness. They spoke of extending the search interstate, and of working with police in Sydney to locate 'persons of interest'. What they were not prepared to reveal, however, was that Casagrande had already turned herself in at Redfern and confessed.

Casagrande's arrest was announced on 15 November, and she was extradited to Adelaide by order of the Parramatta Court. A newspaper photographer caught a brief glimpse of the alleged killer as she was taken away from Adelaide Airport on 17 November. Looking drawn and weak, dressed in a tank top and striped tracksuit pants, Casagrande cowered behind a police officer's jacket and wept. She was held in the City Watch House until 19 November, when she made her first appearance in the Adelaide Magistrates Court. She had been, by this time, given new clothes to wear – jeans, running shoes and a long jacket. She cast an unsteady eye toward the media cameramen who filmed her arrival, and had to be physically led into the courtroom by a sheriff's officer. She was remanded in custody.

One day later, McGuinness was arrested. Police released few details of her apprehension and the public found out little more when she appeared in court on 21 November. At the request of prosecutors, Magistrate Alfio Grasso slapped suppression orders on the images of both defendants – banning the media from showing their faces to a confused public. At the time, no one outside the investigating team had any clue why Lillecrapp had been murdered – including his family.

'I can't assume the remains are him,' Ron told reporters in 2001. 'Obviously, I hope he is still alive. The thing that really hurts me is how someone can do it. They are either cold, callous and brutal, or flying high as a kite on drugs.'

His hopes were dashed on 30 November of that year. Lillecrapp's head and arms were found, burned almost beyond recognition, in a drum at Wingfield dump. Not only had he been butchered, he had been dismembered and decapitated. Coincidentally, the macabre discovery was made just 200 metres away from where teams were excavating for the remains of another murder victim – Japanese schoolgirl Megumi Suzuki, who was killed by escalating rapist Mark Errin Rust. It was a hideous happenstance that further reinforced Adelaide's reputation as the nexus of Australia's bizarrely malicious crime.

The drum had been discovered by an employee of a concreting and restoration business. The man would never be the same again. 'I wished it had never been found there,' he blanched, visibly distressed. 'We just found it there, it had nothing to do with us. We just called the police and they took it away.'

Casagrande's and McGuinness's appearances in court became sporadic. They did not face the Supreme Court until October 2002, at which time both pleaded not guilty to murder. Six months later – in April 2003 – they fronted the court once more. This time McGuinness announced she was changing her plea, and would confess to murdering Lillecrapp. Casagrande continued to protest her innocence.

On 3 June 2003, a near-hysterical Casagrande was brought before Justice John Perry. She began weeping the moment she entered the courtroom, and mouthed messages to friends and supporters sitting in the public gallery. Her composure, however, returned instantly when she was addressed by Justice Perry. The renowned and much-beloved judge and educator, who was nearing mandatory retirement, asked the woman how she intended to plead to the charge against her.

'Not guilty to murder,' Casagrande replied, wiping away her tears, 'but guilty to manslaughter.'

Craig Caldicott, for Casagrande, told the court the months of silence had been put to good use. He said that, by the next hearing date, he would have psychiatric reports about his client. Having worked closely with prosecutors, he would also be in a position to tender a statement of agreed facts – the basis upon which Casagrande was to be sentenced.

Justice Perry was appreciative. 'I'm still looking for a clear understanding of the motive and circumstances around the killing,' he said, echoing the thoughts of many in the public gallery. 'I also want to know what part each of them – Casagrande and McGuinness – played. Quite often that's what these things come down to – which part each of them played, and what they say about the role the other played. I intend to deal with both of them strictly together and hear submissions on the same day.'

That scheduled hearing date – 1 July 2003 – would see an end to the mystery surrounding Joanne Lillecrapp's death. In a rare move for a South Australian judge, Justice Perry dispensed with the secrecy so beloved by his brothers on the bench and released Casagrande's court file to the media. Within the pages of documentation lay a complete transcript of the Redfern interview – and the details it provided were beyond belief. Not only did she detail every moment of the murder, Casagrande also painted a picture of Lillecrapp – whom she always referred to as 'Joanne' or 'her' – quite unlike that given by his family, friends and the police.

'I've been going to Joanne's on and off for years, and she's been coming up to my family's place for years,' Casagrande had told the homicide detectives on 11 November. 'Joanne dobs people into Social Security . . . she's very spiteful. The last summer I was there, I stole her camera and, when I got down there this time, she asked me where it was. I told her that I sold it for heroin in Melbourne. I told her I would get her a new one, and I wanted to leave that day but she locked me in the house and I couldn't get out.'

Later that day, she said, her lover made a discovery. 'Nicole went into Joanne's bedroom and found a piece of paper from the Footscray CIB in Melbourne. That's where I had sold the camera at. She showed it to me.' The women were convinced Lillecrapp intended to turn them over to interstate police because of the camera theft. Knowing he still had $600 of Casagrande's money in the account he had created for them, the women hatched a plot to get it back and then leave Adelaide for good. 'Nicole cooked Joanne dinner and she put a couple of Rivotril in her dinner . . . they're epilepsy tablets,' she said. The highly potent anti-convulsant has powerful muscle-relaxing properties, but also induces drowsiness and impairs the memory. The lovers felt it to be their best tool against someone larger, stronger and healthier than the two of them put together.

'I went out to Joanne and said "You haven't changed at all, you're still the same",' Casagrande continued. 'I said "I'll buy you a new camera" and Nicole kept waving the paper in her face and saying "Well, what's this, what's this?" And Joanne said yes, she was going to ring up (the police) but she hadn't.'

The argument escalated. 'I asked Joanne for my money out of the bank, which I was saving up for my son,' Casagrande said. 'Nicole went into the kitchen and got a stay-sharp blade – you know the ones, the ones with the white handles. She came back into the lounge room and said to Joanne "Just give us our money, and we'll go".' Casagrande insisted the knife was for Nicole's own protection – Lillecrapp was far bigger and stronger than the women. She claimed they feared he would attack them. 'I don't know what happened – Joanne must have thought it was a bluff or something – but it didn't work. So it got a bit more heavy and I flipped out, I said "I just want my money, my son's money, and I'll go". I kept telling her I'd buy her another camera.'

Tempers flared out of control and things turned deadly. Casagrande pushed the weakened Lillecrapp onto the lounge room floor. 'I was holding her saying "Why, why, why?"' she said. 'I just straddled her. Nicole was in the background saying "You lying cunt", and I had my knees on Joanne's arms.'

Unwilling to sit on the sidelines any longer, McGuinness attacked Lillecrapp. 'She had the knife,' Casagrande insisted. 'Nicole sat up on top of her and started punching her. She still had the knife in her hand and she was saying to her "Just give us the money and we'll go, you know how much it means to Donna's son". She said to her "Give us the fucking money, Joanne, or you're going to die today. If you don't give it to us, and let us go, I'm going to kill you". And Joanna wouldn't – she still wouldn't give it back. I don't think she ever had any intention of giving us our money back in the first place.'

Lillecrapp began to fight back. When he couldn't shift McGuinness with the force of his bulk alone he panicked and began to scream. Casagrande punched him in the face, breaking his nose. 'We were yelling and screaming,' she said. 'And then, because she was screaming, Nicole put a pillow over her face and told her to shut up,' Casagrande remembered. 'She said, "Just give us the PIN and we'll go get the money, I'll go get the money, Donna can go get the money. Then we'll leave, and everything will be all right".' Lillecrapp still would not cooperate and so McGuinness threw the pillow aside and began to slap him. Keeping the knife tight in her other hand, she struck repeatedly with her palm, knuckles and fingernails, cutting and scratching her victim's face. 'After a little bit longer of being slapped around a bit, Joanne gave us the number,' Casagrande said.

Leaving McGuinness and Lillecrapp behind, the junkie took her benefactor's four-wheel drive to a pub on Hanson Rd, Arndale. Hands shaking, she tried the PIN. It didn't work. She tried it several times, her anger increasing, before giving up and returning to Norton St. 'I was pissed off,' she admitted. 'When I got back to the house, Nicole was still straddling Joanne, with the knife in her hand and the pillow over her face. And Joanne had four stab wounds in her, right in her temple. They weren't deep.'

McGuinness was infuriated, she said, enraged that they had been tricked – and she was no longer prepared to play games. 'Nicole said, "See? I told you, you stupid bitch, that you weren't going to give Donna the right number! I knew it, I knew she was going to come back and tell me it wasn't the right number! I knew you were lying, I knew you wouldn't give us the PIN, money means more to you than anything!" Nicole was holding the knife up against her throat and Joanne tried to get up.'

Casagrande paused in her retelling, swallowed, and put her head in her hands. Her words began to blur together. 'Then just bang, she stabbed Joanne straight through the heart,' she babbled. 'Nicole put the knife straight through her chest, one through her heart, and four times in her stomach. There was blood coming out of Joanne's mouth. Joanne reached out and grabbed my hand. I held onto it. And then it was too late.'

One of the detectives asked if Casagrande had tried to stop her lover's murderous actions. She admitted she had not. 'I was angry,' she said, 'and I was scared. Then Nicole looked at me, smiled and said, "I can't believe that money can mean more to someone than their own life".'

Casagrande said she began to panic, even though McGuinness 'was pretty calm, actually'. Together they dragged Lillecrapp's body into the bathroom. It was Casagrande's idea. 'The blood wouldn't go,' she said. 'There were pools of blood everywhere. I washed a bit off but I just . . . just kept . . .' Her retelling broke down. 'Blood and all,' she muttered. 'Trails of blood everywhere.'

Composing herself, she continued the story. They had wrapped Lillecrapp's body in a blanket and dragged him out into the backyard and onto the grass. His weight, combined with their poor health and addiction-ravaged muscles, made it impossible to lift Lillecrapp. 'I tried to put her into the four-wheel drive but she was too heavy. We had to get some ropes, tie her up and try to pull her over the grass to the car. And she still wouldn't move! There was no way of getting her into the car, she was too heavy! So Nicole went and got the tool box, because there was an axe inside it, and a hacksaw.'

The stomach-turning series of events that followed would forever immortalise the names of McGuinness – who was still carrying the knife – and Casagrande in Adelaide's rogues' gallery of hideous criminals. 'Nicole kneeled down next to them and looked at the hacksaw, but she said it was too blunt. So then she cut through Joanne's skin with the stay-sharp knife. Then she picked up the axe and chopped off Joanne's head with it. We put that in a bucket.'

The detectives stopped Casagrande, asking whose idea it was to dismember Lillecrapp. 'Mine,' she said, almost too softly for the tape to record. 'Then Nicole said "let me do it", because I was crying too much.'

Casagrande appeared, to the detectives, to be completely disconnected from reality. She was lost in her story, but spoke as if someone else had perpetrated the disgusting act of human butchery. 'We still couldn't pick Joanne up, she was too big,' she went on. 'So then both of her arms had to come off. And after that she was still too heavy, and so big. We tried to lift her and, when that didn't work, both her legs came off, at the groin, so it was just a torso left. The worst bit was the torso . . . she was so fat. Anyway, I got the stay-sharp knife and cut all the fat off Joanne's stomach, and we wrapped her back in the blanket.'

Their bloody work complete, their composure returned, the women became calculating. McGuinness and Casagrande first buried Lillecrapp's stomach and body fat in his prized strawberry patch. Then they wrapped his arms and legs in garbage bags and put them, with the head in a bucket and the blanket-shrouded torso, in the four-wheel drive. They headed to a lake 'about 100 kilometres' from the city. 'Nicole was saying something about putting something heavy on Joanne and putting her in the water, so she wouldn't float,' she explained. The plan went awry when they discovered the lake was a popular fishing spot, already bustling with activity.

Casagrande said they drove into the Adelaide Hills and buried the legs and knife near the Mount Lofty Botanical Gardens. The detectives wanted to know why the women did not bury the body in one location. 'It probably would have been easier,' Casagrande replied, as if realising it for the first time, 'but I thought that, if they found a torso, then maybe they wouldn't know who it was.'

Once Lillecrapp's torso had been safely dumped on a beach at Port Parham, the lovers made their way back to the city. 'We went and bought some petrol and put that in the bucket with her head and arms,' Casagrande said. 'It was about 4 litres of petrol. Nicole took us to this factory at Wingfield, and she went inside. She put the bucket with the head in it in this incinerator, and the arms too, and Nicole was yelling out "Hurry up, hurry up before someone comes!" I ran over to the gate and threw her a lighter. She threw all the petrol in, and about twenty newspapers in there as well, and then lit it up.' She shuddered. 'I keep dreaming about it. Picking her head up by the hair, putting her head in the bucket.'

After that, Casagrande said, the couple 'just drove home'. 'I knew, straight away, we were going to get caught,' she admitted wryly. 'I knew it, and I couldn't stop crying. Nicole gave me some pills so I could sleep. Then, early on the Thursday, we packed our stuff in the four-wheel drive.' Their getaway plan was foiled by, of all things, a minor car accident.

They decided to dump the vehicle and hitchhike their way to Sydney. Though she had no way of knowing for sure that the police were looking for her, Casagrande was pessimistic enough to believe capture was inevitable and a confession might help her score her next fix. She made a triple-zero phone call from a payphone and tried to convince the call centre to swap her confession for drugs. When that failed, she went to the police herself. And, with her sins revealed, she was not happy to learn methadone was not part of the deal.

'I wanted to go get my methadone, I should have gone and got my methadone but I've been trying to build up the courage to do this,' she screamed at the detectives as her addiction savaged her body. 'This is bullshit, this is fucking bullshit! You fucking promised me methadone! I don't have to fucking do this! I'm trying to do the right thing – I came in here to tell the truth, not get fucked around! I've got two kids that I'll frigging never probably see again after this, and all I want is my methadone!'

The truth had, at long last, been revealed. It came as cold comfort to Ron and Lindsay Lillecrapp. Under South Australian law, victims of crime are given an opportunity, during sentencing submissions, to tell both the court and the criminal how they have been affected by the offences in a victim impact statement. Ron and Lindsay had expected to begin the healing process on 1 July 2003 by delivering their victim impact statements and hearing the sentencing submissions for both accused. Only one of those things was to happen. David Stokes, for McGuinness, informed the court he had only just received the results of his client's psychological testing. She also had yet to sign the all-important statement of agreed facts asked for by Justice Perry. 'I'm not in a position to make submissions today for that reason,' Mr Stokes said.

Craig Caldicott, for Casagrande, also had concerns. 'In respect of the victim impact statements, my client hasn't had an opportunity to see them,' he said. 'I was handed them as I entered the courtroom this morning. There are portions of the statements which express opinions from the person which are clearly at odds with the plea that has been entered by Ms Casagrande.'

Mr Caldicott is a renowned and highly regarded member of the bar in South Australia. Until that day, however, no one knew he had a gift for understatement. His comment, as it turned out, was actually more of a warning to which Justice Perry should have given due consideration. He did not, however, and ordered the statements be read.

Casagrande and McGuinness sat, close together and silent, as Lindsay Lillecrapp read her statement to the court. Overwhelmed with emotion, she broke down and cried after just a few sentences. 'Being here today is something I never thought I would have to face in my lifetime,' she continued, 'but I feel compelled to speak up today. Over the past 18 months I have experienced a multitude of emotions, from great sadness to absolute horror. For a member of your family to die in such an unspeakable manner goes beyond anybody's reasoning. I frequently think about Joanne's last thoughts, the terror and absolute betrayal of these two women and the heinous crime they inflicted on Joanne that terrible night.'

Gathering her strength, Lindsay looked up from her notes and glared at the killers. Casagrande began to shake. McGuinness placed a consoling hand on her lover's knee. 'No human being deserves that kind of death – to be drugged, wounded, killed and then dismembered by two women committing this crime for money,' Lindsay went on. 'We, the family, have listened to the facts and the horrors of this crime. We have remained silent. We have even been glared at, had faces pulled at us by the defendants. I myself have never seen one sign of remorse from these two women, and it chills me to the bone.'

Casagrande was fading, ruined by guilt, accusations and heroin withdrawal. She would have much more to endure before the hearing was over. 'Donna presents herself as the less guilty one because she did not stab Joanne,' Lindsay said, staring unblinkingly at Casagrande. 'She participated in drugging Joanne, then she dismembered the body and helped hide the body parts. Her part in this hideous crime deserves to be recognised as horrific, and should be dealt with severely.

'These two women have turned my life, and that of Joanne's family, upside down. The grief and loss they have caused can never be forgiven. The only thing that can help myself and Joanne's family today is that justice is done, and these two women are punished and imprisoned for a very, very long time.'

Ron Lillecrapp locked eyes with his wife briefly, as they passed one another in the gallery. He strode to the podium in a way that suggested power beneath the pain. A tall, strong-looking man – not as large as his brother, but stocky nonetheless – his body language practically shouted that he would not be broken by Casagrande and McGuinness. Twice had he lost his brother to these women – once when the family ruptured, and again when Joanne was murdered. No more would he bottle up his pain. Unlike his wife's measured tones, Ron spoke with venom and volume, and his chin jutted defiantly at the killers as he verbally tore them apart.

'I first met Donna Casagrande in early 1996,' he began. 'John, my brother, had brought her to our house for tea. She abused that privilege by shooting up drugs in the driveway in the presence of my wife and parents.'

Casagrande flushed red, and would be silent no longer. 'I did not,' she shrieked hysterically, stunning those in the courtroom.

'She poisoned John's mind,' Ron continued, refusing to be interrupted. 'After that night they made demanding threats to us. They said they would trash the place if we didn't give them money.'

'You liar, you liar,' Casagrande howled. 'You're a bloody liar!'

'You know I'm not,' Ron shot back, glowering.

'That is a plain lie,' Casagrande yelled again. 'You said you hated him!'

Mr Caldicott's fears had come to pass. Justice Perry moved quickly to regain control of his courtroom. 'I'll have to put you out of court if you say any more,' he told Casagrande, firmly but not unkindly. 'You just have to sit.'

Casagrande did. McGuinness was waiting for her. She pulled her lover into her arms, lowered her head onto her shoulder and began stroking her hair. Her murderous eyes remained fixed on Ron Lillecrapp, as if daring him to say another word against the woman she adored.

Ron did that, and more. 'John was naive and gullible and they played on that as much as they could until a time when he said "enough is enough",' he growled. 'It was okay for them to steal from him but, when he said "no" they killed him. Butchered him grotesquely. That is, in my opinion, premeditated. I see you both equally guilty of the murder and I feel that at no time in these proceedings have I seen any remorse expressed.' He said they deserved more of a punishment than any court could impose – for stealing not only Joanne's possessions and links to his family, but also his remaining years.

'He didn't have you, his family, did he?' McGuinness spat.

'I suggest you have no feelings, considering you could butcher a person,' Ron replied darkly. 'I cannot imagine how anyone could mentally be able to commit that crime, let alone physically. He tried to help both you women get off drugs. He gave you the same credit he gave others in the community – his time and his energy to help you.'

Casagrande pushed away from McGuinness, rose to her feet and strained against the glass walls of the dock. 'He sold me as a prostitute, that's what he did,' she screamed, bringing the old rumour back to life. 'He sold my body, that's what he did!'

Justice Perry had had enough. 'Mr Caldicott, I'll have to put your client out of court,' he said, signalling for the sheriff's officers to take her to the cells. 'There is no way of maintaining the dignity of the court.' Casagrande was removed, still crying and yelling at Ron Lillecrapp.

He took a deep breath and went on, now directing all his pain toward McGuinness. He answered her earlier accusation and admitted he had not always been close to his brother. 'I feel angry and cheated,' he said. 'I will always have to wonder what our relationship as brothers might have eventuated into. I have lost a brother that I could turn to if I needed to.' His voice broke. 'I lost him long before you two murdered him,' he said quietly.

'Yes,' McGuinness hissed.

Her contempt energised Ron. 'You totally shafted him, you stole from him, you killed him and I am so angry for that it is very hard to express,' he raged. 'There's a quote from the Bible – an eye for an eye. A lot of the time when I think about this, I feel it should be a life for a life!'

'Do it,' McGuinness yelled, standing up and leaning toward the glass. 'Do it, do it!'

'You're both guilty of murder,' Ron said, disgusted. 'The worst kind – the kind that scares the whole community, not just my family. The whole population knows what you have done and what you're capable of. They have been reminded that ruthless people like you still exist.'

He returned to his seat in the court, pale but unbroken. It was clear that, despite his best efforts, Casagrande's hysteria had unnerved him. Lindsay clasped his hand tightly as he sat down, and acknowledged the sympathetic glances from those in the gallery. Justice Perry allowed Casagrande back into the court, then agreed to a short adjournment so that Mr Caldicott could speak with her.

'I've been instructed to apply for an adjournment,' Mr Caldicott told the court upon its resumption. 'My client is having difficulty this morning.' He asked all submissions be given on the same day – 17 July – given that he needed time to speak to a cardiologist about Casagrande's ongoing heart valve problems. Justice Perry agreed, and remanded the duo into the custody of the Adelaide Women's Prison at Northfield.

Ron Lillecrapp's words had more effect on Casagrande than he realised. That night, prison officials were called to the killer's cell – she had slashed both her wrists in a suicide attempt. Working quickly, officers and medical staff were able to save her life, and she was kept under close watch until her next court appearance on 17 July.

Mr Caldicott was quick to inform the court of his client's suicide attempt. It was, he ventured, a sign of her true self.

'She is extremely contrite and remorseful as to what has happened and what has occurred,' he said. 'I have been specifically instructed not to take issue with any of the victim impact statements that were read out on the last occasion. She clearly was remorseful, and has been through all of the period, and wanted me to express that to the court.' He said sentencing Casagrande would be a difficult exercise. 'She wasn't the person that did the killing,' he reminded Justice Perry. Were she to be sentenced on the basis she had assisted McGuinness in the murder, then she would have been sentenced incorrectly – a juicy point for an appeals court.

In response, Justice Perry said he felt Casagrande's true crime was 'unlawful and dangerous acts' including drugging and restraining Lillecrapp, breaking his nose and being present when the killing took place. 'There is a slight air of unreality about that,' he said wearily. 'It puts her close to the margin, doesn't it, between manslaughter and murder.'

Mr Stokes, for McGuinness, took his turn at the bar table next. His client, he said, was suffering from rampant memory loss. His claim was supported by psychological evidence suggesting the memory loss was genuine given the murder was committed 'in a haze of drugs'. 'She doesn't dispute the last part of this episode, when the stabbing occurred that resulted in death,' he said, 'because Casagrande remembers it. McGuinness says she can't remember it, but she accepts it and accepts she intended to kill.'

He edged toward suggesting it was a spontaneous crime, but Justice Perry was not interested in hearing that. 'It was spur of the moment, but that is to be considered against the victim being forced eventually to give the PIN,' Justice Perry said. 'When news breaks that the PIN is not right, the situation heats up and culminates in your client stabbing the victim in the heart. So although I have to accept that it wasn't premeditated in the ordinary sense and was spur of the moment, it was the culmination of a relatively long period of restraining and assaulting the victim.'

Stephen Millsteed, prosecuting, argued there was little room for mercy. 'This is a particularly serious example of murder,' he said, 'and there are four serious features about this case.' The first was McGuinness's admission she had a specific intent to kill Lillecrapp, the second was the victim's defenceless state, the third was the motive for the crime. 'In essence, McGuinness killed this man because she and Casagrande couldn't get a few hundred dollars out of a bank account,' he said. 'One couldn't think of a poorer excuse to deliberately take a man's life than to get a few hundred dollars out of a bank account.'

The hideous aftermath of the killing, Mr Millsteed said, was the final factor: 'The gruesome dismemberment of the body is relevant in two ways. First, it sheds some light – indeed, in my submission, a good deal of light – on the callous state of mind the women were harbouring at the time. Secondly, it's an important feature when one has regard to the adverse effects that this crime has had on the victim's family.'

Justice Perry pointed out the butchery was 'logistical, not ritualistic . . . it was a combination of trying to get the body in the car and also trying to conceal the fact that a crime had been committed.'

Mr Milsteed agreed. 'The mere fact they have taken a logistical decision to dismember this man's body is, in itself, an aggravating circumstance.' So, too, was Casagrande's failure to prevent Lillecrapp's death. He said her inaction placed her manslaughter charge 'right on the cusp' of murder. 'The Crown accepts there was no intention, on her part, to cause death or grievous bodily harm to Mr Lillecrapp,' he said. 'But it's quite clear she did not try and stop McGuinness from stabbing the victim.'

Justice Perry remanded the lovers in custody one last time. His task was clear, though working his way through the legal complexity of Casagrande's involvement would require a little extra thought. Seven days were enough; the women were summoned back to the court on 24 July for sentencing. Once they arrived, he did not mince words.

'Both of you are the products of broken homes and had childhoods punctuated by violence and drug addiction,' he said as the women huddled together, their arms around one another. 'You both have spent substantial periods during your adult lives in jail.' The effect on their psyches was evident. Casagrande, he said, had a 'borderline personality disorder' and depression that found expression in her suicide attempt; McGuinness shared her beloved's disorder while also suffering from impulsivity.

'This killing was preceded by an attempt to incapacitate the victim, who was rendered defenceless and then detained,' he continued, relating the story of the PIN argument. 'This killing was followed by the gruesome dismemberment of the body. Not only does this demonstrate the cold-blooded callousness of your conduct, but later it had a devastating effect on the victim's family.'

In the gallery, Ron and Lindsay Lillecrapp held each other close.

'McGuinness, you have conceded you had an intention to kill,' he said. 'Your plea, Casagrande, is advanced on the footing you are guilty of unlawful and dangerous conduct but that you did not have an intention to kill. Even so, you actively participated in the preliminaries to the killing. While present you did nothing to stop McGuinness from stabbing the victim, and you actively participated in the attempts to dispose of the body. For the purposes of sentencing, your crime must therefore be regarded as in that category of manslaughter which is close to murder.'

He jailed McGuinness for life and imposed an 18-year non-parole period. It would have been 24 years, he said, if not for her admission of guilt. Casagrande, he said, deserved a 12-year sentence, of which she had to serve a minimum of ten years.

Casagrande began to weep once more; unusually, McGuinness also started to cry. Their grief was palpable, overwhelming and difficult to watch. They were prised apart by sheriff's officers and led, one by one, back to the cells. That evening they began their long terms inside the women's prison, where they remain to this day.

For Ron and Lindsay, the sentencing was the moment their healing began. 'Today was the first time I noticed their remorse,' Ron said outside court. 'Crocodile tears tend to flow easily but today I think they were finally sorry. I get some small peace of mind from that. We can finally start to find closure.' He was quite happy with the jail terms imposed. 'They deserved what they got, and Justice Perry did the job right,' he said. 'It's finally over, we finally have some closure and we can go forward now that justice is done.'

Lindsay said she hoped some future good could come from the case – particularly for others in her brother-in-law's situation. 'He wanted to be known as Joanne, to be accepted as Joanne, all his life,' she said. 'It's a hard life, so just be very careful how you live it and who you choose to mix with. Just because you choose an alternative lifestyle doesn't mean you have to be shunned and taken advantage of. We accepted it – it was hard, but we never shunned him for the way he lived his life – and other people need to be the same way.'

Deadly Escalation

Mark Errin Rust

When the masked, knife-wielding intruder pushed her to the floor, she did not scream. She did not argue when he ordered her to roll over, did not complain when he stripped her from the waist and laid on top of her. She choked back her fear, her disgust, as he raped her with his flaccid penis, and did not tease him about his impotence. Steadfastly refusing to look at his face, she even held the knife for him while he violated her. His grotesque abuse complete, she handed back the weapon — never once using it in her own defence — and did not try to follow him as he left her darkened office.

Though she would not know it for many years, the woman's submissive attitude had saved her life. On that winter's night in August 2001, she had narrowly avoided becoming the next woman murdered by Mark Errin Rust — a life-long sexual deviant and arsonist who had already slaughtered two women, and was willing to kill again.

•

The people of Adelaide had never paid much attention to Rust. And why would they? An obese, dishevelled, odorous man who expressed his limited vocabulary in a constant monotone, Rust was driven by the most primal of urges. Sex consumed his every waking moment – thinking about it, fantasising about it, becoming frustrated when he could not have it. He was not the sort of person anyone wanted to spend much time with.

Yet, had someone stopped and looked carefully at Rust, years earlier, they would have noticed the killer instinct developing within him. They would have observed his growing hatred of women, his escalating deviancy, his abnormal pre-occupation with his sexual potency. And had they done so, two of Rust's victims – Maya Jakic and Megumi Suzuki – would still be alive today.

Rust was born in Whyalla, 380 kilometres north-west of Adelaide, in 1965. A self-described perpetual loner, his life didn't truly begin until the age of 13, when he first noticed girls. 'He told me that, whenever he saw a pretty girl, he would become so excited that he would follow her whilst fantasising about having sex with her,' treating psychiatrist Dr Narain Nambier said in 2003. 'During his early teens, he first exposed himself to a woman and found this so much more gratifying than masturbating in private. He told me it was more thrilling to masturbate in front of a pretty woman, mainly due to the reaction it would provoke in his victim.'

Dr Ken O'Brien, a forensic psychiatrist, also examined Rust in 2003. 'Rust told me that he used to walk past his would-be victims, stand across the road from them and flash by taking his penis out,' he said. 'He would not say anything to his victim – or, sometimes, victims.'

His behaviour was no secret to his sole friend, who asked to be named only as Craig. 'I had one very, very sick friend and all my mates told me, they said "Piss him off, he's crazy",' Craig said in 2003. He remembered Rust 'liked to scare schoolgirls' at a bus stop in North Adelaide. 'He had his silly ways, of course, but he was a normal sort of bloke,' he insisted. 'If my mum and dad needed help he would be there – he was very helpful.'

Dr Nambier said the horrified responses of women who saw Rust exposed reinforced his behaviour. 'He told me that the urges continued to increase in intensity and frequency, but he would often get into trouble with his teachers and parents as a result,' he said. 'He would continue to expose himself and masturbate until he was caught by the authorities, at which point his behaviour would only be temporarily extinguished.'

As early as 1978, the police and doctors of South Australia had a chance to stop Rust's escalating tendencies. They failed to do so. Neither Dr Nambier nor Dr O'Brien could find any evidence of Rust receiving treatment – or even basic counselling – as a teenager. It was a missed opportunity that would cost lives in the future. Rust did, however, receive Youth and Magistrates Court punishments for his actions – not his sexual forays, but his obsession with fire and resultant bouts of arson. By focusing on property damage, the authorities missed the true crimes forming within the young man's mind. By handing out good behaviour bonds and declining to record convictions, the courts failed to reign in the beast before it could feast on misery.

Flashing was Rust's sole sexual outlet. 'He reported difficulty in intercourse due to either inadequate drive or failure to perform,' Dr Nambier said. 'This often made him angry and frustrated. Although he often had the urge to have sex, he found it difficult to obtain an erection.' That did not, however, stop Rust seeking normal relationships. Little is known about his first marriage aside from the fact it lasted only 18 months, ending just before Rust was sent to jail for causing $642,000 damage to suburban buildings in Norwood and Kensington. The areas would go on to become his favourite haunts for destruction – not of property, anymore, but lives.

The reason for his performance problems was not discovered for another six years, when he and his second wife sought help having children. 'He was diagnosed with Klinefelter's Syndrome, a sex hormone disorder where the male has an additional X chromosome,' Dr O'Brien said. 'Those with this disorder have small testicles and are infertile.' The diagnosis strained the marriage, which had not been the best to begin with. 'Rust told me his wife always wanted him to assault her, to beat her up,' Dr O'Brien continued. 'He claimed she would get abusive toward him and have "fighting fits" to instigate sex. He said he would hit her, and she enjoyed it.' That marriage ended in 1999, when his wife's daughter claimed he had sexually assaulted her. Though he was never charged, Rust attended what was supposed to be the first of several sessions with the Sex Offender's Treatment Program. 'He told me he left halfway through the first day,' Dr O'Brien said, 'because the program was "stupid".'

Once again, no one paid much attention. Rust was allowed to slip through the cracks and avoid the help he so desperately needed. He was now a divorced, sex-obsessed man – working as a taxi driver – who literally lacked the equipment to satisfy his needs. In layman's terms, Rust was a walking powder keg.

'For many years, his sexual offending behaviour was stereotypical,' Dr O'Brien said. 'Between April 1999 and August 2001, however, the character of his sexual offending changed. There was a gradual emergence of aggressive rape fantasies coupled with ever-increasing anger toward women.'

Dr Nambier agreed. 'What's very apparent is that there appears to have been an escalation in the nature of the offending, with offences of increasing severity against other individuals culminating in murder and rape,' he said.

Two months after his divorce, Rust would cross paths with another troubled soul. Maya Jakic was born on 25 January 1969 and grew up in Zadar on the Croatian coast. She was halfway through a photography course in Zagreb when, in 1990, her homeland became embroiled in a war with Serbia. Maya was forced to flee the country, and moved to Adelaide. There, she lived with her mother and stepfather, Jagoda and John Jelic, in the Marden home they had bought two years earlier.

By 1997, Maya's citizenship had been approved and she was working as a sales assistant at the Pierucci fashion store in Rundle Mall. Her employer described her as 'an exceptional employee' and 'vivacious and happy', but there was another side to the woman.

'Maya would call me on the phone at least once a week,' family friend Eda Gregov said in 2003. 'She looked at me as a confidante – I was one of the few people aware that she was suffering from bulimia. I could see there were serious problems within the family, and Jagoda always seemed to be upset as well.'

By 1999 it was clear Maya could no longer live peacefully with her parents. She moved to an apartment in Glenelg – a beach-side suburb about twenty minutes from Adelaide – and became, in her mother's eyes, a loner. 'We didn't know any of her friends,' Jagoda said in 2000. 'She didn't tell us who her friends were.' On 6 April 1999, the family had a particularly bad argument during one of Maya's visits. She stormed out of her parents' home around 4 pm. It was the last time they saw her alive.

Maya's movements between 6 April and her death remain a mystery. Witness reports claim she was seen speaking with staff at the Caltex service station at Bolivar – 40 minutes north of the city – on 9 April. The witness said she was complaining about having been kicked off a bus bound for the regional centre of Port Augusta. Passers-by would later find the remains of a campfire, a pillow, a crocheted blanket and lolly wrappers across the road from the service station. Another person reported seeing Maya at noon on 12 April by the shops on Jetty Rd, Glenelg – not far from her apartment.

What is known is that, later on 12 April, Maya had made her way to Payneham, north-east of Adelaide. The prestigious, upper-class area – full of lush parklands and 1800s architecture – was an idyllic spot for a photographer with a keen eye. Tragically, the exclusive suburb had also become one of Rust's favourite places to leer at women. He was working on his taxi when she walked past. Rust shouted a greeting to her and she smiled politely. 'Want a lift?' he asked, and Maya declined. 'How about a root?' he suggested. Maya said 'no' and walked faster, heading for a nearby bus stop.

Now his blood was up. Rust got into his car and drove further up the road, toward a disused police patrol station on Payneham Rd. He made sure he parked in a spot where Maya would have to walk past him again. It was a grown-up's version of the same game he had been playing since he was 13 – noticing a pretty girl, getting ahead of them and working up the courage to expose himself. He did just that. As he had done so many times before, Rust dropped his pants and bared his shrivelled genitalia to the argumentative, fiery woman who had caught his eye. He wanted a hit of his favourite drug; the horrified look of a disgusted girl. But unlike every other girl whose senses he had assaulted, Maya Jakic took one look at Rust's penis . . . and scoffed.

In that moment, everything changed. Decades of anger and frustration, years of seething hatred for the women in his life, all the loathing Rust felt for his own impotence finally exploded. Without stopping to adjust his pants, Rust moved in behind Maya and grabbed her. 'How about some fun?' he growled, then pulled her down to the ground. There, between a set of bushes and atop dry bundles of twigs, Rust became a murderer for the first time.

'I asked him why he did this,' Dr O'Brien said in 2003. 'He said, "At the time, it was a thrill". He told me that the general purpose of attacking her was to have sex with her, but he decided to kill her at the last moment.'

Jagoda and John had no reason to worry about their daughter. It was not unusual for her to avoid them for days at a time, especially following an argument. 'A week after she didn't return, we started suspecting something was wrong,' Jadoda said in 2000. They searched all of her favourite places, including the Hilton Hotel in Adelaide and the Stamford Grand Hotel in Glenelg, before reporting her missing to police on 12 April 1999.

What followed can only be described as a black comedy of errors, worthy of the Keystone Cops. At 10.18 pm, while Jagoda and John filled in paperwork, Rust drove his taxi 50 metres past the murder scene to a payphone. He called the triple zero emergency phone number and asked to speak to police. Eager for sick gratification, he wanted the body to be found. Maya had not given him the horrified reaction he wanted, so perhaps the police would.

'There's someone hanging around the old Payneham police station,' he told the triple-zero operator. 'There seems to be someone trying to break in down there. I didn't actually see them but they've got flashlights flashing around the place.' Asked for his name, Rust replied: 'I won't disclose it.'

An experienced officer was dispatched from the Norwood Police Station to check things out. Rust watched from afar as the policeman checked the perimeter and left without finding Maya's corpse. Angered that his plan wasn't working, Rust called triple zero again at 11.50 pm, this time from a payphone near the Royal Adelaide Hospital. 'I just walked past the old Payneham Police Station,' he droned. 'There seems to be a body of some sort in the bushes there. I'm not too sure, I haven't gone near it. It's up off Payneham Rd, there. I just seen there's a body there about half an hour ago.' This time, investigators went to the wrong location. They found, of course, nothing.

There were many other opportunities to find Maya's body, and all of them were bungled. Though the patrol station was no longer used for its original purpose, its office space was being used by senior officers engaged in policy review. None of them noticed the half-dressed, decomposing body in the shrubbery – even though Rust had done little to conceal it. The man who lived next door to the station worked in his garden every day, just metres from the body. He saw nothing out of the ordinary. Eventually, the officers noticed an unusual odour and stood less than a metre from Maya's remains without finding them.

At 11 am on 17 April, officers were sent to the old patrol station to handle a domestic disturbance. They did so, yet again failing to discover Maya. Five days had passed since the young woman's grisly demise, and Rust was furious. Gratification delayed was gratification denied; he wanted someone to feel ill at the sight of his handiwork. But not before he himself had enjoyed one last look at it.

At 10.25 pm, nearby residents noticed a taxi park by the patrol base for a few moments, its hazard lights flashing. Seven minutes later, officers at the Norwood Police Station found a handwritten note under the windscreen wiper of one of their cars. Though Rust's words looked like a young child's scrawl, and his spelling betrayed his lack of intelligence, there was no mistaking his lack of patience with police incompetence. 'Their's a dead girl's body in the shrubs of the grounds near the main road of the Pahyhame Police station,' the note read. 'This is no joke!! Take a good look.'

Maya's body had been missed by experienced police officers, senior members of staff and investigators with many years under their belts. It was, however, two newly minted constables who found what remained of Maya Jakic and alerted the world to her demise.

The news all but destroyed Jagoda Jelic. 'My whole world and future was in Maya,' she said in 2003. 'Why would anyone want to kill Maya like an innocent bird and cover her [with] branches thinking no one would ever find her, and that he could cover his dirty crime?'

Sadly, she had completely misinterpreted Rust's intentions. So, too, did the police. To be fair, they had precious little to work with. Maya had no enemies, no dark associations, no hidden secrets that ran deeper than her bulimia. Trying to find a pattern in her movements was already a nightmare – and made worse by the discovery of her handbag, containing her passport and credit cards, at Virginia, even further north than Bolivar. A walker had found it on 10 April, but not reported it until after news of Maya's murder broke. He took detectives back to the bag's location on 21 April but they found no further clues. By early May, they had managed to ascertain that bag was not the one Maya had been carrying on the night of her death, and their only tentative lead dried up.

Appeals for the triple-zero caller to contact police yielded no result. Nor did the promise of a $100,000 reward for information. Major Crime Investigations Branch Detective Senior Sergeant Gerry Feltus decided it was time to think outside the box. 'We may have to resort to releasing the tapes,' he said on 8 May. 'This is a most serious offence and we have to seriously consider courses of action to try and identify the person who called. We are not suggesting that this person was involved in the murder, but he knows something.' It was not a standard police move. 'Releasing tapes doesn't happen very often,' he conceded. 'If we appeal to callers, they normally come forward when they appreciate the importance of them doing so.'

On 13 May, both the note and the first phone call – in which Rust claims to have seen 'flashlights' by the patrol station – were released to the public. Detective Senior Sergeant Feltus played his cards close to his chest. 'The note has been released for the sole purpose of locating its author,' he said. He insisted there was no reason to link the note's author to Maya's killer. 'We believe it's someone reluctant to come forward and be spoken to. He probably believes that he's fulfilled his obligation by notifying us of the fact there was a body in that location. We wish to speak to that person in relation to what else he might know.' His pleas were met with extreme indifference and, on 29 May, the recording of Rust's second call – about a body in the bushes – was made public. The Crime Stoppers hotline received just two responses.

By 11 June, things were getting desperate. Police created a special free-call 1800 number that played, on continuous loop, both of Rust's triple-zero calls. They announced they would refund anyone who called the number from a payphone, hoping to encourage more participation. Hundreds of people swamped the line – more out of macabre curiosity than because they could actually help – and, in another embarrassment for police, the line malfunctioned. After being jammed for three days, it was repaired and operational again on 19 June.

It was too little, too late. Police had once again missed their chance. 'I said to Mum and Dad and everyone in my family, that voice is Mark's,' Craig, Rust's childhood friend, remembered in 2003. 'That was a shock to my system when I heard the voice.' But when he couldn't get through on the number, Craig convinced himself he was mistaken and let it pass.

Voice analysis experts were called in. 'They are 99.9 per cent certain the calls were made by the same man,' Detective Senior Sergeant Feltus said on September 16. He had also come to believe the man was a taxi driver, thanks to the witness reports of the vehicle flashing its hazard lights. 'The taxi driver may have been looking to see if the body was still in the bushes before notifying the police,' he said. 'It's unusual that the caller would ring from Payneham, then from the Royal Adelaide Hospital. One of the leads we are following is that the caller was a taxi driver, and drove to a taxi rank after his first call, then called again. The driver is crucial to our investigation and we are very keen to talk to the person.'

Rust was, at that time, very easy to find. He was in jail. In late 1999, he was given a 20-month minimum sentence for trespassing, giving a false name and address and – unsurprisingly – indecent behaviour in a public place. As had happened so many times before, no one paid attention to the hideous little man with a penchant for flashing pretty women. No one thought, not even for a moment, he could possibly be connected to what had become one of Adelaide's most infamous unsolved murders.

The case was becoming a lost cause. On 10 April 2000, a mannequin dressed in clothes identical to Maya's was put on display at the Police Expo, just outside the city. Detective Senior Sergeant Feltus said the murder was 'one of the most baffling' he had come across, admitting investigators had too many 'unanswered questions'.

Investigations were still ongoing when, in October 2000, a 17-year-old Japanese woman arrived in Adelaide. Her name was Megumi Suzuki, and her fate was to become inexorably tied with that of Rust. Megumi learned all about South Australia through her friendship with a local boy. Chris Hamilton had gone to Shizuoka Prefecture, south of Tokyo, after completing his Year 12 studies and was welcomed into the Suzuki home by her father, Youichi, and doting mother, Masako. 'I had loved my daughter since she was born, only thinking of her happiness and looking after her with love and care,' Masako said in 2003. 'My daughter was my dream and my hope.' Through her association with Mr Hamilton, Megumi would discover her own ambitions. 'My daughter's dream was to become a counsellor for overseas students in

Japan,' Masako said. 'That's why she went to Australia – to study, to help her understand the Western way of thinking.'

She enrolled at Eynesbury College on Franklin Street, in the heart of the city, in its Academy of English. She took a room on the sixth floor of the Torrens Valley International Residence at Modbury, a 15-minute bus ride from Adelaide. One of 20 Japanese students in the complex, Megumi quickly bonded with her countrymen. She was renowned for her love of fashion, late-night karaoke, hamburgers and hot chips. She called her parents once a week and spent much of her time with Chris Hamilton – who, by all accounts, spent much of his time keeping Megumi out of trouble.

Like Maya Jakic, there was another side to Megumi Suzuki. Persistent rumours claimed she often found herself in precarious, dangerous situations. No one seemed to know if it was by naive accident or by design. Mr Hamilton – slightly older than his friend, and much wiser to the cruel ways of Adelaide – passed on his concerns to both the school and the Suzuki family. Megumi went home to Japan – perhaps by choice, likely by demand – but was permitted to return to South Australia in early 2001. In time, everyone who loved the vivacious, outgoing girl would regret giving her that additional chance.

On 23 July 2001, Rust was released on parole. He wasted no time. Ten days later – 2 August 2001 – he attacked an 18-year-old at Cumberland Park, south of Adelaide. The woman had stopped to use an ATM on Goodwood Road when Rust dragged her from her car. For five terrifying minutes, he blocked her escape with his body and masturbated furiously in front of her. Having lacked an outlet for his deviancy for 20 months, Rust had too much fury and too much longing to contain. Finally, the woman summoned up enough courage to push Rust to the ground and leap back into her car. Focused on escape, she reversed down Goodwood Road – a major southern arterial road – at high speed, terrified because Rust had already recovered and begun walking toward her. The woman drove straight to her boyfriend's house, and he immediately notified the police. She was left with life-long scars.

'I have a constant fear of being on my own,' she said in 2003. 'I'm constantly checking doors and windows, and I have panic attacks when I'm driving my car on my own and people walk near it. I constantly feel vulnerable and not safe . . . I don't sleep well, I'm constantly having nightmares and waking up at all hours of the night.'

Rust was back on the streets and back in form. Having already breached his parole conditions, there was no reason to stop. Cumberland Park had already yielded one satisfying experience, and so he decided to try the area again. After all, it was highly unlikely the police would connect him with the 18-year-old's suffering.

On 1 August 2001, Megumi Suzuki spoke to her father on the telephone and said 'don't worry, I'm fine, I'm studying very hard'. It was their final conversation. At 3 pm on 3 August, Megumi left Eynesbury College for the day. Security cameras recorded her walking away alone wearing an ankle-length brown and cream checked dress and three-quarter-length coat. She was carrying her schoolbag and headed in the direction of Rundle Mall – one of her favourite destinations. What the footage could not show was her distress. Friends would later remember Megumi had complained of a recent fight with a close male friend. Her remedy was to go nightclubbing by herself. At 7 pm, she had a friend walk her to a bus stop on Grenfell Street, which runs parallel to Rundle Mall, and was never seen again.

How she came to be at Cumberland Park remains unknown. Her apartment was 40 minutes in the opposite direction, and there were no karaoke clubs in the neighbourhood. Whatever it was that drew her south, it led her to her death.

Rust was at a service station, filling his car with petrol and eagerly searching out his next victim. His time in prison, however, had changed him; no longer was he happy to merely disgust his victims. Rust wanted – needed – sex, and he was not prepared to let anything stand in his way. At around 10.30 pm, he saw Megumi waiting at a bus stop on Goodwood Road. She was listening to her CD player. In a matter of moments he had grabbed the unsuspecting girl – who was far shorter and much, much lighter than he – and pulled her away from the main road. But while he managed to stifle her screams and pull down her pants, Rust's chronic inability to perform stymied his rapist desires once again. He was unable to achieve an erection.

Embarrassed and angry, Rust tried to strangle his victim but failed. Having completely lost his temper, he snatched up a nearby rock and bashed the terrified girl to death. Showing a previously unseen calculating and malicious side, Rust gathered up some plastic sheets that were lying around, used them to tightly wrap Megumi's body and then dumped her in a large, industrial rubbish bin behind a set of shops.

Dr O'Brien would discuss the murder with Rust in 2003. 'He told me that was different from killing Ms Jakic,' the forensic psychiatrist said. 'When I asked him why he killed Miss Suzuki, he replied, "She would've recognised who it was". I asked again why he killed her, to which he replied, "Because I did".'

Megumi's disappearance did not go unnoticed for long. Both the school and her friends reported her missing when she did not attend classes the following Thursday. 'We are deeply worried and distressed,' the school said in a statement. 'Our thoughts are with Megumi's parents, relatives and friends at this time.' Masako Suzuki immediately boarded a plane from Japan. Her husband followed a few days later. 'We love our daughter very much and are desperately concerned for her welfare,' they said in a statement. 'We have been praying for Megumi's safe return and are having sleepless nights.'

So, too, was Mr Hamilton. He found himself in an awkward position – he had some of Megumi's possessions, including clothing, at his apartment. At a friend's advice, he contacted police to let them know. It was a decision he would quickly come to regret.

On Wednesday 15 August, a maintenance worker discovered Megumi's bag – containing her books, ID card, make-up and pencil case – beside the O-Bahn track at Campbelltown. The specially designed concrete 'bus track' links the city with the north-eastern suburbs, including Megumi's apartment at Modbury. Other personal items were strewn across a 500-metre length of the track, giving the impression they had been thrown from a moving bus. Her CD player was not recovered, but her ATM card was found in a nearby street. A check of the bank's records revealed it had been used twice at a Westbourne Park service station. That area was canvassed by officers on foot, while the police helicopter and dog squads searched the rest of the O-Bahn track for more clues.

By 16 August, police had to concede they were looking at a potential murder investigation. 'Every day that goes by, we get more concerned,' Acting Superintendent Neil Tank told reporters. 'We hope for the best but we obviously have to be prepared for the worst. It's now been 12 days since we know she was seen – 12 days since she used her mobile phone.' A 40-man team visited Adelaide's karaoke bars, nightclubs and hotels, speaking with patrons and distributing photographs of the missing teenager. The Crime Stoppers hotline took 90 calls, which detectives began to sift through.

The consequences on Adelaide's reputation as a destination for international students were devastating. 'Because she was Japanese, we feel as if we are in danger,' student Sanae Maekaua said on 17 August. 'It's all over the news back home, it is big news. Parents don't want children studying here because they think Adelaide is a dangerous place.' Fellow student Andre Yosaf said the fear was not limited to the Japanese community. His minders had banned him from going out alone at night. 'It's very frightening to found out someone can literally disappear without a trace,' he said. 'When you are away from home, you have to be very careful and never go out on your own.'

The pressure upon police was enormous. Quite aside from public safety and victim concerns, politicians and educators were beginning to grumble about lost revenue and the damage to tourism. Japan's consul to Australia, Yukinori Amano, also became involved. Based in Melbourne, he understandably wanted answers on behalf of his government.

The case caused a media frenzy in Tokyo. 'Reporters were seen hanging around the front of their house like vultures,' Fusae Simpson, a friend of Mrs Suzuki, said in 2003. 'They tried to photograph inside their house with hidden cameras, taking photos around the house, interviewing neighbours.' Camera crews sent to South Australia were just as determined. 'The Japanese media was looking for Youichi and Masako in Adelaide,' she said. 'The reporters came to the hotel, and they were scared. They were prisoners in their hotel room, and they only left to cooperate with the police search.'

Mr Hamilton was also under pressure. 'Megumi's disappearance was the most traumatic thing that had ever happened in my entire life,' he remembered in 2003, 'but it was only the beginning of the suffering I went through.' By contacting an increasingly desperate police department, Mr Hamilton had turned himself into the prime suspect. 'I had to live, every day, with the terrible memories and outcomes of the blatant investigation focus on me by the police,' he said, dubbing it 'arbitrary harassment'. At one stage he was taken to Sturt Police Station, outside the city, and told that he was either Megumi's killer or 'the reason she's dead'.

He said police demanded an interview with him – a confession from him – and strong-armed him into agreeing to be videotaped and recorded. At the last minute he recovered his senses and asked to call his father – a lawyer – and the interview was terminated. 'It was the equivalent of hell on earth for me,' he later said. 'I was the only suspect in the ensuing investigation and I suffered greatly at the hands of the police. I was their scapegoat. The police all but named me as the killer – even my close friends became suspicious of me.'

Police might have thought they had their man, but a startling claim was to derail everything. On 18 August, witnesses reported seeing Megumi alive and well at the Arkaba Hotel in Fullarton. A man said he and his wife had walked 'to within two metres' of the missing student and called her by name before she ran away. He said she was wearing a wig. Officers swooped on the area immediately, door-knocking every home. No new information was gleaned.

Speculation began to mount that Megumi had simply run away from her parents. Many possible motives were concocted by the public, ranging from the pressures of being a student far from home to a boyfriend of whom mother and father did not approve. Mr Amano, from the embassy, announced he wanted the girl found, questioned and sent home at once. Detective Senior Sergeant Feltus was more restrained. 'It is costing us a lot of manpower and causing stress to her parents,' he said of the search. 'We appeal for Megumi to come forward.'

Inquiries shifted from a murder investigation to a manhunt. Detective Senior Sergeant Feltus demanded Megumi's friends assist his team. 'We're having a great deal of difficulty establishing who her friends are – those people aren't coming forward,' he said on 19 August. 'It may well be someone is assisting her to remain in hiding for various reasons. I don't know why. We know she associated with people in Rundle Mall. We're going to have to go through all the film in Rundle Mall's security cameras.'

Officially, police considered Megumi a missing person. On 19 August they released more photos of her, taken by friends, hoping to jog someone's memory. Major Crime Investigations Branch Detective Superintendent Paul Schramm said the time for games had passed. 'There is now a strong likelihood Megumi is, in fact, still alive,' he told the press. 'I would like to make an appeal to Megumi: you have seen the plea by your parents, you have seen the impact and the response by them. I am aware it may be embarrassing for you to come forward, but I can only say it will become more embarrassing the longer this continues. I would make a plea to her and anyone who may be looking after her to please come forward now. To continue this charade, if indeed that is what this is, can only make things worse.'

It was a waste of time. Megumi was dead and the man responsible – Mark Rust – remained at large. And he was still being underestimated. Once again, police did not pause to consider whether a known sex offender with a taste for pretty women might have any connection with the disappearance of a gorgeous, foreign student. That left the sadistic pervert free to indulge as he saw fit. Realising the Cumberland Park area was now too hot for him, Rust returned to his favourite stomping grounds and began looking for a new target in the Payneham area. While police chased ghosts, Rust tracked down another victim to satisfy his expanding urges.

The woman was working late on Kensington Rd, Rose Park – just nine minutes' drive from where Maya Jakic's body had been dumped. She was beginning to pack up for the night when, at 8.50 pm, the lights in the office went out.

'I thought "stuff it, I'm going home",' the woman said in her statement to police. 'But I looked out the window and saw that one or two other buildings still had their lights on. I saw the computer was still on, and I wondered why.' Rust, thinking ahead, had accessed the building's fuse box and killed the lights. He had made sure, though, to leave himself enough illumination by which to see his next victim's reactions.

'I wanted to leave,' the woman said. 'I hadn't heard anything at all, it was completely quiet. I walked toward the doorway and I sensed a presence to the left. I noticed a black shape and later realised it was a male person. I said "What do you want?" And lifted my hand upwards toward the area I thought his face would be.' Rust had learned from his experiences with Megumi and Maya. He was already wearing a knitted balaclava, and had armed himself with a box-cutting blade. He was also not prepared to wait any longer. Having failed to have sex with Megumi, he needed release immediately. Through body language and short, barked commands, he made that clear to his victim.

She responded in a way Rust had never seen before. 'I don't know why my tone of voice was so calm,' the woman said. 'I didn't know what this person was capable of, so I just used calm, submissive tones. But I was terrified.'

Rust pushed the woman to the ground and laid on top of her. 'I was being submissive and thought that, if I did that, I would not antagonise him,' she later said. 'I suspected that he wanted sex and was going to do something sexual. I decided to comply because I didn't know what he would do if I didn't comply.' She did, however, make one near-fatal mistake – she pulled the balaclava from his face. 'I realised that in doing so, I might make things worse for myself,' she said. 'I then said something like "I'm not looking at you".'

For a moment, Rust was too consumed by lust to notice. He rolled the woman onto her stomach, pushed her legs apart and, with one hand, slid down her stockings and underwear. Then he regained his composure. 'Before he actually engaged in the sex act he said "I will kill you",' the woman said. 'He had something in his hand, and I realised it was a blade of some kind.' Bizarrely, Rust handed the knife to his victim and forced her to hold onto it while he raped her. He trusted – correctly – she was too afraid to consider attacking him. 'I was frightened I wouldn't be able to effectively protect myself,' she said. 'And if I couldn't, I would escalate the situation. He had already threatened to kill me and I was scared he might do it.'

The woman choked back her revulsion as Rust pushed his limp, flaccid penis inside her. He managed a weak ejaculation in just a few seconds. She did not even notice it happen – the sudden end of her ordeal was a great surprise. For a moment, she worried Rust was going to demand 'oral gratification' but he asked instead for the knife. 'I hesitated, as I didn't want to give it to him,' she said, 'but he said it again and I handed it to him.' Rust pocketed the weapon and picked the telephone up from her desk. 'I thought he was going to use the extension line to strangle me,' she said, 'and I kept saying, "I'm not looking at you".' Satisfied, the deviant pulled the phone out of the wall and left his victim alone in the dark. Not knowing where he was, the woman hurried out of the office and summoned help from some passers-by.

The ordeal – and the few things she did know of her attacker – would remain with her for years. 'When he spoke, his voice was very monotone,' she said. 'He didn't have an accent and he was very calm, except when he said he was going to kill me. His voice was soft, and I didn't get the impression he was the type of person who was assertive. But he did have control of what was happening – not angry or hostile, just someone who was fairly calm and in control. My impression was this was not the first time he had done this . . . he seemed very calculating and confident about what he was doing.'

Her subservient and submissive attitude, without doubt, saved her life. Rust would later tell Dr Nambier he'd not considered the incident rape at all. 'When presented with the opportunity and, as he claims, the encouragement by the victim after overpowering her, he could not resist the "invitation" to rape her,' the psychiatrist relayed in 2003. 'He was sufficiently aroused, and used power and force to satisfy his sexual urges.' Dr O'Brien said Rust truly believed his victim was consenting to have sex with him – that she 'wanted it'. 'I asked him why he did not kill the woman,' Dr O'Brien said, 'and he said, "It wasn't on my mind".'

Unlike Maya Jakic, who scoffed at his shrivelled penis, unlike the woman at Cumberland Park who dared to get away, unlike Megumi Suzuki – whose 'sin' against Rust will never be known – the woman gave the sex fiend what he wanted. It is only fitting, then, that she was the reason for his arrest – and that her bravery in exposing her tormentor led directly to justice for the Jelic and Suzuki families.

While running for her life, the woman had kept her wits about her. She memorised the licence plate of all the cars she passed, especially those in the car park of her building. For the first time ever, someone had taken notice of Rust.

It was a simple matter for police to check the details she provided against their database of sexual offenders. In short order, they swooped on Rust's parole address at Gilles Plains and arrested him. After a brief appearance in the Adelaide Magistrates Court – where his name and all details of his offences were subjected to a blanket media ban 'out of an abundance of caution' – Rust was transferred to the Port Augusta prison, 300 km north of the city. He was permitted, under the jail's rules, to bring along a few personal items. He chose Megumi's CD player.

As Rust became reacquainted with the prison system, Youichi and Masako Suzuki went public. In a 100-second video that ran on every news broadcast, they vowed to 'forgive everything' if their daughter simply made contact. 'Megumi, if you are watching this, I want you to come out as soon as possible,' Youichi said, breaking down. 'Sleepless nights for your father and mother continue every day. Family and friends in Japan are all worried about you. If you are really alive, please come out as soon as possible. There is nothing to worry about.' Masako agreed. 'Father and mother will definitely protect you from things to come,' she said. 'Please come out, please.'

There was no response.

On 23 August 2001, police gave up hope of finding Megumi alive. 'We just haven't got anything else since to support the Arkaba Hotel sighting,' Detective Senior Sergeant Feltus said. 'We feel sure someone would have come forward and said "enough is enough". We don't believe she is in hiding, we believe she has come to some harm.' He stopped short of criticising the man who had reported the sighting. 'The guy himself left an element of doubt,' he admitted. 'He said he was 99.9 per cent sure it was her. It's thrown our investigation into turmoil.'

Likewise, Chris Hamilton's life was in chaos. 'The police questioned Chris and bounced him around, telling him that even if he didn't kill Megumi then he was responsible for her death,' his mother, Sue, said in 2003. 'This was a statement that was repeated to him more than once during the investigation.' Just weeks after his 21st birthday, Mr Hamilton attempted suicide. It was only through the intervention of his family and remaining friends that he survived.

On 25 August, Youichi and Masako Suzuki returned to Japan. Life, whether they wanted it to or not, had to go on. Their son was due to celebrate his birthday and Youichi had to return to his work as a maths teacher. The departure coincided with a police admission that officers 'had few clues' as to Megumi's fate or whereabouts. The taskforce was scaled back from 40 officers to 12. Further interviews – including one with the friend who walked Megumi to the bus stop the night she was killed – failed to crystallise the perplexing picture. A final push was made on 10 September, when posters featuring Megumi were pasted across bus stops. Ironically, people in Adelaide began to compare the Megumi investigation with that of Maya Jakic, and spoke of the horror of having two foreigners killed in the same city, years apart, with no hope of solving the mystery of their deaths.

None of this sat well with Mark Rust. His thrills in life came from reaction and revulsion. The only way he could achieve a glimmer of sexual satisfaction was to know people were disgusted and horrified by what he had done. Two unsolved cases, infamous or not, could not provide the release he so desperately craved. There was but one thing to do . . . confess.

Sometime before 21 October 2001, Rust told his Port Augusta cellmate that he had killed both Maya Jakic and Megumi Suzuki. He told his fellow inmate – whose name would, during the resultant court proceedings, become yet another state secret – just enough details to ensure word would spread to the guards, to the warden, to the authorities. He sat calmly on his bunk as his cell was tossed, and made sure he pointed investigators toward the CD player he had taken from the Japanese student's defiled corpse. Prison staff quickly moved Rust to the jail's B-division, home of protected and high-risk inmates. On 21 October, Major Crime detectives attended the prison and formally arrested Rust for Maya's murder. They kept this fact from the public for 24 hours, announcing it only when Rust faced the Adelaide Magistrates Court the next day.

'It highlights investigations such as this are never closed,' Detective Superintendent Schramm said outside court. 'We have spoken to Ms Jakic's parents in Croatia and they are very pleased. It is reassuring for everyone.'

He declined to mention that John and Jagoda had divorced – the strain of the murder too much for their marriage – and that the grief-stricken mother spent her days knee-deep in the snow, weeping over Maya's grave. 'My life is now going to the cemetery every day, no matter if it is rain or snow, no matter if it's 38 degrees or -5 degrees,' Jagoda said in 2003. 'That's my future for the rest of my life – my life is sad and monotonous, always the same.'

On 30 October, the people of Adelaide were stunned to hear an arrest had been made for Megumi Suzuki's murder. Publicly, it seemed as if the case had dropped off the radar. Behind closed doors, officers had been encouraging Rust to give up his secrets and help them locate the teenager's body. And while he had confessed, detectives were taking no chances of having a possible trial prejudiced by media coverage. They asked for – and won – a blanket suppression on Rust's involvement in the crime. While the media knew, from the moment of his court appearance, that one man was responsible for two of the city's most heinous killings, the public would remain ignorant of the fact for two more years.

Not that the public was greatly concerned. The people of Adelaide had but one question: where was Megumi's body? Detective Superintendent Schramm refused to comment, saying only that Youichi and Masako Suzuki were once again en-route from Japan. 'There are things we need to discuss with them face-to-face rather than over the telephone,' he said. 'Investigations are at a sensitive stage.'

It was a massive understatement. Rust had been only too happy to admit to dumping Megumi's plastic-wrapped corpse in an industrial bin. It had, after all, created an entirely new nightmare for police. Like thousands of other bins in and around Adelaide, the bin containing Megumi's body had been picked up and emptied at a site belonging to Integrated Waste Management Services. It was located in Wingfield, a heavy industrial area west of Adelaide, and processed 500 tonnes of rubbish every day. Police began to prepare themselves – both logistically and mentally – for a massive, smelly, disgusting search that could take many months. The official line was that officers were 'cautiously optimistic', though several admitted the chances of finding the body were slim.

Youichi and Masako Suzuki returned to Adelaide on 31 October, traumatised by the latest developments. 'Perhaps now they can at least deal with the circumstances, now that someone has been charged with Megumi's death,' Detective Superintendent Schramm said hopefully. 'This ends three months of speculation.'

Consulate representative Amano also issued a public statement. 'The people of Japan are shocked by Miss Suzuki's death,' he said. 'People in Japan have heard a lot about this, and older people are very shocked. But they are also very grateful to police, because it was a difficult investigation.'

Difficult for none more so than the Suzukis. They faced the media once again on 3 November, clearly distraught. 'We have been praying for our daughter to be alive under any circumstances,' Youichi said, showing the level of desperation the family had experienced. 'This week we received the saddest news we could have.' He struggled on through tears. 'Megumi was only 18 years old, she was at the age when life is beginning to open up. She will not be able to live what should have been the best years of her life.' Recovering somewhat, he thanked police and the public for its support, and asked it continue until Megumi's body had been recovered. 'We desperately wish for her body to be found, we don't want to leave her alone too long,' he said. 'We want to take her back to Japan to be with her family.'

The excavation of Wingfield was to begin on 5 November, but was postponed several times due to weather and manpower considerations. Commitments back home beckoned, and the Suzukis once more returned to Japan empty-handed. More than two hundred police officers and community volunteers finally descended on the dump on 26 November, and their task was grisly.

Megumi had not simply been dumped somewhere amongst the mountainous piles of refuse and waste. Given the time and location she was killed, her body was likely somewhere inside one of dozens of compacted 'bales' of trash stacked around the property. Search teams not only had to dig through trash, they had to break it open and peer within.

Adelaide's weather only made the search worse. In November, the temperature begins to push the 35-degree mark with frightening regularity – three- or four-day stretches of unbearable heat are common. Wingfield is an area without natural shade, surrounded on all sides by freeways and exhaust fumes. The stench of cars mingled, each day, with the pungent wash of garbage. Searchers – many of whom were police cadets – were confronted at every turn by heat, flies and dust from substances many refused to think about. The only respite was a white marquee that was supposed to reflect the sunlight. Its effectiveness was debatable.

It was one of the most horrific tasks a person could be asked to perform, yet the 200-strong force did so with efficiency, courage and determination. Their efforts were rightly applauded by police hierarchy, the government, the public and, most importantly, the Suzukis. Now the mystery had been solved, no one would permit Megumi to continue to lie without dignity – even with the cost of the search expected to pass $1.5 million.

'It's a hard job, a dirty job and a smelly job – but it's a very important one,' Major Crime Superintendent Peter Simons told reporters. 'Finding the body is more important than any issue of cost. We are searching for anything that will give us an indication that Megumi's body may be there including potential weapons, clothing, school books or anything else she had on the day she was killed.' Their efforts were assisted by Integrated Waste Management Services's excellent record-keeping. Staff were able to point the teams to a 50 metre by 50 metre area of the dump that contained all of August's trash. There were 10,000 one-tonne bales to examine.

By day five of the search, 30 November, the teams had developed a system. They met at a local police station at 7 am, boarded buses and were at the dump by 7.30 am. They rifled through bales – spending 15 minutes on each one unless they found something suspicious – until the 10 am break, and continued until their shift ended at 12.15 pm. The second group took over from 12.45 pm, worked until 2.30 pm, then again until their shift finished at 5.15 pm. It was an operation with clockwork precision that produced immediate results – just not the ones police had been expecting.

On day five, an employee of a concreting and restoration business visited the excavation to help out. He found a charred, partly burned human head and arms in a steel drum.

Horrified by what had happened to Megumi, he immediately sought the help of police. A cursory scan was enough to know what DNA tests would later confirm: the severed pieces did not belong to the missing student. It was the head of John 'Joanne' Lillecrapp, a transvestite pro-wrestler and truck driver who had gone missing from his nearby home earlier that month. It was a break for officers assigned to that case but not for the Megumi team. Although, they would not have to wait much longer; Megumi's body was found on 7 December, less than 200 metres from Lillecrapp's head.

Youichi and Masako boarded their final flight to Adelaide. They took possession of Megumi's body after a post-mortem examination had been conducted by forensic experts. 'We realise it was a very difficult task considering the circumstances,' Youichi said. 'It is no exaggeration to say it was a miracle to find her so quickly. We thank the police who cared for us beyond their duty.'

The autopsy confirmed the story Rust had told his cellmate; that he had sexually assaulted the teenager before bashing her head in with a rock. Mourners plastered the front of Integrated Waste Management Services with cards, flowers and hand-made memorials. 'Megumi, we are very deeply sorry, you were a beautiful girl,' read one. 'Our heart goes out to your family. May you rest in peace.'

Youichi said he and his wife were given many 'nice, warm messages' about their daughter. 'We are really lucky that so many Australians supported us,' he said.

On 10 December, consulate representative Amano announced that Megumi would be cremated and buried in Adelaide, during a private ceremony at Centennial Park Cemetery – situated, in a hideous twist, just a few kilometres from the bin in which she had been dumped. This gruesome fact did not escape the Suzukis. They changed their minds on 14 December, opting to establish a permanent memorial to their daughter in the park but take her ashes back to Japan. Leaving the city for the final time, they damned Adelaide with faint praise. 'We don't want the people of Japan to misunderstand that Adelaide, with so many wonderful people, is a dangerous city,' Youicihi said. 'But we hope that Adelaide will prosper further as an ideal city for overseas students to pursue their studies.'

The Suzuki and Jelic families had their answers – but the community did not. Rust's name had been made public only in connection with Maya Jakic's murder. Eager to defend the twisted pervert's right to a fair trial, South Australia's courts obliterated the concepts of open and transparent justice by imposing numerous suppression orders on the case. Seven months would pass before even the briefest mention of the prosecution could be made without exposing the media to legal sanctions, fines or jail time. Even by 27 July 2002, the community could only be told a '37-year-old man from the northern suburbs' had been ordered to stand trial for Megumi's murder. Jury selection was to begin on 2 September.

It never went ahead. Rust's counsel announced he would plead guilty to both killings. He would also confess to the ATM assault and the Rose Park rape. That triggered another avalanche of secrecy. His counsel argued that, out of 'an abundance of caution', it was prudent to keep the public in the dark for as long as possible. The fact no jury would ever be called upon to determine Rust's guilt was seemingly unimportant. Defence lawyers feared for the 'proper administration of justice', convinced it would be 'prejudiced' should the deaths of Megumi and Maya be linked.

The media would not stand for it. On 2 May 2003, reporters sought – and were granted – permission to stand at the bar table and present lengthy, detailed submissions to Justice Margaret Nyland. They argued no one, least of all Rust, would suffer should the connection between the murders be revealed. They urged Her Honour to consider the public's right to know, and that justice must be seen to be done. Reporters found partial support from the Office of the Director of Public Prosecutions. Crown lawyers filed an application of their own – that the existing suppression orders be varied, not removed. They asked Rust's name and image remain a secret, but his involvement in both crimes be publicised.

It was a nonsense submission, but it met with Justice Nyland's approval. She made the order, then listened calmly as Rust pleaded guilty to every charge levelled against him. He showed little emotion as he did so, barking out a monotone 'guilty' after each count was read. Wasting no time, Justice Nyland imposed mandatory life sentences for each count of murder, ordering Rust serve them concurrently. She remanded him in custody 'to a date to be fixed' for sentencing on the other two offences.

Though severely hamstrung by the court's caution, the media was nonetheless able to give the community some insight into the events that befell both Maya Jakic and Megumi Suzuki. Members of the public who had been diligently following each case remembered Rust had been named in connection with Maya's death when he appeared in court the previous October. Despite Justice Nyland's orders, the name of Mark Errin Rust became an open secret in South Australia. Anyone who truly cared to know the killer's identity was easily able to figure it out. His name spread through the community like wildfire, exposing the base hypocrisy and utter uselessness of the state's obsession with suppression orders. The Supreme Court had, in truth, only hobbled itself by clearly demonstrating its lack of acumen and failure to understand how the world beyond the bar table truly worked.

Rust had what he'd always wanted – the attention of a disgusted audience. The woman he assaulted at the ATM was shocked to learn Megumi had been killed the night after her ordeal. 'It could have been pure luck, or he decided it was the rehearsal for what he was going to do the next night,' she said in 2003. 'Or he might have thought "No, it's not the right time". You just don't know what's going through their head. But it's been really hard for me to keep hearing people say how lucky I was. At times, I resent people for reminding me.' It did not help her healing. 'I was brought up to believe the world is a wonderful place with worthwhile people in it,' she wept. 'Unfortunately, I found out through this crime that I cannot always trust people. There are people out there who can and will hurt or change your life. This has put a tarnish on the way I see the world and the people in it.'

Craig, Rust's sole childhood friend, was wracked with guilt. 'The thing that will always be in my head is that, if I had come forward in 1999, Megumi Suzuki wouldn't have got killed,' he said in 2003.

The impotence of the court's secrecy order was obvious by 21 May. It was quickly dropped, and Rust's name and face became public knowledge. During that hearing, prosecutor Geraldine Davison tendered a thick bundle of documents including Rust's 18-page criminal history and victim impact statements written by Youichi and Masako Suzuki. 'They were prepared in Japanese and have been translated,' she said. 'It's their wish that these be read to the court at a later stage when sentencing submissions occur.' They would not, she noted, be returning to Adelaide for the case.

Her next application was unexpected. 'We ask that Your Honour embark upon an investigation under Section 23, and that Your Honour order two reports to be prepared by psychiatrists,' she said, nominating doctors Nambier and O'Brien for the task. 'They should inquire into Rust's mental state and his capacity – or incapacity – to control his sexual instincts.'

It was, at the time, relatively untested legislation. Section 23 of the *Criminal Law (Sentencing) Act 1988* states that a person convicted of an offence that has a sexual component – be it rape, unlawful sexual intercourse or a lust-driven murder – can be imprisoned indefinitely as an uncontrollable sex predator. To make such a ruling, the court must have psychiatric evidence supporting the conclusion that the offender is 'unwilling to control their sexual instincts' and therefore poses a 'significant risk' of re-offending in a similar manner. It is one of the harshest and most crushing penalties a court can impose, as the indefinite detention does not begin until after the expiration of the prison sentence. In the case of Rust, Ms Davison was effectively asking the court to lock him up and throw away the key. Someone had finally paid some attention to the danger he posed.

Michael Boylan, QC, for Rust, was caught unawares. 'I don't have instructions to oppose that course at this stage,' he said, asking for a three-week adjournment. 'There are other inquiries which I wish to make, and I require an adjournment at least until we decide whether we are opposing the Section 23 application.' Going one step further, he asked

Justice Nyland to not even contemplate such a penalty until he had instructions.

She declined, saying Rust's was an 'appropriate case' for analysis. 'It would be difficult for you to persuade me not to embark upon that course,' she said levelly.

'With respect,' Mr Boylan said coolly, 'I'm not surprised about that.'

Dr Nambier filed his report with the court on 21 August, based on two sessions spent with the killer. He found Rust co-operative, but noted it was difficult to clarify some details of his past. 'I originally took this as being related to deficient memory and poor verbal skills,' he said. 'However, having interviewed him on two occasions, there were some inconsistencies in his accounts for some events which suggest a reluctance to provide details or, at least, gave the impression that he was weighing things up in his mind before providing answers.'

Notably, Dr Nambier did not discuss the murders with Rust, feeling that was beyond his mandate. He focused instead on the man's childhood, sexual history and 'very abnormal behaviour patterns'. 'His offender record shows underlying antisocial aspects to Rust's personality,' he explained. 'This has gradually crescendoed, over time, to more and more serious offences against the person, culminating in two murders.' Those crimes, he said, haunted Rust. 'Since being incarcerated, Rust has been feeling "down and out",' he reported. 'He once said "I wish I was dead" and that he had contemplated suicide.' Rust told the doctor he had considered suffocating himself, or using a razor blade, but lacked the courage for either. 'He recalled having visions of the murder victims in his dreams, as well as intrusive images of the victims, dead, while he was awake,' Dr Nambier noted. 'He also alluded to voices that talked to him during his dreams.'

Parallel to this was the fostering of 'deviant sexual behaviours' that had left Rust 'driven by an absolute preoccupation with sex'. 'His need for sexual gratification is continuing to escalate,' Dr Nambier said, 'and he is a man focused on surrendering to his sexual impulses. It became the focus of his life.' The more confidence Rust had in his sexual potency, Dr Nambier said, the more heinous his crime would be. 'In my opinion,' he concluded, 'Rust remains a great risk of being unable to control his sexual impulses.'

Dr O'Brien's report, filed a short time later, backed up those fears. Unlike his colleague, he had encouraged Rust to speak about his crimes in great detail, and so gained a different – but equally chilling – insight into the murderer. 'I asked Rust what his fundamental problem was,' he said, 'to which he replied "I don't know, that's what I want to find out". He told me he felt terrible about what he had done and was "disgusted". He conceded that if he had not been apprehended, his exhibitionism would have continued and even maybe more killings.' Dr O'Brien said Rust's issue was the 'gradual emergence of aggressive rape fantasies' coupled with his 'ever-increased anger toward women'. 'It's my opinion that Rust is an extremely dangerous individual with a high probability that he would re-offend in a similar manner should he be released from custody,' he concluded. 'I do not have any alternative other than to state that, at the present time, Mark Errin Rust is unable to control his sexual instincts.'

On 27 November 2003, the Supreme Court reconvened. Justice Nyland had yet to decide whether she was prepared to jail Rust indefinitely and so wanted to give those affected by his crimes a chance to tell him, face to face, of their pain. Jagoda Jelic did not attend the hearing. Nor did Youichi or Masako Suzuki. The parents were all overseas now, spending much of their time at the graves of their lost children. Youichi and Masako had kept Megumi's ashes in their home for almost two years, only interring her in the family plot when begged to by their friends, family and religious leaders. Their grief was overwhelming.

Jagoda's friend, Eva Gregov, confronted Rust in her stead. She could not keep the fury from her voice. 'I can only say to you that you have not only killed and taken the life of Maya, you have also completely destroyed the life of her family,' she spat before sitting back down.

Fusae Simpson, who served as translator for the Suzukis during their multiple trips, read their statements to the court. 'It drives me insane when I think about Megumi being treated like rubbish and buried in a rubbish dump for four months,' Masako's statement read. 'My heart becomes filled with bitterness and anger when I think about how my daughter's dreams and future were stolen. Why did she, who wanted to help others, have to be killed? I hate Rust so much as to feel I could kill him. The law should be more severe to murderers.'

Hatred also filled her husband's statement. 'Can you understand a father's feeling that I will never again be called "Papa" by my beautiful daughter?' it read. 'I'm so sad that I will not hear her voice again. Rust brutally ended our daughter's precious life when she was just about to blossom, and left an eternal scar on our hearts. For this reason, I will never be able to forgive him.'

They were not the only ones touched by Rust. Chris Hamilton had attended the hearing, armed with a statement of his own. His rage and fury at the murder and at the way he had been treated by police finally had outlet. 'My life has been all but destroyed since the murder,' he yelled, edging toward hysteria. 'I'm a mere shadow of who I used to be and I now have nothing left to live for. You did the most despicable and awful thing anyone could do to such a beautiful young person. You took her life, and ruined the lives of those who cared for her. You have as good as killed me, too – just know that I will spend whole days at her grave at Centennial Park, crying and retching.'

Though he struggled valiantly against the destructive feelings within his chest, much of the fiery abuse he targeted at Rust from the bar table was lost in amongst his choking sobs. 'Because of your disgusting nature and the incapability of the police team who handled her case, I have now become as a dead man would be – having no desire to live and no dreams left,' he yelled at the killer. 'There is no way you can be punished sufficiently for all you have done, for the horrors you have brought into this world of horrors. May you outlive me in your life of suffering.'

Rust was taken back into custody and remained there for another five months. Clearly struggling with her decision, Justice Nyland did not reconvene the court until 27 April 2004. Maya Jakic had, by that time, been dead for five years and 15 days. Megumi Suzuki had been murdered two years, eight months and 25 days earlier. Her judgement was well worth the wait. First, she refused to give Rust a non-parole period. Then she jailed him indefinitely as an uncontrollable sex predator. The only chance he would ever have of release was to convince psychiatrists he had reigned in the beast within, and then apply to the court for the setting of a non-parole period. Given the hundreds of pages of evidence condemning his grotesque nature, such a chain of events was so unlikely as to be impossible.

It was a punishment most fitting for Rust – and one he had earned a long, long time before. But he had slipped through the cracks so many times – escaped prosecution, dodged jail time, evaded psychiatric analysis – only because the authorities had failed to properly identify the extreme danger he posed. As much as any of his institutionalised cellmates, Rust was a product of the system; a mad dog who had been allowed to assault and disgust, to rape and kill, because no one had paid attention to his deviancy.

The deaths of Megumi Suzuki and Maya Jakic, the suffering of the women at Cumberland Park and Rose Park, were as much the fault of South Australia's flawed criminal justice system as they were the depraved killer himself. Of this, Masako Suzuki had no doubt. 'My daughter's life would not have ended in this wasteful way,' she said in 2003, 'if Mark Errin Rust had not been free to walk the streets.'

Z for Zorro, D for Devotion
Roman Jadrych

Three angry, red scars on her cheek formed the letter Z. Her neck, shoulders and arms were hideously tattooed with another 37 deep cuts, each one at least 12 centimetres long. The tiny, slightly built woman moved stiffly, but commanded the attention of everyone sitting in the Holden Hill Magistrates Court. For the first time, Janina Jadrych was going to speak publicly about the ultimate betrayal – about being attacked, in broad daylight, by a man she trusted with her life. About being savaged by her tall, powerfully built husband of 20 years. The spectators waited to hear her denounce Roman Ignatius Jadrych; to ask he be kept far away from her, their daughters and their grandchildren.

Instead, Janina Jadrych faced the court on 16 January 2003 insisting prosecutors drop all charges against her husband and allow him to return, immediately, to their marital home.

◆

The story of Janina and Roman Jadrych is unique, even amongst Adelaide's macabre criminal history. It is, on the surface, a tale of shattered trust – of a husband using the ultimate level of force against the mother of his children, of a man deliberately and viciously spilling the blood of his wife. But it is also a tale of love, between both a couple and the members of a family. In the face of one of the most appalling crimes in the city's history, the Jadrych clan banded together and would not allow anything – including the law – to come between them and the life of which they dreamed. Janina, especially, refused to compromise and would accept nothing but the restoration of the status quo. Even if that meant facing down the Director of Public Prosecutions, the Magistrates Court and the Supreme Court by herself.

Prior to 2002, the Jadrych family had lived a quiet life in Wynn Vale, an upper-middle-class suburb 20 minutes north-east of the city. It is one of several neighbourhoods that make up the City of Tea Tree Gully – a council that, since the early 1980s, has experienced an unending boom of good fortune. International development powerhouse Delfin chose the area for one of their mass-housing creations. A once-rural area known as Golden Grove became a high-class housing estate complete with shopping malls, fancy cafes, recreational facilities and three high schools. Eager to attract families, Delfin created large tracts of open green space and kept them heavily watered – no mean feat in forever drought-ravaged South Australia. Their lack of environmental concern paid big dividends; Golden Grove was named the 'world's best residential development' by the International Real Estate Federation in 1998, and 'Australia's best master-planned development' by the Urban Development Institute of Australia in 2003.

It was an idyllic place for the Jadrych clan, who originated from Poland. Roman worked as a psychiatric nurse, tending to both the heartbreakingly vulnerable and the criminally insane. Janina was a housewife and mother, caring for the couple's daughters and their grandchildren. They bought their groceries at the Golden Grove Village Shopping Centre, north of their home, and often ate at the nearby, Italian-themed Cafe Primo restaurant. On Roman's days off, the couple would take their dog for a walk down one of the many pathways through the parks.

So it was on 8 November 2002. Roman and Janina took their dog for a walk to Civic Park – a multi-use open space area adjacent to the Tea Tree Gully Council Chambers. Though a popular area for families, Civic Park was not overly busy that day. The couple nodded and gave polite greetings to the four adults and one child they passed as they walked. Roman lagged behind his wife momentarily; thinking nothing of it, she continued on.

Without warning, Roman rushed Janina from behind and forced her to the ground. He then produced a 40-centimetre carving knife and stabbed Janina 40 times in the arms, shoulders and neck. In a gruesome finale, witnessed by the passers-by and the child, Roman held his wife very still, turned her right cheek toward him and carved the letter Z into her flesh.

Roman stood up, leaving his wife in a spreading pool of her own blood, and turned to walk away. The stunned witnesses did not follow the knife-wielding man, choosing instead to check on Janina. Amazingly, she was still alive. Roman was completely unaware of this fact, as proven by his subsequent actions. With the bloody weapon still in his hand, he walked a few hundred metres to the council chambers and stepped inside. His face a mask of unnatural calm, Roman attracted the attention of staff behind the counter and asked they call the police. 'I've just killed my wife,' he told them.

Police soon arrived, with the media following closely behind. Through radio reports – and, later, television and newspaper stories – word of the grisly encounter quickly spread. Tea Tree Gully residents were shocked and appalled. Many had moved to Golden Grove and its surrounds to get away from violence. They had 'traded up' from dingy, crime-ridden areas like Elizabeth, Salisbury and Munno Para in order to have a new lease on life. They and their children were supposed to be safe now, from knives and assaults and madmen. They had thought – naively, hopefully, incorrectly – that the steep, four-laned curve of the Grove Way was enough to separate them from crime. The stabbing of Janina Jadrych was a wake-up call for the world's best address; an unmissable reminder that no suburb of South Australia, irrespective of its standing on the world stage, was immune to Adelaide's bizarre and blood-thirsty influence. Worst of all, there seemed to be no explanation as to why the crime had occurred.

Roman was loaded into the back of a van and taken to the Holden Hill Police Station, where he was interviewed at length and charged with attempted murder. In a surprising development, he was granted bail and released to live with his parents at their Fulham Gardens home. Police were not, at the time, prepared to justify nor explain their decision. They did, however, insist on pointing out the strict conditions attached to his release. Roman was not to see, contact or approach Janina – who had been rushed to hospital and successfully treated – in any way.

On 16 January 2003, Roman appeared before the Holden Hill Magistrates Court. He arrived in a car with his parents and one of his teenage daughters. As soon as the group passed through the security station at the front of the court, a second car arrived carrying Janina and the couple's other daughter. It was an exercise in clockwork precision that would be repeated many times before the prosecution against Roman had been completed. Janina entered the court building and took a seat near the doors of courtroom two. Roman was 200 metres away, as per his bail conditions, sitting by the doors to courtroom four. They shared a quick, distant smile before their daughters began crossing the space between them, whispering into the ears of their parents. It was the closest husband and wife had been since the attack – Roman's bail address was almost 30 kilometres from the home he had once shared with Janina.

Just after 2.15 pm, Roman's matter was called on before Magistrate Charles Eardley. A tall, gangly adjudicator with a shock of white hair, a gravelly voice and a neatly trimmed moustache, Magistrate Eardley was a well-liked eccentric. A lower-back problem made it difficult for him to sit down for long periods; he would stand at the head of the court and pontificate from a lectern. It was an impressive and unusual sight, even for Adelaide's courts. Possessed of a sharp mind and even sharper temper, Magistrate Eardley suffered no fools in his court and had little time for sentimentality. Unfortunately, he was about to encounter both.

Prosecutor James Stewart wasted no time in outlining his difficulties. 'Janina Jadrych has refused to comply with police requests for a declaration or statement,' he said. 'She is, therefore, not going to be a witness for the prosecution.'

Magistrate Eardley looked down in clear disbelief. 'This cannot go on,' he boomed, already annoyed. 'I don't want to just be reading witness statements – I've already spent weeks reading witness statements.'

Mr Stewart reassured him that, from his perspective, the matter was ready to be committed for trial. 'It's no secret between the Crown and defence counsel that Mrs Jadrych has not been co-operating,' he said. 'We do not have permission, from Mrs Jadrych, to access her medical records without a subpoena. We do, however, have eyewitnesses who saw her being stabbed. And we say the act of a knife going into the victim's body 40 times is enough for Your Honour to find there is a case to answer before the Supreme Court.'

Roman's lawyer, Stephen Ey, did not share that confidence. 'Without the medical records, I don't know how my friend can prove there are 40 stab wounds,' he smiled. 'I find the Crown's attitude in this matter quite difficult.' He suggested a different approach – throwing the case out entirely. 'I am therefore prepared to have the matter set down so that I can argue there is no case for my client to answer,' he offered helpfully.

Magistrate Eardley's temper red-lined. 'Today's hearing was for Jadrych to enter a plea,' he growled. 'If you want some more time to read the statements, Mr Ey, then I will adjourn the case and order your client enter a plea in one month's time. And if you want to do anything else in the meantime, then I suggest you do it quickly.'

Defence counsel, as it turned out, already had a goal in mind – altering his client's bail so he could return home and live, once again, with his wife and daughters. Janina had prepared a declaration, he said, in support of this goal.

Mr Stewart would have none of it. 'This was a savage and unprovoked attack upon the victim,' he argued. 'There has been no indication, from either the victim or defence, as to why it happened, aside from numerous references in the record of police interview to "mental health" and "medication". The Crown does not know the current state of Jadrych's mental health, and nor does the court. We hold grave fears for the safety of Janina Jadrych, given she was not adequately able to defend herself on the last occasion. There's simply nothing before Your Honour to alleviate those fears.'

Mr Ey said the Crown had no heart for romance. 'The prosecution is putting itself in the way of the renewal of their relationship,' he said, blind to Magistrate Eardley's puzzled expression. 'I don't see how the prosecution can stand in the way of that.'

Nor, it appeared, did Janina Jadrych. She stood up and walked, stiffly, to join Mr Ey at the bar table. She held several pieces of paper in her right hand. 'This is a declaration,' she began, but was quickly cut off.

'Mrs Jadrych, I'm not disposed to vary your husband's bail today,' Magistrate Eardley said, waving away her protests. 'You are the alleged victim in this case, and there is no justification for allowing you and your alleged attacker to live together in the same home. If you will not look after your safety, then the court will.'

Disappointed, the family split into two groups and left the court. Roman emerged first and returned to his car with his daughters. Janina left almost a half-hour later, and made a point of smiling at photographers and cameramen waiting in the car park. Her mother-in-law spoke briefly to reporters. 'It's a terrible thing,' she said, 'that Roman spent so much time with sick people, only to end up sick himself.'

The case returned to court on 27 February 2003. Once again, Janina and Roman made their carefully timed arrivals, one after the other, and sat the requisite distance apart in the courthouse. This time, the space between them was repeatedly crossed by a kindergarten-aged relative. The little girl happily moved from lap to lap, chatting all the while. Mr Ey arrived some time later, and spoke with both husband and wife before the case was called on.

If Magistrate Eardley had hoped for a plea, he was to be disappointed. There would be no plea, Mr Ey informed the court, owing to the need for further time to deal with materials relevant to the case. Instead, in a display of his tenacity – and Janina's determination – he renewed his application to alter his client's bail conditions. 'We have here a husband and wife who need to be able to communicate at what is a difficult time,' he said. 'The Director of Public Prosecutions is trying to prevent that husband and wife from establishing contact. It's not for the DPP to play God with relationships, like they're endeavouring to do here.'

Mr Stewart had reached the limit of his tolerance. 'It's an act of God that Mrs Jadrych is still even here,' he interrupted. 'While we respect her wishes to have contact with her husband, the application is still opposed simply for her safety.' The adjournment had done wonders for the Crown's storehouse of information. 'We have witness reports of the alleged attack, saying they saw a man holding her down and stabbing her,' he said. 'We have photos of the stab wounds that are significant and multiple, and declarations from staff at the council chambers that Jadrych came in and told them he'd murdered his wife. What was the motivating factor behind this attack? It was savage and macabre. The facial injuries were disturbing – he carved a Z, like Zorro, into her face! It's a serious, serious matter.'

Magistrate Eardley was somewhat moved by the situation. 'The court isn't satisfied that there's justification, at this stage, for a variation of the conditions of bail,' he said, turning to look at Janina. 'The application is refused – however,

I'm prepared to vary another of the conditions to enable communication between Mr and Mrs Jadrych.'

It was a start. Though still banned from being within 200 metres of one another, Roman and Janina could now speak on the telephone. Again, Roman left the court first. He carried the little girl in his arms – the little girl covered his face with her own head and hand. Once he was safely in his car, she ran back across the car park and into the courthouse. Moments later, the little girl resumed her 'human shield' duties for Janina, covering the woman's face with her long, curly hair.

Janina's determination earned the couple another victory two months later. In April, Magistrate Eardley permitted Roman 'supervised access' to his wife twice a week. The couple were to be chaperoned, at all times, by his bail guarantors – his parents. Their court-enforced old-fashioned 'courting' continued, without incident, past Roman's appearance in court on 15 May. During the brief hearing, he pleaded not guilty to one count of attempted murder and was ordered to face the Supreme Court the following month.

Timing their arrivals at the Supreme Court was not as easy as it had been north-east of the city. Unlike the Holden Hill Magistrates Court, the central seat of Adelaide justice does not have its own car park. Located in, quite literally, the centre of the CBD, the Sir Samuel Way Building shares a block with the Central Market shopping precinct. On 16 June 2003, Roman and Janina once again arrived separately and within minutes of one another, all without breaching the 200-metre barrier. She came first, having parked north of the courthouse. He came from the south about five minutes later. By the time Roman arrived, Janina had taken a seat on the north wall of the building, roughly 200 metres from where he chose to sit. The only time they came closer to one another was when it was allowed by law – when each took their seat within the courtroom itself.

The hearing, before Justice John Perry, was incredibly brief. Roman repeated his plea of not guilty and was remanded on continuing bail for two months. Janina did not speak at all, and left seemingly without acknowledging her husband. Speculation was rife – had there been some form of lover's quarrel? Had prosecutors somehow managed to change Janina's mind, or elicit some form of evidence from her?

The answers came on 26 August, when Janina read a pre-prepared affidavit to the court. In such a huge courtroom, she looked even tinier than she had in the Magistrates Court, but her words were impossible to ignore. In precise and eloquent terms, her affidavit summarised the feelings of a woman who, quite clearly, put her role as a wife and a mother well ahead of the concerns of the criminal justice system.

'I have been married to Roman Ignatius Jadrych for approximately 20 years,' Janina said. 'We have two daughters together, aged 18 and 17. Since his arraignment, I've only been allowed to see my husband twice a week whilst under supervision. I wish to see my husband on more than two occasions each week, however.' It was often difficult, she explained, to arrange a convenient time for the family to be together. 'I've found contact with my husband has been of great benefit to myself and my children,' she continued. 'I believe that it's important for our relationship and the unity of our family that we are able to see each other without supervision. I believe it's important for our daughters to see both myself and Roman together without supervision in order for them to feel they are part of a family that loves and cares about each other.

'Roman Jadrych has been a wonderful husband to me, and father to his daughters. I believe our relationship is strengthening, and will continue to do so. These proceedings against Roman are causing me much anguish and I feel tender emotionally. I feel that strengthening my relationship with him will be of great support and benefit to me. Thank you.'

Mr Ey insisted it was time for the supervised access to end. Jane Abbey, prosecuting, strongly disagreed. 'Without stating the obvious, this is a very serious and violent offence,' she said. 'There are serious concerns for Mrs Jadrych and her ongoing safety. The psychological reports we have so far recommend contact, but only if it is supervised.'

The court ordered a follow-up report, saying it wanted time to consider its decision. Roman left the building immediately – there was a car waiting, its engine running, in the taxi rank outside. He pushed past the waiting media, covering his face with his arm, and leaped into the back seat.

Photographers and cameramen readied themselves to film Janina. She did not appear. For more than an hour, the media waited to get a glimpse of the wife willing to forgive the unforgivable crime. Still, she did not emerge from the building. It was later discovered she had found herself a quiet spot in one of the witness waiting rooms on the building's fifth floor. There she remained until 5 pm, when the court closed and the media was long gone.

The couple repeated their now-familiar synchronised entrance on 5 September. Mr Ey was also stuck on repeat – he wanted to continue the bail variation argument immediately. Ms Abbey, however, said there was a more important issue to deal with. 'We have just received a psychological report saying Jadrych has a mental incompetence defence,' she said. It was the first clear sign of a motive for the crime – that Jadrych may have been insane, at least temporarily, when he took the knife to his wife's face. 'The Crown is still considering its position and needs to investigate the matter further, given both reports attribute his behaviour to anti-depressant medications.'

Justice Margaret Nyland said she saw benefit in being cautious and waiting 'for another few weeks' and more tests before allowing the couple to be alone together. But Mr Ey would not be silenced. 'Our psychological reports say Jadrych no longer suffers from psychosis, and has not since early this year,' he insisted. 'They say he is safe, and the authors of those reports are in the best position to assess that because they've been seeing my client for quite some time now.'

He said it was for Janina, not the prosecution, to worry about her safety. 'We are at the point, now, where unsupervised access is crucial to their ongoing relationship,' he said. 'They are Polish, and obviously the family unit is quite important to them. It is the family's opinion their relationships can be furthered only by unsupervised contact. Janina Jadrych feels quite safe with her husband. There is no reason this change to the bail conditions cannot be made right now.'

Ms Abbey was unmoved. 'The Crown continues its opposition,' she said. 'If that causes a delay in the repairing of their relationship, then that's an unfortunate consequence – but it's not a proper reason to grant a bail variation and let this couple be alone, unsupervised.'

Justice Nyland – an expert in mental health cases, renowned for her emphasis on rehabilitation – split the decision down the middle. 'I'm inclined to make a partial variation and let there be one occasion of unsupervised access per week for an interim period,' she said. 'If there are no problems in that time, there will be a situation where supervision could be completely abandoned. I think I would feel more comfortable with that.' She then spoke directly to Janina. 'I understand your enthusiasm,' she said, 'but I'm still concerned about your safety given the seriousness of the allegations. This is a moderate approach, and might be unduly conservative, but it's what I feel comfortable with.' Janina's expression did not change. She simply nodded.

Roman and Janina had finally achieved a real victory – not that it was apparent from their behaviour. Granted the right, at last, to be together, the couple left court separately once again, each running to a different waiting car. Their hard, closed expressions betrayed no happiness – no hint of emotion at all – and served as a preview to the course the case would take for the remainder of the year.

Given the sensitivity of the possible mental health defence, the prosecution of Roman Jadrych was shifted into the 'directions' list – South Australia's politically correct term for secret, closed-court hearings. Not only were the public banned from attending the next few court appearances, the media was banned from reporting what went on during them. Even now, years after the finalisation of the case, the details of Roman's 19 September and 17 October appearances cannot be published. Further, the transcripts from both hearings cannot be accessed by the public, and are not included in the Supreme Court's own file on the matter. Such is South Australia's obsession with secrecy – once a matter is classi- fied, it remains that way forever.

As a result, Roman's 18 March 2004 court date was some- thing of a surprise. Justice Tim Anderson held the matter in open court, and began by announcing he was prepared to find Roman not guilty of attempted murder by reason of mental incompetence. In South Australia, insanity defences are governed by part 8A of Section 269 of the *Criminal Law Consolidation Act 1935*. It holds that a person found to have been mentally incompetent at the time they committed an offence is not guilty of said offence because one must have knowledge, and intent, to commit a crime. However, it does not erase the crime altogether – the person is still found to have done the thing with which they were charged, they are merely not to be criminally sanctioned for it.

In the case of Roman Jadrych, the court was therefore prepared to say he did stab Janina 40 times, and he did carve a Z for Zorro into her face – but none of those acts were a crime because he was insane at the moment he perpetrated them. Because of the secrecy blanket thrown over the case, one can only speculate as to the cause of Roman's madness, how it had been cured, and whether it was a temporary 'psychotic break' or the final manifestation of a long-term, undiagnosed problem. As with many matters that pass through South Australia's shuttered justice system, the public will simply never know.

On 18 March, the Crown was represented by its third prosecutor, Adele Andrews. She tendered a bundle of nine reports – authored by three separate psychiatrists – which she said proved Roman was mentally incompetent when he stabbed Janina. Justice Anderson accepted them, saying he was satisfied with their diagnosis. He further found the 'objective elements' of the case – the number of stab wounds, the manner in which they were delivered, the observations of witnesses and the statements of council staff – proven beyond reasonable doubt.

He remanded Roman on continuing bail until August, at which time he intended to set a 'limiting term'. Under Section 269, a 'limiting term' is a period a person is to be under the care and supervision of mental health professionals. The law requires it be equal to the jail sentence that would be imposed for the same situation had the person been mentally competent. In the case of murder, for example, an insane killer would be subject to a lifetime of psychological and psychiatric treatment in an institution. Roman's circumstances – including his supposed rehabilitation – would likely lead to him being counselled as an outpatient while living in the community.

It would have been the end of the hearing, had it not been for Mr Ey. He had been instructed, by both his client and Janina, to make one final push on behalf of their love. 'This matter has a long history and over a long period of time there have been a number of bail variations,' he said. 'Now we've come to the stage we are at, it's my application that there be a further variation, and that my client be permitted to reside in Wynn Vale – that's the matrimonial home.' He said there was no longer any reason to keep husband and wife apart. 'She and his guarantors have indicated they agree with the variation of bail. And I understand the prosecution has no objection.'

Ms Andrews confirmed the Crown's opposition had ended – to a point. 'My only concern is there is no indication, in any of the psychiatric or psychological reports, as to whether a move back to Wynn Vale is appropriate at this time,' she qualified. 'I'm a little concerned from a mental health point of view.'

She was not alone. 'So am I, Mr Ey,' Justice Anderson added. 'I just wonder whether this is a bit premature.'

Mr Ey argued the move should have happened long before. 'There have been previous relaxations of the bail, so much so that Jadrych is entitled to be with his wife daily,' he explained, hinting at events that had transpired within the directions hearings. 'That's been the wish of Janina Jadrych, and it's her wish her husband now be reunited with both her and their family.' The decision, he argued, was a no-brainer. 'He's currently entitled, really, to spend an indefinite time with his wife.'

Justice Anderson did not miss the point. 'What you are putting to me is that, effectively, Jadrych can be at the home already,' he said. 'He can spend 23 hours a day there and go home to his parents for an hour, technically, and not be in breach of his bail.'

'Your Honour is quite right,' Mr Ey agreed. 'Effectively, my client is entitled to be with his wife for 23 hours and 59 minutes of every day.'

Justice Anderson then asked Janina to stand up. 'You have heard what we've been talking about and you are content with this course?' he asked.

'Yes,' she replied, finally showing the court a slight hint of a smile.

His Honour turned back to Ms Andrews. 'I understand your initial apprehension, which was the same as mine,' he said, 'but I think with having it explained by Mr Ey, I'm content to make the variation.' He then spoke to Roman. 'Just in case there's anything you do not understand about what has happened today, you make sure you ask Mr Ey,' he warned. 'If you do not understand anything, or you are not sure about something, you make sure you ask Mr Ey.'

Like his wife, Roman smiled. 'No, everything is quite clear, thank you,' he said from the dock.

The final restriction on Roman and Janina – which, truthfully, existed in theory only – had been removed. When Justice Anderson adjourned the court, Roman left the secured area and walked straight over to his wife. She looped an arm around his waist and stood close to him, chatting with their family and with Mr Ey. For the first time since January 2003, there were no games outside court. Janina and Roman left the building side by side and walked slowly toward the northern car park.

The couple came to court hand-in-hand on 24 June for a status hearing. Justice Anderson wanted to know how things had progressed since the bail variation. Janina was more than happy to tell him. 'There's no change from the way we were before all this,' she said under oath. 'My husband works and does the normal things we used to do.' Indeed, Roman had returned to work within the medical profession – but not as a psychiatric nurse. He had taken a position at Ashford Hospital, a private health facility just south of the city, and was there most days. The couple had also resumed their routines around Wynn Vale and Golden Grove, and were regularly seen dining at Cafe Primo. Roman, notably, refrained from sampling the wine list – Ms Andrews had successfully sought to have him banned from drinking alcohol both before the setting of, and for the duration of, his limiting term.

That term was imposed by Justice Anderson on 12 August 2004. In a three-page document, he ordered Roman to remain under mental health care and supervision for ten years, back-dating the term to his arrest on 8 November 2002. Roman was required to regularly see his psychiatrist and obey all of his directions, especially blood tests to monitor his compliance with medication. Aside from medication prescribed by his psychiatrist, Roman was banned from using, possessing or administering any other form of drug – including alcohol – and was subject to random urine and blood tests to ensure he had not broken the rules. Finally, Justice Anderson ordered Roman liable to immediate detention in an asylum at the discretion of his doctors or because of any breach of his release conditions. Roman happily signed his name to the last page of the document, no doubt eager to continue his rehabilitation and his life.

It was to be the final court appearance for Roman and Janina Jadrych. They had come alone, unaccompanied by family or friends, and were blind to the waiting media. Utterly unconcerned by the attention they garnered, the Jadrychs could have been any couple going for a stroll through the city. Neither sought to shield their face, and Janina did not blink when cameramen zeroed in on her right-hand side. The scars, by that time 16 months old, were still visible – and likely always would be. They would remain forever etched into her flesh, an indelible reminder of the love she felt for her husband, the forgiveness she was able to provide to him, and her unflagging determination to turn the other cheek to his unprovoked violence.

A Monster Unmasked

Trevor John Brooks

Note: the names of victims and their families have been changed.

Hayley spent eight years terrified of a man whose face she had never seen. 'When you've been raped, you fear for your safety,' she said in October 2003. 'You don't go anywhere on your own and you certainly don't stay home alone at night. The worst thing is looking over your shoulder at everyone, or staring at people in queues. You fear he might be out there, the rapist, and you don't know what he looks like.'

From 1995 until 2000, the northern suburbs of Adelaide were stalked by a masked madman. Each of his deviant, frenzied attacks followed the same pattern: he would undress outside his victim's home, break in while naked, force his victim to perform humiliating and grotesque sex acts and then flee. Three women suffered his sick excesses; a fourth endured far worse. On that occasion, the rapist brought along a friend, and the duo – clad in Ku Klux Klan hoods – victimised her for more than an hour. Between each crime, the pervert would all but vanish. Months, sometimes years, would pass before he would strike again. The only evidence of his passing was broken women, crushed souls and DNA samples.

On television, they tell you DNA is a crime-solving miracle; a wondrous scientific advancement that puts every depraved animal in the cage they deserve. Television, sadly, does not match up to the twisted reality that claimed those four women. Samples taken by police did nothing more than link each of the masked man's crimes to the other; he existed on no offender's database, making a match impossible. There was nothing anyone – victims, police, the courts – could do but wait for a breakthrough. For almost a decade, they waited. And when the rapist was finally unmasked, he immediately pulled on another disguise – that of an amnesia-stricken, doting husband and father.

◆

The sexually charged rampage began on 25 January 1995 in Elizabeth. Located 28 kilometres north of Adelaide, the suburb was established as part of a 1955 'satellite city' plan. The object was to create safe, reliable, low-rent housing over 3000 acres of former farming land, thereby encouraging the spread of the state's rapidly increasing population. Many of the thousands of new dwellings were controlled by the Housing Trust, an authority responsible for finding homes for low-income earners. The problem, so obvious in hindsight, was that the Elizabeth development placed many struggling families of incompatible ethnic and social beliefs next door to one another. The result was violence and high crime rates. The very name of the area quickly became a derogatory term.

Nevertheless, good people still lived in Elizabeth. Hayley, who shared a modest home with her husband and two sons, was one of them. 'My life was one that would present to the community as made up of a loving and devoted husband, good children, a nice family home and a working mum,' she said in 2003. 'My life was generally one of contentment. I had a family that worked together to achieve its goals, and a family that played together to develop relationships.'

Play was very much on the family's mind in April 1995. Hayley's husband and sons had decided to use a long weekend for the time-honoured tradition of a fishing trip. Hayley waved them goodbye, thrilled to see her boys 'all packed up and excited' for the adventure to come. Her own plans were very simple: taking a well-deserved break by indulging in books and television.

Late that night, Hayley heard a man's voice coming from somewhere inside the house. She called her husband's name, wondering if he and their sons had returned unexpectedly. The voice responded, claiming to be her husband. Instantly, Hayley knew that could not be so – the voice was alien to her, utterly unfamiliar. Before she could panic, a naked man leaped upon her. He was in a frenzy, breathing heavily and muttering, and all he wore was a mask that obscured his features. Shrugging off her attempts to defend herself, he tore Hayley's clothes from her body. Ignoring her pleas, he raped her – savagely, viciously – twice.

'I felt petrified,' Hayley said later. 'I feared not only for my safety but for my life. I remember pleading with the man not to harm me. I remember explaining that I had two young sons and saying, "So please, don't harm me". But harm me he did. No one can see the scars . . . the scars are in my heart and my mind. Scars that, to this day, are there and I cannot ever imagine them going away.'

His cruel urges satisfied, the masked man left Hayley cowering and fled. By the time she regained her composure and called the police, he was long gone. Investigators found little trace the man had ever been there. DNA was collected but, worryingly, did not correspond to that of any known sex offender. To their horror, detectives from the Elizabeth Criminal Investigations Branch realised they had a brand-new criminal on their hands. Given the brazen nature of his actions and his penchant for disguise, they feared he would strike again immediately.

A second assault, however, did not come. Though other crimes occurred – as they always did in Elizabeth – none were a match for Hayley's bizarre rapist. The lack of a follow-up only increased her family's pain.

'Can you imagine the confusion and devastation they felt?' she asked in 2003. 'Can you imagine the difficulty I had, explaining to two young boys what had happened? Can you imagine their fears, anger and frustration when, within 24 hours of the rape, their lives were turned upside down? My husband blamed himself for not being there to protect me. He lived as a guilty man, yet he was not guilty.'

Two years passed, and Hayley's rape remained unsolved. Detectives' initial fears of a serial sex predator had proven to be unfounded. A sick individual had perpetrated a horrific crime, but at least he had struck but once. The immediate threat to the community, to the people of Elizabeth, had lessened.

In March 1997, the masked rapist returned. His target was Aleisha, who lived just kilometres from Hayley's home. 'It's hard to remember life before I was raped,' Aleisha said in 2003. 'That place was my first home. It was where I bought furniture for the first time and cooked meals. I didn't have much, but I was proud of my little home and what I had achieved by the age of 21. Most people don't have the responsibility of a home by the age of 18, so having what I had made me proud.' She was proud, also, of her relationship with her new partner. They intended to marry.

Aleisha had taken an all-too-rare night off from being a mother when she was assaulted. 'One of my best friends and I had enjoyed a 21st birthday party with friends,' she said. 'Due to the cold night, she dropped me at my place on her way home so I could get changed. I was planning on going to a friend's house later, as I didn't like being in the house alone, but I fell asleep in front of the television. My first awareness of the intruders in my home that night was when someone standing in my bedroom doorway awakened me.'

The details of Aleisha's ordeal have never been made public. Her statements to police, and evidence tendered against her attackers, remains sealed by court order due to their intensely graphic nature. What is known is Aleisha was confronted by two naked men, each wearing a Ku Klux Klan hood. For more than an hour, they subjected her to multiple acts of oral, anal and vaginal rape. Two more attempted sex acts failed. Only after binding and blindfolding her did they leave the scene.

'Can you possibly imagine having your house broken into, being repeatedly raped by two strangers, made to participate in indecent acts against your will?' Aleisha said in 2003. 'Can you imagine having your phone lines cut and mobile phone hidden, so a call for help would go unheard? Irreplaceable personal belongings were stolen from me, and I was left tied down, face up, with a pillowcase over my head.

'I can honestly say I know what it feels like to have your life flash before your eyes. I had heard the saying before, and couldn't imagine what it would feel like or at what point in your life it would occur — if ever. I can only explain that I felt like I was going to die that night. It is beyond words to be able to explain the feeling. I never want to endure that feeling again.'

Hours later, Aleisha's friends and family discovered her plight and freed her. As police began their investigations, her life spiralled out of control. She was diagnosed with post-traumatic stress disorder. Though she took anti-depressants, they did little to control her mood swings and irritability. She developed phobias about the dark, about crowds, about confined spaces and being alone. Media coverage of the crime – and its links with the 1995 offence – left Aleisha feeling exposed. Several of her co-workers matched her long absences to the newspaper stories and realised what had happened. Aleisha felt embarrassed and ashamed as a result.

'I had to endure the possible outcome of a pregnancy test and had to wait three months for the outcome of an AIDS test,' she said. 'During that time, my friends and family were very cautious around me. They started to judge me, and I felt I was being scrutinised. One of my best friends lives with the guilt that she dropped me home, on that night, to an empty house. My partner helped me through all my problems, but was still suffering immense guilt for not being with me the night I was attacked. We cancelled our wedding plans six weeks before the wedding day. I sold my home.

'How do you explain to someone your sudden outbursts, or not being able to go shopping or to a movie because you are frightened every moment? How do you explain what happened without someone feeling sorry for you, thinking of what you did to deserve the attack or asking "why can't you just get over it?".'

Kilometres away, Hayley's once-happy family was also falling apart. 'My youngest son refused to go to school and displayed violent outbursts,' Hayley remembered. 'He wanted to be with me all the time – it was his way of protecting me.' Psychiatrists eventually diagnosed post-traumatic stress disorder and obsessive-compulsive disorder. 'As if the family did not have enough to deal with,' Hayley said. 'For me as his mother to see this was, to say the least, very distressing. Every day I ask the question "Did this have to be?" and "Could I have dealt with it better?" and "Could I have prevented it by managing the process of explaining the rape and home invasion in a better way?" I will never know the answers to these questions.'

Hayley herself was suffering acutely. 'Before the rape I was comfortable being physically close to people,' she said. 'Now I stand away from them, especially if I do not know them very well. I stand sideways in queues because I am fearful of the person behind me. I used to like nothing better than to sit in the dark and gaze at the stars – now this is scary for me. I had my hair cut very short, did not wear make-up, spent many hours in the shower because I felt dirty and wore clothes that I considered to be unattractive.'

Police were dealing with a nightmare of their own. DNA testing confirmed one of Aleisha's attackers was the same man who had raped Hayley two years earlier. The idea the masked lunatic had found himself an accomplice was disheartening – and made all the worse when the partner's DNA failed to generate a match within the police database. Detectives now had two naked, masked, unidentifiable, vanishing rapists with whom to contend.

Once again, the masked predator disappeared off the radar. None of the rapes, sexual attacks and indecent assaults that occurred in Elizabeth between March 1997 and November 1999 lined up with the monster's methods. There were no sightings of a naked man wandering the streets, nor of a hooded figure peering into windows. Thousands of criminals were arrested across Adelaide, but none of them provided a DNA sample that could link them to the tortures Hayley and Aleisha had survived. There was no respite, no relaxation, for detectives this time. They knew the masked rapist would strike again – the only question was when.

On 14 December 1999, a young girl – whose name is suppressed – spent the night alone in her Elizabeth home. She was 17. 'I was an outgoing, happy person,' she said in 2002. 'I was carefree, bubbly and easygoing. I loved going out, I wanted people around me all the time. I was very sociable. I was completing Year 10 at school and thinking about my future. I didn't know what I wanted to do, but I had my life ahead of me.'

Among the girl's many interests was playing the guitar. Taking advantage of an empty house, she eased back on her bed and strummed away. Lost in both the melody and thoughts of the future, she did not notice the nude, masculine frame filling her doorway. When she did look up, it was too late to escape. He advanced upon her, his face wrapped in a green mask with two small cut-outs she would later describe as 'peep holes'. Roughly, he demanded oral sex. Once satisfied, he left.

'I was too scared to sleep for two months afterwards,' the teen said later. 'When I started sleeping, I had nightmares. I started scratching myself and cutting myself until I bled. I stopped eating. I felt that my life was in ruins . . . I was too scared to go anywhere and just wanted to lock myself in my room. I didn't want to have anything to do with anybody.'

Like Hayley before her, the girl took drastic steps to accomplish this. 'I tried to change my appearance – to disappear, so he couldn't find me,' she said. 'But I always feel like I am being watched. I am still looking out for him, watching my back, and am scared of being by myself in the dark. I listen out for noises and feel really paranoid. I dropped out of school as I was too scared to keep going. I couldn't work, I couldn't do anything.'

Seeking a way to cope, she turned to extreme measures. 'After the crime I hated myself, because I felt that I had let it happen,' she said. 'I felt that no one cared, and that the world was against me. In order to forget about what happened I started taking drugs. It made me feel better about everything. But I was suicidal, and attempted to commit suicide by overdosing on drugs or strangling myself.'

Though she did not know it, the teenager's plight was echoed kilometres away. Two years had done nothing to ease Aleisha's pain. 'There was not much compassion and support available for victims,' she remembered in 2003. 'If I took the opportunity to seek help, there were always hurdles. On one occasion, when I was at the point of taking my life for the second time, I made a phone call to a counselling service. Even after my pleas for help, they advised me the earliest appointment available was in six weeks' time.' Thankfully, Aleisha chose to bury herself in her work – allowing her to make it through another day. Her professionalism was a positive outlet for her stress; others were not so helpful. 'My stress release turned to food and I gained 24 kilograms,' she said. 'I was now unhappy with the way I looked and the person I had become.'

Aleisha, Hayley and the teenager did not know each other, nor did they realise there were others in the world going through the same horrific emotional turmoil. Those investigating the crime – hunting the monster – did, however, and it tore them apart inside. Hoping an arrest would bring the women even the smallest measure of closure, they redoubled their efforts. It came, sadly, to naught. An analysis of the teenager's ordeal yielded no new information. Once again, police had a DNA sample that matched the previous rapes and nothing else. Investigations stalled once more.

Waiting was, for Aleisha, the worst thing. 'For years I lived in fear, and I had to rely on my partner to support me,' she said. 'I never let him leave me in the house alone, especially at night. We limited our socialising, as I did not know who the offenders were and so didn't trust those around me. We disowned many friends due to lack of trust. In six years, I lived in eight different houses.'

The teenager also struggled to cope. 'I was not happy with myself, and I had low self-esteem,' she said. 'I used to live each day as if I had the rest of my life to live, but now I live each day as if it is my last. I have a big fear of dying, and I am still scared.'

The 1990s ended with the masked rapist still at large. Police had no leads to follow, no suspects to interview. That would change, for all the wrong reasons, on 1 October 2000. On that night, the pervert took his fourth victim – a mother of two known as Ginsh.

For 29 years Ginsh had been married to Trevor. Theirs was not a smooth relationship. 'Ginsh was an alcoholic, and she'd had a problem with alcohol since she was 13,' Trevor said in a statement to police, filed in 2000. 'She didn't drink between 1992 and 1998, but then commenced drinking again. That placed a great deal of strain on our relationship, and we often argued.'

Hoping to ease tensions, the couple had hit upon a deal. If Ginsh had been drinking, Trevor would spend the night with friends. That way, she could sober up without them fighting. The deal, sadly, did not prevent tempers from flaring. On 1 October, Ginsh came home and admitted she had been drinking. 'She was very upset when I told her that I was leaving to go out,' Trevor told police. 'She began to cry. She was trying to grab me and saying "Come back, you shouldn't go, I'll go instead." I told her that, if she had been drinking, she couldn't go anywhere.'

Trevor would never forgive himself for what happened next. 'She followed me out to the car, grabbed hold of me and tried to turn me around so I would face her,' he said in his statement. 'I reached out and pushed her away from me. I placed my hand in the middle of her and pushed her fairly hard. I left, and I didn't speak to her again that night.'

Guilty and grief-stricken, Ginsh did not remain at the couple's home. She made her way to the nearby Elizabeth Motel, rented a room for the night and cried herself to sleep. When she woke up, there was a man lying on top of her.

'I started to fight yelling "no",' Ginsh would tell police the next day. 'That's when he put a pillow over my face and punched the pillow. He said, "Be nice, be good or I'll have to tie and gag you." But I kept screaming "Get off me" and "Who are you?" and "Why?". All he kept saying, in a very calm way, was "Because you're cute".'

Ginsh refused to co-operate. She struggled violently with the masked man; he tore her bra off and ripped her pants from her legs. 'I know he was getting really frustrated when I kept screaming and yelling, because he started pressing really hard down on the pillow and I couldn't breathe,' she said. 'He kept saying "Be a good girl, just let me do this, just let me".' Desperate for air, Ginsh tried another tactic. "I thought I was going to die, I didn't have any breath left in me,' she said. 'It disgusts me to actually think I said this, but I said to him "Don't rape me, just come on my breasts". And that's when I blacked out.'

Minutes passed. Ginsh had the vague sensation of being 'thrown around like a rag doll'. When she regained consciousness, she discovered the rapist had put his penis in her hands. 'I could hear the police banging on the door,' she said. 'It was like a flaming gangster movie, it was so ridiculous. They were saying "Police, open up" and the guy shot off toward the bathroom.'

Police had, at long last, caught their first break. The Elizabeth Motel is situated on Main North Road, and shares an intersection with the Elizabeth Police Station. Motel staff had heard Ginsh's screams and alerted detectives. They had responded immediately – some in cars, some on foot – to her plight. Despite the rapid response time, the rapist was quicker still. Startlingly, he managed to escape the dragnet.

The rapist had made a mistake, though; in his haste to rape Ginsh, he had not stopped to pull on his mask. 'He had long, shoulder-length, wavy, dark hair,' she told detectives. 'He was unshaven and he had small, dirty genitals.' What seemed, at first, to be a vital breakthrough turned out to be false hope. 'I close my eyes and try to form a photo-fit of him in my head, but I can't,' Ginsh admitted. 'And I didn't get to hurt him as much as I would have liked to. I couldn't even knee him in his tiny balls or bloody push him away . . . he was so damn persistent and strong.'

Trevor learned of the incident the next morning, when Ginsh called him from the police station. He was completely unprepared for how their lives were about to change. 'I had heard of cases such as this on many occasions and, whilst feeling disgust and sadness for the victims, I had no idea what effect such a trauma could have on a person,' he said in 2003. 'I spent night after night trying to console my wife with no effect – she had become a different person. Slowly, I began to realise our life could never be as it was. Physical injuries can heal, but mental injuries are another story.'

Despite her alcoholism, Ginsh had a personal reservoir of strength upon which to draw. 'My wife was not one to give up easily,' Trevor said with pride. 'She tried every avenue open to her to get the memory of that – in her words – "filthy creature" out of her head. Her sleep was short, her nightmares were terrifying, and she became more and more mentally exhausted. If the nightmares I have suffered are any indication of what she went through, then I am not surprised that she was fighting a battle she was slowly losing. She told me, over and over, that she "could not get the vile stench of that person" out of her memory.'

Ginsh started carrying a knife with her at all times – to bed, around the house and on the one and only occasion she left the house. 'She managed to summon up enough courage to take the dog for a walk around the block,' Trevor remembered. 'She did so with a knife in her possession. She had become paranoid. She asked herself "Who was this attacker?" and if he was at the shops when she was there. She wondered if he was watching her. I can only try to imagine the terror that was in her mind.'

Any hope police had that Ginsh's rape was an isolated incident was dashed by DNA testing. Again, frustratingly, they had the same phantom match. Though he had left his mask at home, the monster had indeed struck again. The case no longer made any sense. The time lag between crimes was so huge it defied logic. Why would a predator so vicious, so frenzied, so twisted and detailed in his fantasies wait so long between sex acts? How could a pervert show such restraint, then explode so horrifically? What kind of mind, of mentality, were police dealing with – and how did he manage to disappear so completely between crimes?

It was that lack of sense, of cohesion, that would ultimately solve the case. On 23 December 2000, Elizabeth police were called to investigate a break-in. A knife-wielding man had forced his way into the home of a woman named Joanne Tanner, terrified her, then left with some of her property. Foolishly, the robber had left the knife behind. Passers-by saw the burglar's car as he left, and took note of its licence plate.

When the knife was swabbed for DNA, as was routine, alarm bells went off. The robber's genetic signature was identical to that of the masked rapist. It also matched samples taken from a series of crimes that occurred while the testing was underway – at a nursery, a trophy store and the head office of a freight-liner trucking company. And the car driven by the alleged thief was registered to a man named Trevor John Brooks.

Brooks was a 37-year-old father of two, and the youngest of five children. He had spent much of his life working for his father, and had been in a stable, committed relationship with his de-facto wife for ten years. There was nothing in his limited criminal history, nor any records attributed to him, that so much as hinted he could be a disgusting serial rapist with a flair for the dramatic. For three months, police consolidated their evidence. Officers investigating the break-ins combined their efforts with the detectives who had waited six agonising years to catch a predator.

On 16 March 2001, police stormed Brooks's home, determined to arrest him. The man who had so successfully hidden his identity for half a decade refused to go down without a fight. He did not answer the door, and so officers kicked it down. Brooks was nowhere to be found; he had removed a manhole cover in the ceiling and crawled into the roof space. Determined to escape, he had pulled apart the iron roofing and jumped onto the house's veranda. With disbelieving police in pursuit, Brooks leaped from rooftop to rooftop, eluding them. Refusing to play games, officers drew capsicum spray from their belts and doused the pervert with blinding foam. He dropped like a stone and was immediately handcuffed. Somewhat appropriately, Brooks was half-naked; he had not stopped to dress before running.

The police then informed Hayley, Aleisha, Ginsh and the teenager that they at last had a suspect in custody. The women's reactions were not what officers had expected.

'Detectives visited my home, unannounced, and asked me to go over my statement again,' Aleisha remembered. 'Reliving the night of the rapes was a torment, and I could not even finish reading the statement. The pain became so unbearable and I just wanted the feelings of despair to be gone. That evening, I attempted to take my own life.'

Hayley felt herself victimised a second time – by the courts process. 'Had Brooks not chosen to break into my home and rape me, I would never have had the unfortunate experience of the justice system,' she said in 2003. 'The system allowed what was a feeling of elation, upon Brooks's arrest, to turn into what became the longest, most controlling, evasive and frustrating sequence of events I have ever had the horror of being a part of. This is not about the people within the system – the police detectives or the public prosecutors. It is about the legislation, and the rules in which these people have to work.'

For Ginsh, news of Brooks's arrest coincided with her impending 30th wedding anniversary. 'My wife fought hard, she was a fighter and she had a will to live,' Trevor said in 2003. 'That was to change. Not long before our anniversary, she could bear the memories no more and decided to end her life rather than live with the nightmare in her head.'

Ginsh committed suicide on 12 October 2001. She left behind a hand-written note, her pain-wracked words printed neatly on floral paper. 'Please make sure my sons and husband know I love them dearly,' her note reads. 'I can't live with Trevor John Brooks in my life any more. He is in every breath I take. I'm so sorry – hopefully I'll find peace. I am so sorry.'

Trevor said Ginsh had been drinking on her last day alive. 'I got a phone call from her in the morning, we had an argument and I hung up,' he said. 'The last word I heard her say was my name. I learned, later, that the hospital then received a call from my wife saying, "Goodbye, I've taken an overdose." They called me, and I got in my car and went to her.

'I got there 30 seconds after the police arrived – Ginsh was alive, but unconscious. I was entirely numb . . . nothing seemed to work, nothing seemed to make sense. I'm sure I felt as helpless as I did the night my wife was raped. I realised that all was lost when I saw she had carved the word "sorry" into the back of her hand. Why should she be sorry? The wrong person was saying sorry. She just could no longer live with the memories in her head.'

Trevor believed learning the name of her personal demon was the final straw for Ginsh. 'A wife was lost, my sons lost their mother,' he said. 'In retrospect, we lost a wife and a mother long before she took her own life and I live with the guilt that I was not able to do anything to help her. I live with the thought that, had I been able to stop her taking her own life that day, would I have been fair to her? The effect of this attack was so great that death was, in her mind, a better option.'

Hayley, too, was plagued with questions. Months passed between Brooks's arrest and his appearance in court. 'That may not seem like long but, when you are at this point still referred to as an "alleged victim", it is a very long time,' she said. 'Nights are longer due to lack of sleep, nervous habits reappear, the pure energy required to stay on task and concentrate at work left me feeling sick and constantly fatigued.

'Finally, Brooks appears once again in court and pleads not guilty. What happened during this time span is anyone's guess, I sure as hell do not know. I remember, at this stage, hitting a wall, screaming and generally feeling like I had no control over myself or the events that were occurring. As an "alleged victim" it appeared as if, in fact, nothing had happened and closure was a long way off.'

Appearances were deceiving; the long delay was the result of a sudden success. Research into Brooks's life and associates had identified Aleisha's other rapist. His name was James Trevor Birmingham and he was in the very last place anyone would have thought to look – a cell at Mobilong Prison, where he was serving a five-year minimum term for killing a man.

Birmingham's story begins in February 1996. An easily angered man with an explosive temper, he had become embroiled in an argument with a young man named Shannon Burke in North Adelaide. Determined to win, Birmingham pulled out a knife. Burke leaped into his car and drove away but Birmingham, in a rage, followed in his own vehicle. He pursued his foe for 18 kilometres, driving at speeds of up to 150 kilometres per hour, to Bolivar Road at Salisbury.

Desperate to escape, Burke risked turning around and driving into oncoming traffic to shake Birmingham. But the hunter would not be denied; he caught up to Burke's car and rammed it ten times until their bumpers locked. Burke spun out of control, crossing the median strip and flying off the Port Wakefield Bridge. The vehicle hit the ground and exploded, incinerating Burke.

The next day, his anger abated, Birmingham surrendered himself to police. He was charged with murder but, eventually, pleaded guilty to the lesser charge of causing death by dangerous driving. In June 1996, he was released on a $1000 bail, pending sentencing. Soon after his release, he formed a friendship with Brooks.

Their mutual history would come to light in a psychological report compiled by Dr Allen Fugler in August 2003. He wrote that, on the night before the rape, the duo had gone fishing at St Kilda – a mangrove area near Elizabeth. 'Birmingham was on bail, at the time, on a charge of causing death by dangerous driving,' Dr Fugler wrote. 'He remembers having a headache and taking a few pills he discovered in the glove box of the vehicle being driven by Brooks. He thought they were Panadol. His next clear memory is Brooks telling him the tablets were Rohypnol.' Also known as the date-rape drug, Rohypnol is a hypnotic drug with sedative and amnesic properties.

'Birmingham claims to have no memory of the sexual assaults,' the report continued. 'He doesn't recall there being a plan between himself and Brooks, and he had no explanation for the two hoods used during the rapes. He has no clear memory of the crimes he perpetrated.' One way to view it is that Birmingham was also a victim of Brooks's twisted ways.

Detectives were, nonetheless, horrified. Birmingham had raped Aleisha in March 1997, while he was on bail awaiting sentencing for killing Shannon Burke. One man had destroyed two young lives, in completely different ways, and only been punished for one of those cruel acts. Worse, he was due for release on parole in August 2002. Officers were not about to let that happen. They visited Mobilong Prison on 19 June 2002, and formally charged Birmingham with three counts of rape and two counts of attempted rape, all pertaining to the attack on Aleisha. His parole was cancelled.

The case was handed to the Office of the Director of Public Prosecutions. The decision was made to file fresh allegations with the court, accusing Brooks of all rapes and jointly charging Birmingham with the attack on Aleisha. The matter was scheduled for trial in the District Court on 28 January 2003.

Hayley panicked. 'I thought "A trial, my God, I will have to stand up in court,"' she said. 'This seemed like a life sentence to me all by itself.' She spent the next eight months preparing herself, physically and mentally, for the ordeal to come. 'I had a court visit and was supposed to make rational decisions on matters such as speaking in an open or closed court, giving evidence through closed-circuit television, having a security screen or not. It was this event that really threw me. I remember going into the room where the CCTV operated from and the lights going out, leaving me in total darkness. I remember the fear that took over my body.'

On 18 December 2002, the scheduled trial was abandoned. For Hayley, it was another kick in the heart. 'I was not coping with all these delays,' she said.

The teenager, too, was shaken. 'I felt very anxious about the trial and going to court,' she said in 2002. 'Bringing all this up again caused me to be so stressed that I lost my job. The crime had made my life so difficult, and I just wanted it to go away.'

The three survivors of Brooks's sick perversions needed support – and they found it in one another. At the insistence of police, Aleisha met with Hayley and the teenager in a secure location early in 2003. 'I was really hesitant at first, not knowing what to expect,' Aleisha said. 'I didn't know what had happened to them.'

Hayley greeted the others with a mounting sense of horror. 'I thought, "My God, he's done this to other women, he needs to be stopped",' she said. 'When I heard Aleisha's story I realised that, while I'd been raped, she had endured more and suffered far worse in the years since.' Older than her new friends, Hayley took on a maternal role within the group and, together, they began to heal.

'It was like we had been friends forever,' Aleisha said. 'Finally, there was someone who knew exactly what I had gone through, because they were going through the same thing. With time, I started becoming a stronger person and slowly rebuilding my life. Some of the effects eased, but they were never gone.'

While Aleisha, Hayley and the teenager looked to the future, experts pulled apart Brooks's past. On 30 September 2003, his counsel announced he would plead guilty to all charges. In preparation for his District Court sentencing, Brooks had been visited by a plethora of psychologists and psychiatrists. One question had loomed large since his arrest: how had Brooks managed to escape detection for so long? What was it within his psychological make-up that allowed him to 'switch off' the monster and live an unassuming life between such hideous crimes?

Psychologist Jack White had interviewed the prisoner first. The cracks in Brooks's psyche were on show almost immediately. 'Brooks described his de-facto partner as a "money-sucking jealous woman" and said their relationship had always been rocky,' Dr White reported. 'He perceives himself to be a warm and friendly individual who is attracted to activity and excitement. However, he is a person who is highly submissive in interpersonal relationships and readily dominated by others. He has high levels of irritability associated with feeling very frustrated, he is a person who is easily angered and perceived by others as being hostile with an angry temperament. He is highly belligerent.'

Brooks's coping mechanism, he said, was drugs. 'When he was 18, he had a breakdown which he attributed to using too much amphetamine,' Dr White said. 'He said that, when he was younger, he liked using drugs "too much".' Brooks admitted spending up to $600 a day on heroin and Rohypnol at various times in his life. 'He used them to "forget about life" and said that he often binged on drugs and did not remember what happened afterwards,' he said.

Psychiatrist Craig Raeside had next assessed Brooks. His conclusions were almost identical to those of Dr White. 'Brooks said he had "got sick" of his partner who was "just an idiot" and "a jealous bitch",' Dr Raeside wrote. 'He said he had started seeing some other women "on the side" and said that had given her a reason to be jealous.'

Dr Raeside found Brooks was "dismissive" of the rapes. 'He said he "wouldn't be here" in jail if he "didn't touch the stuff", meaning drugs,' he wrote. 'He understood the charges but said he had no memory of the incidents as he was "in a drug-induced state". He thought that was due to the effects of Rohypnol. He said he was ashamed – if he did it. He said he "couldn't remember" and "didn't want to remember", and that he would plead guilty "because I've got no choice". Brooks said "I will just do the time and be 60 when I get out, get a pension, maybe have something with my kids then".'

On 1 October 2003, Brooks and Birmingham appeared in the District Court and pleaded guilty to all charges. Eight years, eight months and six days had passed since Hayley was raped. Never, in all that time, had she known what Brooks looked like behind his mask. On that day, she sat in the middle row of the court gallery and stared at the man who had haunted her for so long. What she saw was a slightly chubby, nondescript man with long, dark hair and small eyes.

'His face wasn't at all what I had pictured, and maybe that was a good thing,' she said after the hearing. 'I don't think anyone could explain the feeling of seeing a face you've been afraid of for so long. It was a very psychological confrontation.' Far more satisfying was hearing him confess to his crimes. 'Even when they've been arrested, there is still trauma because they're only accused of the crime,' she said. 'You still feel very much like the guilty party. To hear the word come out of his mouth, to hear him say "guilty", that was good.'

Judge David Smith ordered prosecution and defence to prepare sentencing submissions for a 3 December hearing. Rosie Reed, for Brooks, took her cue from the psychological and psychiatric reports. She intended to paint her client as a modern-day Dr Jekyll who, against his will and control, was transformed by illicit drugs into a savage, woman-raping Mr Hyde. But to do so convincingly – and secure a lesser jail term for Brooks – she needed second opinions and, therefore, another adjournment.

'I sent a fax to the prosecution last week, saying there were many issues my client still wanted to address through an up-to-date psychological report,' she said on the day of the hearing. 'We want to explore a treatment program for him.'

Aleisha, Hayley and Trevor were sitting in the court's public gallery. The possibility of yet another delay upset them badly. Fortunately, they had an empathetic and powerful ally at the bar table – Crown prosecutor Liesl Chapman.

'There have been too many adjournments in this case,' she said coolly. 'Ms Reed already has a number of psychological and psychiatric reports, and she's supplied none of them to me. If it's the case she needs more reports, then I say it's simply too late. We've been waiting months, now, for this matter to be finalised. I urge the court to proceed today.'

Her forceful submissions found support in Judge Smith. He ordered the hearing go ahead as scheduled, beginning with Hayley's victim impact statement. Having been silent for almost a decade, Hayley wasted no words. She spoke of her husband and children, and how they had been changed by Brooks's actions. She spoke of her own struggles and torment. She told of her anguish in dealing with the justice system. Above all else, she confronted Brooks on her own terms.

'Now we stand here today – you the offender, me the victim, and I inform the court of the impact your act had on my life,' Hayley said, staring directly at her rapist. 'But no matter what your sentence is, Mr Brooks, it can never be equal to my sentence. I will take my sentence to my grave. You chose to violate my body and break into my home, and this has left me with a life sentence. To this day I feel a sense of fear, violation, confusion and disgust. No, Mr Brooks, I do not want revenge. I want justice.

'Be rest assured, nothing has ever given me greater pleasure than to stand up here today, look you in the eye and speak these words to you. I wanted you to hear and see that I may always be affected by the rape but I am free – free of you, free to walk the streets, free to make my own decisions, free to enjoy the wind in my face. I am free to enjoy the greatest pleasure of all, and that is freedom. You, Mr Brooks, are not free. Your imprisonment will protect me and others.'

Hayley stepped down from the bar table and let out a loud, cleansing breath. As she made her way back to the gallery she crossed paths with Aleisha, and the women shared a brief, silent moment. Hands shaking slightly, Aleisha took up position at the front of the court and read out her own statement. She referred to her night of horror as being 'attacked'. To call it rape, she said, would be to acknowledge 'this has really happened to me'. That out of the way, Aleisha found the strength to look both Brooks and Birmingham in the eye, and speak of the upheaval she and her son had experienced since March 1997.

'For nearly seven years, I have not had a stable home,' she said. 'With time I am becoming a stronger person and am slowly rebuilding my life. I am certainly not the person I was seven years ago. I would like to imagine that, without the setbacks I have endured over this time, I would be a more confident and more successful person.

'It would have been easy for me to give up on life after this attack. I can honestly say that I had to convince myself to continue living on many occasions. There are ailments I will always suffer due to the impact of this crime but I do have a beautiful home filled with love that I can share with family, friends and pets.

'I will not cry, as it would be wasted tears. My life is not a waste because of this. My father certainly summed it up for me when he said of Brooks and Birmingham "what a waste of a life".'

A court orderly read out the teenager's statement. She, too, had moved on with her life. She had returned to high school and completed her studies, earned hospitality qualifications and found love with a 'happy, supportive' man. Her physical health continued to suffer, however, and she remained 'moody and unpredictable'.

Trevor was the final person to give a statement to the court. He half-walked, half-staggered to the bar table, his entire body vibrating with rage. His gaze bore holes in Brooks, who averted his eyes and could not bear to look at the grieving husband. Trevor spoke, at first, in a dangerously low voice, but his volume rose as his anger grew. Emotion spilled from him, threatening to drown the monster who had ruined his wife and his life.

He told the court of his suffering, of how his sons had tried to cope with the loss of their mother. But that was only part of his purpose that day. Trevor's true goal was to share – with the court, with the victims, with Brooks – his wife's final words. He took from his pocket a single piece of paper. On it was a poem, written by Ginsh just before she committed suicide. It was titled 'Stripped of Soul'. The wrenching verse re-told the night of the rape, moment by moment, and her losing battle with depression.

Terror, indescribable pain
My soul has been ripped apart
Tears fall like acid rain
While blood drains from my heart

Months have passed and the memories remain
I see no respite in sight
Living daily with the pain
Of that horrendous night
My body erupts in tremors
While my thoughts remain inept
My mind chooses to remember
While my heart fights to forget
The faceless shadow, and rancid smell
mine forevermore
His voice will haunt me till he rots in hell
His power too great to ignore
My journey is eleven months old
and I am becoming weak
Hope is my destination
and there, it's sanity I seek
Each torturous step I take
I yearn to be free
But my heart and soul remains in the hell
That the devil has cast upon me
Evil will not destroy another woman's heart
Because I won't share this pain I own
This is my weapon against his will
And it will remain mine and mine alone.

His voice hoarse with grief, Trevor returned to the public gallery. Aleisha and Hayley were waiting for him, and the trio embraced. A little more healing had occurred; they had moved one step closer to closure. But their torment, sadly, was yet to conclude – Ms Reed announced Brooks wanted to give a public rebuttal to the victim impact statements. He wanted to argue some of the claims made against him, and sought to question the victims about their physical and mental health.

As the victims' faces drained of colour, Ms Chapman again leaped to their defence. She was not prepared to let the deviant draw another moment's pleasure from those he had already tried to destroy. 'The victims don't want to hear that reply,' she said. 'I'm sure Your Honour understands that feeling.'

Ms Reed was insistent. 'My client is the one facing charges in relation to all of the victims, and he would like a chance to respond to what they have said here today,' she said. 'He has had to listen to them for the last hour, I've made three pages of notes and I submit it's very important for the victims to hear what he has to say. It seems they want to make very sure he knows their pain – therefore it's necessary he be given a chance to respond to that.'

Judge Smith was unmoved. 'The victims don't have to tolerate that,' he scowled, 'and I don't blame them for not wanting to hear it. Your request is denied.'

The sentencing submissions continued on 5 December. Tim Dibden, for Birmingham, was eager to distance his client from his callous co-accused. 'What is quite clear, from the victim impact statements, is not only the impact of these offences but the impact of the judicial process upon the victims,' he said. 'Mr Birmingham has asked me to emphasise to the court, and to these women, that he came into these proceedings much later than Brooks. He pleaded guilty at the earliest possible time.'

Birmingham, he said, had no recollection of the attack upon Aleisha. He said this was due to the 'hypnotic effect' of the Rohypnol he had inadvertently taken. 'This type of drug causes memory loss,' he explained. His first memory, after taking the tablet, was walking along the streets of St Kilda hours later, with no idea where he had been during the missing time. 'That said, my client certainly accepts full responsibility for his involvement in this offence. He wants that conveyed to the court today. Mr Birmingham is shattered, and deeply embarrassed, by his involvement in this assault, because he has two daughters himself and two close friends who have been raped. He has expressed empathy for the victim and remorse for his behaviour.'

A hand-written letter of apology was tendered to the court. 'I feel very hurt and disgusted with myself for what I have done,' it read. 'I just cannot express the feelings and thoughts that are going through my head. I have recently completed a victim awareness course, and I feel that it has opened my eyes and has helped me understand that one wrong action causes so much pain and hurt. I am truly remorseful and very, very sorry for the devastating impact of my behaviour.'

Mr Dibden said his client 'knew' he was going to receive 'a substantial jail term', and that it would be added onto his death by dangerous driving sentence. Parole was no longer an option for Birmingham, and he said the rapist willingly accepted that as a consequence of his drug-addled crimes.

Ms Reed took the opposite approach. Brooks, she said, had lived through the 'domination' and domestic violence suffered by his mother. As a child, he was 'very much under his father's thumb' and so lashed out, bashing a schoolteacher with whom he disagreed. He had risen above all that – experiencing 'great success in his working endeavours' – but his entire lifestyle, from his anger toward women to his copious drug use, was someone else's fault. Even the rapes, she argued, were the fault of forces beyond Brooks's control.

'He was working as an automaton and not remembering anything,' she said, likening her client to a robot. 'He used amphetamines and then Rohypnol. His behaviour, then, was completely disinhibited. He was not operating in his usual manner – which was [as] an upstanding member of the community, a loving husband and father. Indeed, he asked for a second opinion on the DNA evidence because he was struggling to believe he was involved at all.'

Judge Smith, who had read the psychological and psychiatric reports, was not about to swallow that. 'He has a five-page criminal history,' he balked. 'You seriously cannot be putting to me that he is a fine, upstanding member of the community. That is very hard to accept. In each of these attacks there were conversations, there was premeditation, there was overwhelming evidence of his consciousness of what was happening. It is inexplicable and very horrifying, and none of what you've said here today even approaches explaining how these crimes could have happened.'

Sensing she had the advantage, Ms Chapman kept her response short and sharp. 'The fact Brooks pleaded guilty was inevitable because the case against him was overwhelming,' she said. 'His plea did nothing to speed up proceedings, nor facilitate the proper course of justice. The victims have spent considerable time waiting while Brooks has dithered, trying to determine whether he can change the inevitable. His actions, throughout the investigation, represent no willingness to accept responsibility, or remorse, whatsoever. Trevor James Brooks is not a person to whom leniency can be extended.'

Brooks and Birmingham were remanded in custody until 19 December. It was an unusually short break for a South Australian court, which would normally spend months deliberating on a decision. Judge Smith, in contrast, had very clearly made up his mind early in the case. He completely rejected Brooks's claims he was an automaton, ruling the rapes were premeditated and planned. 'The offending defies description; the rapes were horrific, despicable and cowardly,' he said. 'No words of mine could adequately paint the picture of the degradation and terror to which you subjected your victims. To be so abused, by the two of you in that fashion, beggars belief.' Though both men had pleaded guilty, neither was to receive any credit for their confessions. 'Birmingham, you simply bowed to the inevitable,' Judge Smith said, 'while Brooks's plea was motivated by an acceptance of what is indefensible.'

His hard-line stance thrilled Hayley, Aleisha and Trevor. Prosecutors and police had prepared the trio for the worst – that the men may receive credit for their 'honesty' and their attempts to show remorse could find a sympathetic ear on the far side of the bench. To hear their tormentors dismissed so coldly, so studiously ignored, warmed them. All that was left, now, was the sentencing.

Birmingham was dealt with first. He stood ramrod straight, ready to face his fate head-on. He barely blinked as Judge Smith jailed him for eleven and a half years and denied him any chance at parole for nine and a half years. Showing some level of insight, he did not try to meet Aleisha's gaze as he left the court and did not say a word.

Brooks, now alone in the dock, was next. For his crimes, Judge Smith ruled, no less a sentence than 53 years was appropriate. The decision finally broke through the rapist's uncaring facade; he paled noticeably, perhaps thinking of the treatment jailed rapists receive from other prisoners. Because of a South Australian law that prevents judges from handing down 'crushing' sentences, Judge Smith was obligated to reduce Brooks's term to a 'more realistic' 27 years. It was clear from the judge's attitude that he was not impressed with the requirement. He more than made up for it, though, by imposing a 23-year non-parole period.

Reality sunk in. Brooks was an animal, and his cage was now ready. He would be 60 years old before he had even the chance of release and, given his outlook on life and utter lack of remorse, it was doubtful authorities would be prepared to consider parole even then. His final attempts to hurt his victims – by questioning their pain, by seeking to provoke them into a courtroom confrontation, by disputing the DNA tests – had failed. Desperate for something to warm his cold future, Brooks did the only thing small, pathetic, cowardly men know how to do. He turned to his victims, grinned maliciously, and showered them with mocking applause.

He wanted to have the last laugh. Hayley, Aleisha and Trevor refused him even that grotesque victory. As one, the trio rose and gave Brooks a standing ovation as he was led toward the cells. It was the perfect revenge – the rapist lost all composure, his grin warped into a frown, and his eyes grew red and puffy. He had not merely been jailed, Trevor John Brooks had been broken.

'I'm happy with 23 years,' Hayley said outside court. 'He didn't get what he deserved, but any more years on the sentence would just have given him more chance to appeal. Judge Smith was brilliant, and he restored my faith in the judicial system a little. He was very compassionate and factual, and that was a really important part of the healing process – that the system finally understood how we felt.

'I feel really relieved, and I'm going to try not to give that man another thought. He's wasted so much of my life, deprived me of so much time and energy, so I'm just going to say "see you later" and not think about him at all.'

Aleisha left court ashen-faced, but said time would brighten her mood. 'It's all a bit confusing,' she admitted. 'I want the sentences to be longer, but I understand what the judge was saying. When I first heard the sentences I didn't think they were enough. But when I think of what I can achieve in the next 23 years that they will not be able to, I feel better. The pain they've caused will never be gone but I'm lucky – I'm alive.'

Trevor's mood was dark. It was some time before he was ready to speak – and even then, he offered his opinion only after he had been comforted by Hayley. 'I don't think there is a sentence long enough for someone like Brooks,' he said. 'Part of his brain is missing, you see – the part that creates compassion, and regret, and the ability to follow the law. He doesn't possess any of that. He's been put behind bars but I honestly don't believe that, when he comes out, he's going to be any different.'

His thoughts turned to his wife, and his gradual acceptance of her decision to end her life. 'There's nothing anyone can do that's going to bring back what's been taken from these women,' he said. 'Looking back on Ginsh's life after the rape, I couldn't have possibly asked her to suffer another day like that. Her every waking moment was complete misery, and that was unfair. I think she would have looked at this sentencing as I do: that it's the best anyone could have hoped for.'

Trevor paused. It was a warm summer's day in Adelaide, and the sun shone brightly down on the courthouse. 'There are probably things I should have said to my wife before she took her own life,' he said softly. 'Such as there was nothing anyone could do to change how I felt about her. I would urge all partners of the victims: if you have something to say, say it straight away and, after that, do not let this creature have any more effect on you at all.'

Enemy of the State

Paul Habib Nemer

I t was a simple crime – and, in the minds of some, perhaps
no crime at all. Believing he was defending two girls from
a vicious sex predator, a wealthy young man fired a single
shot at a mysterious panel van. His bravado destroyed the
right eye of an innocent newsagent who had merely been
on his morning rounds. It was a tragic, regrettable mistake
borne out of the best intentions. And it was just one bullet.

The people of Adelaide tend to forget those facts when
they reflect on the case of Paul Habib Nemer. Issues of race,
class, wealth and perceived entitlement twisted and mutated
the case – exaggerated it, heightened it – until it became a
symbol of the deep, ugly divides that run through the southern
capital. The name 'Nemer' became, unfairly, synonymous
with the notion one could buy justice. It also became a
political buzzword for a populist, rhetoric-happy government
that refused to allow justice to be the responsibility of the
justice system. Paul Nemer's bullet not only ruined a man's
eye, it decimated the career of a top prosecutor, forever
rent asunder the tenuous relationship between Parliament

and the legal fraternity and exposed Adelaide's ridiculous small-mindedness on a national stage.

•

Prior to 2001, the Nemer family lived an opulent life in Springfield. The exclusive hills suburb, 18 minutes south-east of Adelaide, consists of less than a dozen streets lined with expensive mansions. Of Lebanese origin, the family made its money through a dry-cleaning franchise, as well as its interest in a number of petrol stations. Paul Nemer, then aged 19, was the youngest of their three sons. He lived at home with his parents, George and Rita, and was in his second year at the University of Adelaide. He dressed in designer suits, wore patent leather shoes and lived under some very strict rules. Nemer's parents would claim their son was not allowed to drink alcohol, go to nightclubs or stay out past midnight – even on weekends. He was expected to focus on his studies, on his Catholic faith and on the charity work his family undertook.

That did not mean, however, Nemer lacked the company of pretty girls. Two of those were Brooke Annan, 16, and Lillian Mavromichalis, 17. The willowy, dark-skinned girls – who many mistook to be sisters – had come to know Nemer through his circle of friends and cousins.

At 3 am on Saturday 19 August 2001, Nemer had a phone conversation with the girls. They were planning to walk from the city to their home in Ashford because they had run out of money and couldn't afford a taxi. He urged them not to make the trip. It was a wise suggestion – Annan and Mavromichalis would have to travel through the city's notorious southern parklands, an area renowned for rape and gay sex. Nemer suggested they hail a taxi and come to his place, where he was hosting an all-nighter for his friends and cousins. The gathering was a violation of his parents' rules – but George and Rita were in Melbourne for an AFL game, while Nemer's brothers were out for the night. Two more guests, he felt, couldn't hurt. The girls declined, insisting they would be fine and would speak to Nemer the next day.

The boys went on with their night, watching television and playing video games until the early hours, before piling into the mansion's many beds. At around 4 am, Nemer's 15-year-old friend was woken by a call on his mobile phone. A woman, claiming to be a 90-year-old resident of Arthur Street, Unley, said she was ringing on behalf of the girls. In the background, the 15-year-old could hear them screaming.

Arthur Street is, for someone walking, almost 40 minutes west of Ashford. Annan and Mavromichalis had gone vastly off-route, and fear was the reason. As they had crossed the southern boundary of the CBD, they had become convinced they were being followed. They would later describe their stalker as a bearded man, wearing a beanie, who drove a large white van. Remembering Nemer's warnings and fearing rape, they panicked and began turning randomly down the leafy streets, hoping to lose their pursuer. Every time they thought they had succeeded – and began to turn back toward Ashford – they would see the van again and start to run east. When the van drew very close to them, Annan and Mavromichalis jumped the fence of the 90-year-old's home, rang her doorbell and begged for help. Though suspicious and distressed, the elderly woman listened to the girls. They were being stalked by a rapist, they cried, and could not call for help because their phones had run out of pre-paid credit. They asked the woman to call Nemer's 15-year-old friend so they could get a ride out of their nightmare.

Minutes later, the teenager woke Nemer, saying Annan and Mavromichalis were being 'threatened by a rapist'. Adrenalised, worried for his friends, Nemer made what was to be the biggest mistake of his life. Instead of calling the police, he went into his parents' bedroom and dug out a box from beneath their bed. Inside was the 9mm Browning handgun – complete with ammunition – that belonged to his grandfather. Once a competitive shooter, Nemer's grandfather had turned his back on guns in the 1990s. He had sold his armoury save for the Browning and its Shobra ammunition, made in Cairo, Egypt. Nemer's parents were unaware their son knew where the gun was. He had found it by accident, months earlier, after dropping a television remote onto the floor. Now armed, Nemer and the teenager got in his mother's Mercedes Benz and drove to Unley.

It was an 11-minute trip – more than enough time for the situation to degenerate. The girls' hysteria infected the woman until she, too, feared for her life at the hands of the mysterious van driver. The man was still lurking in the area, visible through the window of the house. At 4.20 am, the elderly woman called triple zero and requested police assistance. A recording of the call, later tendered in court, is almost inaudible for the screaming of Annan and Mavromichalis in the background.

Nemer and the teenager arrived on the scene at 4.30 am. Unable to locate the elderly woman's house, the 15-year-old called one of the girls. He heard nothing but screaming before the line went abruptly dead. Terrified for the girls, they pushed the Mercedes faster. As they neared the Unley Shopping Centre, less than 1 kilometre from the woman's home, they received a call. The girls were now inside with the 90-year-old, and they were all panicking. 'He's back,' they shouted down the line. 'He's back, he's come back!' Nemer pulled over on the northern side of Arthur Street. The girls left the house and ran toward his car, pointing at a white van that was travelling slowly down the street. 'That's him,' they shouted, before the 15-year-old told them to get in the car and stay down.

What happened next – and, especially, where Nemer stood when he fired – became the subject of debate so great that it dominated the state's courts for years.

Annan said she saw Nemer run toward the van, which was by that time reversing out of the driveway of a block of flats. She claimed Nemer's arms 'were both straight and pointing' toward the front of the van. 'I believed that he had a gun, I couldn't see but you could tell,' she told police. 'The split second after I saw this, I heard the shot and the window break. This all happened very quickly and I'm not exactly sure of the sequence of events. It's possible I heard the shot and looked up to see Paul still in the position with his arms up. I did not see the flash of flame, or anything else, at the time of the shot.'

Mavromichalis said Nemer was horrified after he fired. 'Paul kept saying "I shot at him, I shot at him",' she told police. 'He said "I can't believe I shot at him. I hope I didn't hit him".'

Annan shared his disbelief. 'I didn't even see the firearm, I only heard the shot,' she said in her statement. 'I said to the 15-year-old, "Was that a fake gun?" He said to me, "No, it's not. We're Lebs, we don't have fake guns".'

Had Paul Nemer shot a pervert, a stalker or a rapist, that would likely have been the end of the matter. He may even have been hailed a hero by certain members of the public, who would have called for any court penalty handed down to him to be light. But Nemer did not rid the world of a sick person, a sadist. Instead, he had fired a 9mm handgun at a hard-working 44-year-old named Geoffrey Williams.

The father of two could not have been more different to Nemer. A thin, rapidly balding man with an untidy beard, Williams worked diligently for every cent his family made. He owned and operated a small newsagency and on that morning in August 2001 he was delivering newspapers to his subscribers. Williams had no idea why the girls he passed, several times during his rounds, reacted to him with such fear. Nor did he pay them much attention – he had work to do. In particular, he had to take four copies of the Sunday newspaper to a block of flats on Arthur Street, Unley.

Two weeks after the incident, Williams would tell police he had turned his head to reverse the van out of the block's driveway when he saw somebody standing near his van. 'The next thing I know, I see a hole up against that window,' he said. 'I presume it was the barrel of a gun that the person must have had very close to the window. When I saw this hole, the window of the van was intact. Immediately after this I felt an intense stinging pain in my face and noticed blood immediately. The blood was spurting around the cabin where I was sitting and coming from my face. I thought to myself, at that time, that I had been shot.'

Half-blind and in agony, Williams somehow managed to drive away from the scene. He stopped one minute later on King William Rd at Unley, and called triple zero. Police and ambulance crews arrived quickly and rushed Williams to the Royal Adelaide Hospital. Emergency department doctors found a bullet wound through the bridge of Williams's nose, leading to the shattered remains of his right eye. They prepped him for immediate surgery but it was too late – they could not save the vision in his right eye. Strangely, there was no sign of the bullet. A few days later, as Williams's wife, Judi, was doing the family's laundry, she heard something clanking in their front-loader. The bullet had exited his skull and become lodged in the wool of Williams's beanie.

While Williams recovered, Nemer spent five days in consultation with lawyers. Sparing no expense, his family hired arguably the best barrister in Adelaide – David Edwardson. A handsome man with a sharp wit and charming smile, Mr Edwardson had made a name for himself by taking on controversial cases. He also originated the 'zig-zag defence', a legal tactic used in cases involving head-on car crashes. Through a carefully worded cross-examination of police experts, Mr Edwardson would leave jurors in doubt as to who had crossed onto the wrong side of the road – his client or the victim. Acquittals were the inevitable result, the jury too vexed with reasonable doubt to return a guilty verdict.

On 24 August 2001, Paul Nemer surrendered both himself and his grandfather's gun to police. He was held in custody and interrogated. 'On behalf of my lawyers, I wish not to answer any questions,' was all he would say. After five hours of that, he was taken to the Adelaide Magistrates Court. Nemer's tailored suit was a stark contrast to the attire of most overnight arrests, but the charge against him was not. Police prosecutors accused him of attempting to murder Williams.

Mr Edwardson was quick to point out the allegation was no more than a 'holding charge', and asked Nemer be released on bail. 'My client has participated in police inquiries in any way he can,' he stressed. 'He has signed a statement admitting he was the person who fired the gun in this matter. At no time did he intend to kill or cause physical harm to the unfortunate victim.' He said Nemer had handed over his passport and the clothes he wore on the night of the shooting. 'The fact he has provided his passport, without being asked, is a pretty good indication he is prepared to help police,' he said.

Ian Press, prosecuting, opposed bail. He said Nemer had 'cooperated so far', but warned that might end were he released. Indeed, the Office of the Director of Public Prosecutions feared the young man would impede investigations. He also objected to Mr Edwardson's downplaying of the attempted murder charge. 'The victim was sitting in his car at the time of the shooting,' he said. 'The gun was held extremely close to the car when the victim was shot. Someone being out at 4 am with a pistol and shooting someone to the head is hardly indicative of a holding charge.'

Magistrate David Gurry ruled bail was appropriate – but only under strict conditions. Nemer was confined to his parents' home between 11.30 pm and 7 am. He had to report to the nearest police station twice a week, and his father would forfeit $10,000 should his son disobey his bail.

Immediately, the case caught the public's attention. Nemer, with his slick style of dress and well-to-do family, seemed like the rich kid everyone loved to hate. Williams, on his first public appearance, was a typical Aussie battler now missing an eye through someone else's irresponsibility. Within the community, battle lines were being drawn. The case started to play on very deep, very ugly sentiments of race and class. The Lebanese community closed ranks around the Nemers, while many Australian-born citizens began to look sideways at the wealthy businesspeople.

'I was born and bred in Adelaide, and baptised in the church in the city,' George Nemer remembered in 2009. 'Growing up in the mid-1960s, I was called "wog" and "spag" and "dago" . . . it was a pretty racist time. But things were worse after Paul was charged. When my wife went to the shops, people would point at her and say "She's the mother of that shooter".'

The case began its slow progress through the justice system. A ballistics report, completed and filed on 16 July 2001, cast an early shadow over Paul Nemer's co-operation with police. Forensic scientists had examined the 9mm Browning pistol Nemer had surrendered, as well as several Shobra rounds. They formed the opinion the bullet that struck Williams could have been fired by the Browning – but they could not 'exclude' the possibility it had been fired by another gun. In addition, bullet fragments recovered from the scene had not been fired through the chamber of the Browning that had been handed in by Nemer. An essential question arose: had the young man swapped the 9mm's chamber for that of another 'clean' gun prior to his voluntary arrest?

Nemer hired senior counsel to work with Mr Edwardson – Lindy Powell, QC. Famed for her passionate closing addresses, renowned for her rapport with juries, Ms Powell was an invaluable addition to the team. Highly respected within legal circles, Ms Powell had literally grown up with the rest of the state's top lawyers – both prosecution and defence – and those relationships ran deep. Most importantly, Ms Powell forged strong bonds with her clients and would sacrifice much for their cause. It was a quality that would be necessary, time and again, in the months to come.

Nemer's motive for shooting at Williams was not made public until 22 April 2002, during committal proceedings. After hearing evidence from Annan and Mavromichalis, Magistrate Charles Eardley ruled it appropriate Nemer stand trial, in the Supreme Court, on charges of attempted murder, wounding with intent to do grievous bodily harm and endangering life. Ms Powell disagreed. 'My client did not intend to kill or injure Mr Williams,' she argued. 'The charge against him should be dropped. Specific intent must be proved for the charge of attempted murder to be upheld.' Magistrate Eardley, however, would not be swayed, and Nemer had a date with the state's highest court.

Before that came about, there were negotiations to be had. Mr Edwardson and Ms Powell hoped to draft a plea bargain for their client. They took their petition to the Director of Public Prosecutions himself. Paul Rofe, QC, was the first and only man to hold the position since its establishment in 1991. A tenacious litigator with a gravelly voice and dogged determination, Mr Rofe was justifiably proud of his office. The DPP, as it was known, was a well-balanced blend of eager legal graduates and experienced counsel, working together to process in excess of fifteen hundred cases each year. Under the *Director of Public Prosecutions Act* (1991), his office was autonomous from everyone in the State Government – including the Premier and the Attorney-General. That meant the final decision on every one of those cases – including whether they would go to trial or be settled through plea-bargaining – was the sole responsibility of Mr Rofe.

'My client offered to plead guilty to a charge of unlawful wounding,' Mr Edwardson said in 2003. 'That offence carries a maximum of five years' jail. The offer was rejected. Then, I think, there was an offer to plead guilty to committing an act likely to cause grievous bodily harm. That carries a 10-year maximum. That was rejected, too. Finally we made the offer to plead guilty to endangering life, which has a 15-year maximum. We started at the bottom and moved up.'

For 15 months, the Nemer case disappeared from public view. When it re-emerged on 7 July 2003, it was markedly different. Mr Rofe personally appeared before Justice John Sulan and formally withdrew the allegations of attempted murder and wounding with intent. Nemer immediately pleaded guilty to endangering life. Ms Powell asked her client receive a suspended sentence, saying he had fired a hasty 'warning shot' through the back window of the van while running toward it. Mr Rofe said he would not oppose such a penalty.

Justice Sulan wanted them to slow down. 'How can a shot pierce a man's eye when it's fired from behind the vehicle, and the victim is sitting in the vehicle?' he asked.

The problem, as His Honour saw it, was that paperwork filed by both sides contained conflicting versions of events. Ms Powell did her best to ease Justice Sulan's mind. She said Nemer was 'eight metres away' from Williams's van when he fired 'a warning shot'. 'He had received a hysterical phone call from two girls and decided to be their knight in shining armour,' she quipped apologetically.

Justice Sulan was not convinced. He pointed to Williams's victim impact statement. 'He says, "I remember seeing the barrel of the gun pointed at me, and the next thing I knew there was blood everywhere",' Justice Sulan said. 'That conflicts with your "warning shot" submission.'

Ms Powell countered it was 'not uncommon' for victims of crime to be mistaken. 'People who have been through traumatic situations can convince themselves of things they thought they saw,' she explained. 'We know that's so in the courts, because that's human nature.'

Her submission did not impress Justice Sulan. He ordered the hearing continue after the luncheon adjournment, strongly advising Ms Powell and Mr Rofe to get their stories straight before he returned to the bench.

His suggestion went unheeded. At 2.15 pm, Ms Powell presented His Honour with a document written, by both parties, at a cafe around the corner from the courtroom. 'It is our position, and indeed the position of the prosecution, that whether or not Mr Nemer was 2 metres away or 8 metres away matters not,' it read. 'What is important is that Mr Nemer has accepted that, at the time the gun was discharged, that act was likely to endanger the life of Mr Williams.'

The document sat poorly with the broader community. Many perceived it to be less a plea bargain and more of a plea to sweep the matter quietly under the rug. Given the high price tags Ms Powell and Mr Edwardson placed on their services, and their long-standing personal relationships with Mr Rofe, some began to mutter unhappily.

Tensions were high on Friday 25 July 2003, when Justice Sulan was due to pass sentence. Nemer – dressed immaculately as always – stood quietly in the dock. The public gallery had overflowed with spectators, ranging from the Williams and Nemer families to interested, irate members of the public. Extra court sheriff's officers had been rostered on in case of incident. Mr Rofe left the bar table to speak quietly with Williams, and to shake his hand.

The room fell silent when Justice Sulan entered. His Honour's sentencing remarks made it clear he knew, all too well, the sort of powder keg with which he was dealing.

'I consider it is appropriate to make some general remarks because it appears, to me, that there is among members of the community some misunderstanding about the function of the courts,' he began. 'It is fortunate we live in a society where the system of justice is transparent, but public comment about what we judges say or do should be fair and balanced. Any criticism should be informed, balanced and proportionate with regard to the facts. I regret that is not always the case.

'It is the role of prosecutors, not judges, to determine whether a person will be prosecuted for criminal offences. The judge is bound by the charges that the prosecution elects to bring. It is not right for a judge to require a prosecutor proceed with a higher, rather than a lesser, charge. Judges should not be involved in the functions of prosecution or defence counsel. Judges should not jump to conclusions.'

The mood in the courtroom was distinctly sour. Shorn of its flowery language, Justice Sulan had, in the only manner available to him, publicly denounced the plea bargaining system and declared himself to be just as much a victim of it as Williams would soon consider himself to be.

'Mr Nemer, you must consider yourself to be very fortunate because the Director of Public Prosecutions has deigned to accept your lesser plea,' he continued. 'The DPP and defence counsel are agreed as to the circumstances surrounding this offence and, in the absence of other evidence, a sentencing judge has no alternative but to sentence on those facts. The DPP would have been mindful of the principle that a court can only sentence on facts proven beyond a reasonable doubt.'

Several people in the gallery shifted uncomfortably. Justice Sulan's candour was difficult to listen to, and his thinly veiled rebukes of Mr Rofe were incredibly potent.

Justice Sulan told Nemer his crime – as outlined by prosecution and defence – lacked specific intent to harm and was therefore 'reckless' and 'immature'. He said Nemer had been 'indifferent' as to whether or not Williams's life would be threatened by the shot he fired. He criticised his desire to rescue Annan and Mavromichalis. 'It was wrong that you did not telephone the police, and it's unfortunate that you decided to act as the girls' saviour and protector,' he said. 'On the other hand, you were relatively young and chose to act in the way you did on the spur of the moment in this chaotic and frightening situation.' Justice Sulan did not, however, blame him for the gun. 'You cannot be held responsible for it being under your parents' bed,' he said, shifting to look at Nemer's father momentarily. 'But you did make the decision to take it with you, and that had disastrous consequences.'

Williams, he felt, had 'shown great courage and great presence of mind' in the situation. 'Since then, Mr Williams has suffered enormously, both physically and psychologically,' he said. 'Technically, he should not even be here – he is fortunate that he did not lose his life. Nemer, your act has caused acute hardship to both Mr Williams and his family. He has been left with permanent physical injuries, but he is a man of extraordinary character and resilience, and has shown this by getting on with his life.'

Justice Sulan noted that Nemer had also suffered. 'You had been an outgoing young man at the beginning of adult-hood,' he said. 'You should have been approaching some of the most rewarding years of your life. You had exceptional school results and good support from a loving family. You are regarded as a person with great empathy for others who are underprivileged. You have a great deal going for you. Now, you have been left with a feeling of shame and remorse. You feel helpless because you feel you cannot explain, to Williams and his family, how much you regret what this has done to them. You have pledged to compensate him when you can. I accept that you are truly sorry, and this was something that was completely out of character for you. This incident will stay with you for the rest of your life.'

Saying he would have imposed a four-year jail term, had Nemer denied the allegations, he instead ordered the young man serve three years and three months, with a two-year non-parole period.

The mood in the room settled. The Nemer family had long believed their son was bound for jail, and quietly accepted the decision. Williams, flanked by his wife and children, smiled broadly. The sense of relief was only short-lived, and shattered irrevocably when Justice Sulan announced he was suspending Nemer's imprisonment. The rich young man, he said, would go free on condition of a three-year, $100 good behaviour bond.

Reporters, sitting in the front row of the gallery, paused midway through their note taking. Muffled surprise rifled through the spectators. Everyone was sure they had misheard Justice Sulan's order. Surely the Supreme Court had not imposed a mere $100 bond on a man whose family was exceedingly wealthy? But that was indeed the case. Whatever his reasons, Justice Sulan had ruled Geoffrey Williams's shattered right eye had a monetary value of $100.

The result was chaos. Several people vented their frustrations vocally and were ushered outside by sheriff's officers. George Nemer approached Williams, hand outstretched, with an apology and an offer of $200,000 compensation. Williams refused both. The newsagent left court silently, pushing past reporters eager for his comment. Asked if he was happy with the sentence, Williams simply shook his head and kept walking.

Mr Rofe told reporters he was satisfied with the outcome, and dubbed Justice Sulan's unusual comment 'very considered and proper'. 'I don't subscribe to the belief that every case has to result in a long jail sentence,' he said. 'Is it better to have kids with no previous convictions, even if their offences are serious, in jail? Or is it better to have them becoming proper members of the community? That's what the judge had to decide, and it seems to me he did so properly.'

Nemer and his family emerged soon after, and were surrounded by television cameras. Unperturbed, they made their way across Victoria Square and headed for the nearest Catholic Church. There, they prayed and offered thanks to God for what they felt to be their unexpected good fortune. George Nemer told his family not to celebrate. He was concerned the case was far from over . . . and he was right. The paltry sum attached to Nemer's bond had made the family an enemy in the form of the single most powerful man in South Australia – Premier Mike Rann.

Born in the United Kingdom and raised in New Zealand, Mike Rann moved to Adelaide in 1977. Upon his arrival, he served as press secretary for then-Premier Don Dunstan, writing his speeches and advising him on policy. Rann would go on to perform the same role for Dunstan's Labor Party successors – Des Corcoran and John Bannon – before moving into politics himself in 1985. By 1989 he was a minister responsible for a number of portfolios, including tourism and state services. After Labor lost the 1993 election, Rann became the party's deputy leader and, with the support of right-wing power brokers, was named leader 12 months later. His charismatic, populist style was popular with voters – causing a swing to Labor in the 1997 election – but was not enough to win Parliament. Every inch the Premier-in-waiting, Rann focused his attention on the upcoming 2002 election. To win, he needed to court the favour of powerful, influential

South Australians. It was at this time he was contacted by George Nemer.

'I got to know Mike Rann when he was the opposition leader,' George said in 2009. 'I needed some help getting a permit to establish a petrol station at Old Noarlunga. From there, we developed a personal relationship. He would come to our family parties, he would come to our charity functions, and quite often he would speak. He once said to me that "without the Nemer family, this state would not be where it is today".'

Mr Rann's opinion would change. In 2003, he was less than a year into his first term as Premier. He presided over a minority government that relied on the preferences of independent politicians. The controversy surrounding the Nemer case provided an opportunity for him to emphasise his goal of delivering law and order to South Australians. On the day Nemer received his suspended sentence, Mr Rann became the first Premier in state history to openly question the justice system.

'I would like to express how deeply shocked I am by the outcome of the Paul Nemer case,' he told reporters. 'It is difficult to imagine circumstances where someone involved in a serious shooting can escape jail. A message must be sent to offenders that criminal behaviour is unacceptable.' He said the Attorney-General's department would compile a 'comprehensive report' on the case. 'I am particularly interested to know the views of the victim and I sympathise with him and his family,' he said. 'I want to discover the process by which a plea was negotiated, the factual basis upon which the sentencing judge imposed sentence, and whether the prosecution accepted the factual basis.' Rann said he particularly wanted to know 'whether Mr Rofe intended to appeal against the sentence'.

Legal identities scoffed at that. All it proved, they felt, was that the Premier had no understanding of the justice system. There was no need for an Attorney-General's report – the answers Rann sought were in Justice Sulan's sentencing remarks. Clearly, Mr Rofe was not going to appeal against a deal he had personally brokered.

The Director of Public Prosecutions spent three days studying Justice Sulan's comments. On 28 July, he announced there would be no appeal. 'There is no prospect of success,' he said. Mr Rofe said his decision had nothing to do with Nemer's affluent background. 'It wouldn't matter who the person was,' he said. 'Providing he had the same good character and no convictions, as this boy did, I would have expected much the same result.' He also said firearms charges would not be filed against George and Rita Nemer, and acknowledged a mistake had been made. 'Police, quite understandably, were focused on the shooting and so was my office. Probably, if we had the time over again, I'd do it differently.'

Public sentiment was grim. An editorial in *The Advertiser* newspaper claimed an 'overwhelming majority of South Australians' had come to believe 'the law is the plaything of people with wealth, privileges and connections'. It said citizens 'look with disbelief at the justice dealt to Mr Williams', and called on Rann to intervene. The rest of the media zeroed-in on the Nemer family. Camera crews camped outside their mansion 24 hours a day, desperate to capture even a glimpse of the convicted gunman. Much was made of George Nemer's attendances at the Sky City Casino.

'It was hell, absolute hell,' George Nemer said in 2009. 'It just made us feel like we were outcasts, hated and unwanted.

To be honest, we felt like shit. Wherever we went, people would point . . . we had to hide Paul under a blanket, in the back seat of the car, just to get him in and out of the house. I just can't express properly how stressful life was. For the first time, I just wanted to pack up my family and leave Adelaide – the place I was born, my hometown – and move overseas.'

While the Nemers suffered the community's wrath, Geoffrey Williams found himself elevated to near folk-hero status. He made his first public statement on 29 July, and began by thanking South Australians for their 'support and genuine wishes of concern'.

'Myself and my family have whole-heartedly agreed with the sentiments of the community in relation to this offence,' his statement read. 'This malicious shooting of an innocent man while he is going about his business can only be viewed as one of the most despicable and cowardly crimes open to another human being. Had I not turned, I would almost certainly have been shot in the back of the head and would no longer be here.' It was for this reason, he argued, people had questioned Justice Sulan's 'disgraceful, absolutely and utterly rubbish' sentence.

However, Williams felt His Honour deserved something of a break. 'In criticising this sentence, we would like to acknowledge the position of Justice Sulan, who quite clearly was left with his hands tied behind his back,' the statement continued. 'The mere fact he went to such lengths to explain his role in the sentencing process demonstrates his reluctance to accept the facts which were put forward to him.'

The blame, Williams said, fell solely and squarely on Mr Rofe. 'I find it hard to comprehend the circumstances under which the plea to endangering life was accepted,' he said.

'The fact that the Crown, through Mr Rofe, did not oppose a suspended sentence shows to us his lack of concern and understanding. My feeling is that the actions of a small few let down the work of many others. I feel it is not only my family which has been let down by this process, but the community at large who now live, work and play with people like Mr Nemer amongst them.' He concluded with a bombshell. 'The only way I feel this can be addressed is through a judicial inquiry into the matter. I have no doubt than an inquiry would ask serious questions of the Director of Public Prosecutions.'

On 30 July, Williams had a private meeting with Premier Rann. Afterwards, the two men posed for the media, and Mr Rann said he strongly believed Nemer should have been jailed. That statement fanned the flames of discontent into an inferno. Media outlets – in particular, Channel 7's controversial current affairs show, *Today Tonight* – backed Williams's calls for a public inquiry. Mr Rofe found himself followed, at every turn, by television cameras. Footage was aired, almost nightly, of his visits to the TAB betting office near his chambers, of him smoking, of his nights out at pubs. The Liberal opposition asked, in Parliament, whether Mr Rofe had the support of the government. Callers to talkback radio stations made their views clear. One elderly woman said she 'knew' Mr Rofe was 'a bad person' because 'when he comes on the television, that awful, nasty music plays'.

Mr Rann had, in the eyes of the legal fraternity, crossed the line. Although concerned by the Premier's initial comments on the case, counsel on both sides of the Bar had chosen to bite their tongues. Now that he had called for Nemer to be jailed, the legal fraternity felt it had no choice but to actively defend its institution. The South Australian Bar Association told the media its members were concerned any government inquiry into the Nemer case would blur the lines between the State and the judiciary, and compromise the independence that was Mr Rofe's under the law.

The Nemers, meanwhile, had become prisoners in their own home. At the end of July, they received an anonymous letter in their mailbox. 'Scum must pay,' it read. 'Always look over your shoulder.' Frightened, they sought to smooth things over once again. Through Ms Powell, they contacted Williams and asked for a private meeting. The idea was that Paul Nemer would apologise to his victim, face to face, and express his remorse.

Williams took their request public. 'I said "no",' he told *The Advertiser* on 1 August. 'They asked me but I had to say no. How could I accept? I didn't want to see him.' He was, however, pleased with the 'enormous' public sympathy he had received. 'I have people stopping me in the streets, wishing me well,' he said.

His 16-year-old daughter, Courtney, felt her father deserved even more adoration. Following Mr Rann's lead, she circulated a petition calling for Nemer to be jailed. 'I had to do something, I want justice to be done,' she said on 1 August. 'It's been very emotional – our family has been through a lot – and because I'm so close to Dad, it's been really hard.'

The Liberal opposition, previously supportive of the government's stance, flipped on the spot. It accused Mr Rann of 'whipping up public hysteria', saying he could not guarantee the independence of an inquiry. Only the hiring of an interstate lawyer could do that, opposition MPs argued, not the 'cosy arrangement' of having Solicitor-General Chris

Kourakis – the government's top counsel – dig into the Nemer matter.

The Premier, buoyed by the sharp spike in his approval rating, was unconcerned. He announced that Mr Kourakis would conduct an inquiry to determine whether an appeal against the sentence could be filed. He dismissed the suggestion he was feeding dissent as 'absolutely puerile'. 'I'm not encouraging lawlessness,' he insisted. 'Anyone that's a vigilante, let's lock them up and hopefully they will be in the cell next to Mr Nemer.' He was unimpressed, also, by the Bar Association. 'Why are they so terrified of having a look at the way things have been done for years and seeing if we can't improve them?' he asked rhetorically. 'Why are they being so defensive?'

The usual rules of politics and justice had gone out the window. Every side was issuing public statements – the Nemers, Williams's family, lawyers, political parties. In such a bizarre climate, the only thing Mr Rofe could do was go public himself. On 2 August, a memo from his office to the Attorney-General was leaked to the media. It damned the government for 'undermining' his authority, and demanded a public declaration of 'your support for this office'. It also revealed Mr Rofe's team resolved 80 per cent of their case load through plea bargaining because 'the court system simply cannot handle' the sheer volume of cases waiting to go to trial. 'You are undermining the community's confidence in this office to adjudicate and prosecute our files properly and according to law,' the memo read. 'We are making approximately 30 decisions per week on complex and emotive matters. Negotiations are an inevitable part of our work.'

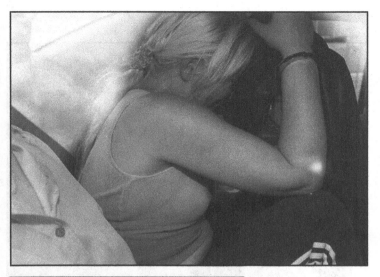

Donna Lee Casagrande being taken from Adelaide airport after surrendering herself. (Newspix/Mark Calleja)

Mark Errin Rust, sex pervert and murderer. (Newspix/Michael Milnes)

Police search the Wingfield Dump for Megumi Suzuki's remains and find Joanne Lillecrapp's head as well. (Newspix/Campbell Brodie)

Roman and Janina Jadrych reunited outside the Supreme Court.
(Newspix/Michael Milnes)

James Trevor Birmingham, the second masked rapist, flees media outside the District Court prior to his road-rage sentencing. (Newspix/Chris Mangan)

Jean Eric Gassy being ferried, by heavily-armed officers, out of the Supreme Court during his trial. (Newspix/Michael Milnes)

Hayley, one of Brooks's victims, after the sentencing.
(Newspix/Michael Milnes)

Paul Habib Nemer. (Newspix/David Cronin)

Photo taken by Anthony John Smith, the 'Artful Dodger', while hiding out in a luxury hotel. (Newspix/Michael Milnes)

Rebecca Jane Clarke – who made pornographic movies with two 14-year-old girls – outside court at the start of her pregnancy. (Newspix/David Cronin)

Joseph Higham, aka 'the running man'. (Newspix/BURTON)

The memo received the attention of Mr Rann's spokesman. He said the Premier felt there was 'no reason to question the DPP's capability because of one particular case'.

The government wasn't questioning Mr Rofe – it was content to simply override him. On 12 August, at the recommendation of Mr Kourakis, the DPP lodged papers with the Court of Criminal Appeal. It sought a hearing for permission to appeal against Nemer's suspended sentence and $100 bond. Sticking to his guns, Mr Rofe refused to conduct the appeal. He was ordered to brief Mr Kourakis, who would do so in his place. Mr Kourakis, of course, was an employee of Mr Rann and the Labor Government. Therefore, for the first time in South Australian history, the State Government would be directly prosecuting a criminal case. The office specifically designed for such a task had been cut out.

Mr Kourakis intended to argue four main points. He would ask the court to find Justice Sulan failed to properly take into account the fact Nemer had fired the gun 'knowing he might kill' Williams. He would claim the sentence failed to have regard to 'the fact the gun handed in by Nemer was not the entire gun used in the offence'. He would tell the court Justice Sulan erred by ruling Nemer had fired into Williams's van 'while running toward it'. Finally, he would argue the suspended sentence and $100 bond was 'manifestly inadequate' punishment for so serious a crime.

Police were given the job of serving Nemer with the appeal papers. They had little success. Visits to the family mansion and another address failed to locate the young man. He was not hiding from the police – he was trying to avoid mass public scrutiny. On 18 August, a meeting was arranged at a secret location, and the paperwork was handed over. With that done, the appeal hearing could go ahead the following month.

The South Australian Bar Association then made its move. Concerned at what it perceived to be the government's strong-arming of the DPP, representatives said they would seek to appear at the hearing as *amicus curiae* – a Latin phrase translating as 'friend of the court'. A successful *amicus curiae* application would see the association given a seat at the hearing to present information on points of law relevant to the case. Specifically, the association wanted to talk about the independence Mr Rofe had under the *Director of Public Prosecutions Act* (1991). Their goal was to convince the Court of Criminal Appeal that, because Mr Rofe did not want the appeal to go ahead, it had no standing and should therefore be thrown out. It was a matter of public interest, they said.

Mr Rann, however, believed it was a matter of protecting their own. 'To me, *amicus curiae* means enemies of the victims, enemies of the public,' he said on 28 August. 'My message to the lawyers is this: I have accused you of being a club and I have been criticised for doing so. If ever there was an example of a club in action, trying to defend its own interests, then here we have got it. The question I would ask of the legal fraternity is this: when are you going to stand up for the victims of crime? When are you going to be on the public's side, rather than the lawyers' side?'

Almost immediately, the association backed down. The application was not filed. A spokesman pithily denied the change of heart had anything to do with 'any so-called club'.

The argument, however, was not about to go away. David Edwardson and Lindy Powell took up the association's cause and added it to the appeal hearing. On 12 September, they filed suit with the Full Court of the Supreme Court, accusing the Rann Government of breaking the law. The government acted invalidly, they argued, by forcing Mr Rofe to appeal and had therefore breached the *Director of Public Prosecutions Act* (1991). 'The act guarantees Mr Rofe the right to perform his duties entirely independent of direction or control by the Crown, or any minister or officer of the Crown,' the document read. 'The government's actions constitute control. We seek an order directing the Attorney-General to withdraw the direction to appeal to the DPP.'

It was an attempt to torpedo the government's appeal before it even began, and it was only partially successful. In another legal first, Supreme Court Chief Justice John Doyle said both cases would be heard at the same time. He, Justice Graham Prior and Justice Ann Vanstone would conduct a 'double-header' and sit as both the Full Court of the Supreme Court and the Court of Criminal Appeal.

The make-up of the double bench was fascinating. Prior to his appointment to the Supreme Court, Chief Justice Doyle had served as Solicitor-General from 1986 to 1995. A Rhodes scholar, Chief Justice Doyle had spent many years as a highly regarded lawyer and was thought to be an expert in complex constitutional cases. That background would serve him well when hearing Nemer's claims the government had acted illegally.

Justice Prior had also been Solicitor-General – from 1976 to 1984. Senior, opinionated and possessed of a razor-sharp tongue, he was a fearsome judicial force that terrified many lawyers. Justice Vanstone had been the Deputy DPP – second only to Mr Rofe – until joining the District Court bench in 1999. She had only recently donned the red robes of the Supreme Court, but she had earned the reputation of being both firm and fair. It was an ideal panel for an incredibly complex case.

The appeal was listed to be heard on 18 and 19 September in courtroom three. It was the first time the high-tech, ultra-modern, computerised chamber – refurbished at a cost of $3 million – had been used since the trial of the Snowtown serial killers. Nemer did not attend the hearing – his presence was not required, and would likely have caused a scene. Williams, accompanied by his family, entered the court just before the hearing started. They jostled for space in a large public gallery already overflowing with media and gawkers.

Ms Powell's opening gambit was unexpected – she asked Mr Kourakis be removed from the case due to a conflict of interest. 'The DPP had made a decision not to pursue this appeal,' she said. 'Mr Rofe has not been given a platform upon which to defend, to this court, his position. The Solicitor-General must, therefore, be in conflict – he cannot be said to be acting for the Office of the DPP because of their fundamentally different positions. There's no conflict with Mr Kourakis representing the government – that's no problem at all – but he cannot represent the DPP, whose position is diametrically opposed to that of the government.'

Mr Kourakis said there was no problem – he had been briefed by Mr Rofe. Whether that briefing had been given willingly or not was of no consequence. 'My professional responsibility is to attend to this criminal appeal as best I can,' he said.

The court agreed, and the hearing went on as planned. It was announced the Justices would commence by sitting as the Full Court of the Supreme Court. The legality of the government's position would be decided before the appeal against Nemer's sentence.

Ms Powell was more than ready to begin. 'Clearly, Parliament intended to create a Director of Public Prosecutions with the power, the discretion, to appeal or not appeal as he saw fit,' she said. 'That must be sacrosanct. It would be pointless and fruitless to have an entirely independent DPP who can be told to reverse his decision by the Attorney-General. The Attorney-General cannot say, "I'm taking away your discretion and substituting my own".'

She agreed the government must be allowed to give 'general directions' to prosecutors – they were, after all, public servants. But she insisted there was a line that could not be crossed. 'The DPP can be given directions in respect of how to do things, not whether or not to do things,' she said. 'Once the DPP had exercised his power and decided not to appeal, it was not open to the government to substitute its opinion for that of Mr Rofe. That so fundamentally undermines the law as to make it nonsense.'

Mr Kourakis said the key was what the law did not say. 'There is nothing that says the Director can determine there will not be an appeal,' he said reasonably. 'It would be of great inconvenience if the decision to prosecute or not prosecute, to appeal or not appeal, could be made once and for all in a way that was not subject to second thoughts or better consideration over time.'

It was an incredibly powerful argument – the legal equivalent of a backhand across the face. Tellingly, the judges decided to transform themselves into the Court of Criminal Appeal and move on to the challenge to Nemer's sentence.

Mr Kourakis began by outlining all the evidence against Nemer – information that was, he said, 'utterly inconsistent' with the plea bargain drafted by Mr Edwardson, Ms Powell and Mr Rofe. He pointed to the ballistics report, and the likely swapping of the gun barrel. He argued that this information, coupled with Annan and Mavromichalis's statements, Williams's recollections and other forensic evidence, led to one inescapable conclusion. 'Nemer must have been aware of the very high risk to Mr Williams's life when he fired,' he said. 'The evidence is inconsistent with the version of events he told the court, and with the leniency he was shown'.

Nemer, he argued, already knew this. He tendered a letter written by the young man that had been attached to the Browning he surrendered. 'Nemer says, "My only intention was to scare him because I believed he posed an immediate and serious threat to the girls",' he read. 'Well, the way you scare someone when you have a gun is by endangering their life. He deliberately decided to shoot at Mr Williams. Calling his actions reckless, stupid and dangerous are not enough – the decision to shoot someone at close range, knowing the high risk of injury, can only properly be described as callous.'

Then he dropped a bombshell: Nemer had a criminal history. 'Just six months before the shooting, Nemer made a false report to police,' he said. 'Nemer had a car accident while driving his father's car, then reported it stolen. He was fined $400, but no conviction was recorded. His father punished him by refusing to buy him a car as he had been planning to.'

The revelation cast Nemer in an entirely new – and entirely unfavourable – light. His few supporters had considered Nemer a 'good boy' who went to church, listened to his parents, obeyed his curfew and made a poor decision. Mr Kourakis portrayed him as a liar whose virtuous life was the result of punishment for an earlier transgression. It capsized Mr Rofe's much-publicised belief Nemer deserved to stay out of prison and become a 'proper' member of society.

That Justice Sulan had not taken these matters into account, Mr Kourakis said, was a 'fact-finding error'. 'There are errors serious enough to allow an appeal,' he argued. 'Mr Rofe appears to have proceeded on facts that were inconsistent with the evidence. The prosecution failed to appreciate the full significance of this material.'

Mr Edwardson then took the bar table. He urged the court to ignore Mr Kourakis's submissions because none of his concerns had been an issue at the original case. The government, he said, should not be allowed to bring in new evidence – to shift the goal posts, as it were – simply to prove its point. It would be unfair to a young man who was already suffering much. 'Due to unprecedented publicity, this man is now an outcast from society,' he said. 'What is most important is that Mr Nemer handed in the weapon, that he accepted he had acted recklessly and he accepts responsibility for his actions.' In those circumstances, he argued, a suspended sentence was warranted.

Chief Justice Doyle, and Justices Prior and Vanstone, spent 48 days deliberating. The parties gathered in courtroom three, once again, on 7 November 2003. The court's 53-page decision was fascinating – and spoke of a deeper dissent.

Chief Justice Doyle, the constitutional expert, said the government had overstepped its bounds. 'The idea of directing the Director to make a particular decision is, I consider, an odd one,' he said. Saying the government had no right to interfere in Mr Rofe's decision-making, he sided with Mr Edwardson and Ms Powell.

He was overruled by his colleagues. Justice Prior said the situation was not odd but 'exceptional', and that the government had the power to make prosecutorial decisions 'whether the Director has made a decision or not'. Justice

Vanstone's decision was a surprise. Mr Rofe's former offsider went against her erstwhile boss and had 'reached the firm view' the government had acted properly.

The findings on the government's appeal were even more chaotic. Again, history was made – the Court of Criminal Appeal found itself in a three-way split.

Chief Justice Doyle agreed with Mr Edwardson, deeming it 'unfair' the court had been able to consider evidence not presented to Justice Sulan. While that was far from satisfactory, the 'risk of injustice' to Nemer convinced him it was best to maintain the status quo, and leave the sentence as imposed.

Justice Prior strongly disagreed. 'I do not think it is in the public interest to permit the sentence to stand,' he said. 'The proper administration of criminal justice requires an appeal to be granted.' He warned he was ready to impose a replacement sentence immediately unless Nemer took the stand and gave evidence, finally, on what really transpired that night.

Justice Vanstone was not about to wait. 'The sentence imposed was manifestly inadequate,' she said. 'It was far below that which should have been imposed. A sentence of no less than four years and nine months imprisonment is the very lowest sentence that could properly have been imposed in this case. And suspending that sentence would be inappropriate.'

However, she said she had come to agree with Justice Prior, and would allow Nemer the chance to speak for himself. It was 'too late', they said, to examine Nemer's intent in firing the gun. What they wanted clarified, once and for all, was the distance between the gunman and the van at the time the shot was fired – 2 metres or 8 metres. That, they felt, would give them the information they needed to decide an adequate sentence.

Nemer was remanded on $15,000 bail to appear in court, and give evidence, in one week. The writing was on the wall: Paul Habib Nemer was going to jail. The only question was when, and for how long.

Williams left court smiling. 'I'm not going to say anything until next week,' he told reporters. Ms Powell also declined to comment, saying she was saving her submissions for court. Mr Rofe, by contrast, was quite vocal.

'I'm confident I did my job properly, including full consultation with the victim,' he said. 'Throughout the case, I sought to act in good faith and in accordance with the law. The sole function of the Office of the DPP is to seek justice – it is not about winning, or losing, or maximising results.'

Mr Rann was eager to talk as well. 'This is a victory for victims, a victory for common sense and a vindication of our decision to intervene in the case,' he said. 'That decision proved to be totally justified. The law is very important but, for me, justice is much more important and, last week, justice prevailed.' He said he had already phoned Williams. 'He seemed very pleased, although there's still some matters to get through,' Mr Rann explained. 'I said, "I think we should have a beer next week".'

Pundits claimed the Premier was in a 'win-win' situation, but one that carried a severe financial cost. 'It is all well and good to talk about being tough on law and order, because increasing penalties for crimes does not cost anything,' columnist Greg Kelton said following the decision. 'It is the aftermath that costs millions of dollars. The cost of getting tough on crime, during the next decade, could be as high as $500 million.'

Nemer's family had believed, all along, their son was bound for jail. They had hoped to spare him that fate, but had never liked their chances of success. Their devotion to their youngest son had cost them all dearly. 'Wherever we went, people would point,' George Nemer said in 2009. 'Never in my life had I thought Adelaide – my hometown – could be so cruel. There's always been that undercurrent of darkness, yes, but you think that if you stay away from certain places, avoid certain people, then Adelaide stays a nice place to raise a family. And what kept me going was the support of those sorts of people. They would come see us at the petrol stations and say, "You didn't deserve what happened". I'd have people come up and ask, "Are you related to Paul Nemer?". I'd get worried, but I'd say, "Yes" and they'd reply, "You poor bastard, you've been screwed by the government". This happened many, many times and it restored some of our faith in Adelaide.'

Defence counsel were not about to meekly accept a jail term. On 10 November, Ms Powell made the most dangerous submission of her long career. Facing down the entire Court of Criminal Appeal bench, Ms Powell confirmed Nemer would give evidence – provided Justice Vanstone disqualified herself from the case. In a bold move, she accused the newly minted judge of bias. 'Justice Vanstone cannot sit on this sentencing matter,' she said, earning a vicious glare from the bench. 'Her Honour has pre-determined what the result would be, even if Mr Nemer did not give evidence.'

Her Honour's response was frosty. 'I don't think I've said anything like that,' she replied. 'But you go on, and we will not bother to disagree.'

Sensing the battle had been lost, Nemer approached Ms Powell and whispered something into her ear. The QC then said her client was prepared for the matter to go ahead as scheduled.

The lawyers had one last trick up their sleeves. Nemer was due to give evidence before the Court of Criminal Appeal on 13 November at 10.15 am. Less than two hours before that – at 8.30 am – his lawyers made an emergency petition, by video-link, to the High Court of Australia. Justice Dyson Heydon was told the Full Court was wrong to side with the Rann Government, that Justice Vanstone had revealed her 'irrevocable bias' against Nemer, that sentencing should be deferred until after counsel could bring the matter before the full bench of the High Court. There was a 'high risk', the lawyers said, Nemer would be 'immediately jailed' and spend months behind bars before a full High Court challenge was heard, exposing him to 'great suffering'.

Justice Heydon was unmoved. 'It would be exceptional if the High Court were to interfere with a part-heard criminal case,' he intoned, 'and this case is not exceptional enough to warrant that. This case is unusual, but that does not make it different from a wide range of criminal defendants before the court. This application is a back-door way of gaining bail, prior to sentencing, in circumstances where the front door is – if not locked – at least difficult to open. It is not to Mr Nemer's advantage that uncertainty as to his punishment be left hanging over his head for another year.'

There were no more escape routes, no more trapdoors. His final avenue exhausted, Paul Habib Nemer had no choice but to take the stand, in the Court of Criminal Appeal, and submit to intense questioning about the case that had divided South Australia.

At 10.15 am, the public gallery of courtroom three became a microcosm of that divide. One side of the public gallery was taken up by the Nemer family and their supporters. It was a sea of immaculately dressed, heavily gilded young men and women. Each sported high-end designer suits and the latest hairstyles. They greeted one another with raised voices, bear hugs and firm handshakes. The other half of the room was taken over by Williams and his supporters. Moderately but neatly dressed, this group sat in near silence, staring at the front of the courtroom and ignoring the antics of their opponents. Williams, in the back row, was the lone voice in the group, muttering derisively on occasion. Between the factions lay a small demilitarised zone where Adelaide's media were permitted to sit. It was a rare thing for reporters to be used as a buffer between rising passions.

The disquiet was palpable, and worsened unexpectedly. One of Williams's supporters – an elderly man, unconnected to the family save for shared ideology – crossed the gulf and took a seat between Nemer's friends. Just metres from the convicted gunman's parents, the elderly man took a deep breath and loudly expressed the opinion that Nemer 'deserved 10 years' jail'.

Several young women shifted uncomfortably, while a few men tensed but, thankfully, no one rose to the bait. Undaunted, the man repeated his view three more times, increasing the volume with every retelling. Finally, a Nemer supporter barked 'shut your mouth'. The man refused to oblige and, instead, shoved the owner of the dissenting voice. Further pushing and arguing ensued, attracting the attention of a court sheriff's officer. With steely politeness, he invited the elderly man to join him outside the courtroom for 'a little chat'. They returned several minutes later. The antagonist looked defeated and regretful, and was more than happy to take a seat on the pro-Williams side of the court instead.

The exchange unsettled Nemer himself. Appearing nervous, he separated from his friends and paced the room, checking in constantly with Ms Powell and Mr Edwardson. He then approached a court orderly and asked whether he would be required to sit in the dock during the hearing. When told yes, Nemer broke completely away from everyone and sat on an office chair that had been left near the dock. He slumped forward, rumpling his crisp suit, and twiddled his fingers anxiously. Nemer cast a gaze across the courtroom, as if taking in the emotions he had unleashed. Then the judges entered the room and Nemer took the stand.

'The first thing I heard was screaming,' he began. 'I thought it was from both girls . . . loud screaming saying, "That's him, that's him, he's back." I saw a van with its lights on, proceeding up the middle of the road. My friend started running after the van, I just followed him. I could see the van was being driven by someone – just a silhouette, no actual features. I recall that person looking over their left shoulder and staring at me. We were screaming things at the man, telling him to "fuck off" and "get out of here". I was too scared to get near the van, not knowing who was in it. That's when I raised the gun.'

Nemer leaned back in the chair of the witness box, took a sip of water and continued. 'I took it out of my right-hand pants pocket, on the front of my thigh. When I was running, I just started to fire it in the vicinity of the van, over the top of it, hoping it would just scare off whoever was there. I was between seven and nine metres from the van, looking at the left side of the back of it. Then, like, a second or so later, the van drove off.'

He paused. 'I never had the intention to, never wanted to, endanger someone's life,' he said emphatically. 'Things got a lot more scarier, if I can use that word. I was hoping I would miss. I wanted to scare him, and thought it would be the quickest way to scare anyone off. I thought that he had just attacked two girls . . . and now saw two more people and just kept staring, not caring, like he was crazy or something.'

He had spoken in a low, slow voice during his testimony, keeping his posture relaxed and submissive. Nemer's remorse certainly seemed genuine, and he appeared to be accepting of his fate. His appearance changed markedly, however, under cross-examination. Faced with Mr Kourakis's rapid-fire, sarcasm-laced questioning, Nemer's posture became more defiant, his responses more arrogant and his attitude very snide. If he had been a penitent 21-year-old before, he was now a prideful, defensive young man.

But the game changed again when Mr Kourakis asked that Nemer be shown one of the prosecution exhibits. An orderly passed a small object, wrapped in brown paper, first to a sheriff's officer and then to a policeman stationed in the court. Both men inspected the item, nodded, and handed it back to the orderly. She then took it to the witness box, stood in front of Nemer and unwrapped it – revealing the 9mm Browning handgun used to shoot Mr Williams.

Nemer leaped to his feet like he had been electrocuted. 'I don't want to hold it,' he yelped, recoiling from the weapon. 'No way, I'm not touching that thing!' He stayed as far back from the gun as he could, his complexion pale and his hands shaking slightly. Mr Kourakis tried to ask a question, but Nemer was not listening. 'Your Honour,' he said to Chief Justice Doyle, 'can I ask that it not be left in front of me?'

The young man's supporters were equally shaken – two women, one old and one young, wept openly. Williams, still in the back row, smiled broadly. Chief Justice Doyle swiftly brought the room under control. The gun, he said, would remain in front of Nemer. The questioning would go on. Nemer sat back down, but did not look at the weapon unless specifically directed to do so.

The Browning, Mr Kourakis said, could not have fired a bullet without first being primed. He explained that a shooter would have to cock the gun's firing hammer, by pulling back its slide, thereby drawing a bullet into the chamber. He asked Nemer to try pulling the gun's trigger, now, without first cocking it – the young man once more refused to touch the weapon.

Mr Kourakis would not be denied. 'Did you cock the gun?' he asked.

'No, I did not,' Nemer replied.

It was highly unlikely the gun, Mr Kourakis said, would have been stored in a ready-to-fire position. That would be 'too dangerous', he suggested reasonably. It would have been something Nemer, raised in a family of marksmen, would have noticed.

'Sorry,' Nemer cut him off, 'but I did not cock it. I did not touch the thing to cock it. I'm not here to lie to you.'

'The gun can not be fired,' Mr Kourakis insisted, 'and the trigger cannot be pulled without the weapon being cocked. Did you cock it?'

'Sorry, but I did not cock it,' Nemer repeated. 'I did not cock it at all, Mr Kourakis. That's your suggestion but it's wrong . . . I've told you that three times now, and I cannot say it any other way. I just pulled the trigger. It's going to sound weird, and maybe it's because of adrenalin, but I don't think I even heard the gun fire.'

A short adjournment was called. Nemer stepped out of the witness box and joined his supporters, who were already filing out of court. He and several of his friends – all male, all dressed in dark suits and sunglasses – left the courthouse and headed to a nearby coffee shop. They walked five abreast, forming a human wall with Nemer at the centre, presenting a massive target for waiting newspaper and television cameras. They looked, unmistakably, like gangsters.

When the hearing resumed, Nemer took his place in the dock while Williams replaced him in the witness stand. Mr Kourakis informed the court Williams would not be giving oral testimony – the prosecution would rely on the statement he gave police two weeks after the incident. Williams, he said, maintained Nemer had fired the shot while the barrel of the gun was pressed against the van's window. The victim insisted he had seen a 'shadowy figure' pass by in the moments before the shot was fired.

The way was open for Ms Powell's cross-examination – and, like Mr Kourakis before her, she was not inclined to be gentle. 'I suggest to you that your statement is, in fact, a reconstruction based on what people were telling you, and assumptions you made about what happened to you,' she said.

Williams held a copy of his statement up like a shield. 'No,' he said firmly. 'This is exactly what I saw.'

It was the only straight answer Ms Powell would receive. She cross-examined him for more than two hours, never abandoning her allegations of reconstruction. Williams answered in short, clipped, monosyllabic sentences. He often appeared confused and asked, repeatedly, for questions to be rephrased. Increasingly hostile, he refused to look directly at Ms Powell, and directed most of his answers toward the judges.

'Is it safe to say this was the last thing you expected to happen that morning?' she asked.

'Yes,' he replied.

'The first unusual thing you heard were screams . . . you thought you should stop your van and see what was going on?'

'I can't answer that.'

Ms Powell changed approach. She took up the sworn testimony of the ambulance officers who had attended Williams after he fled to King William Road. It was those paramedics, she said, who informed Williams he had been shot and that there was a hole in the window of the van – contrary to his long-standing claims. He had never mentioned any gun, she said, to the ambulance crew.

She went on, saying Williams was understandably disoriented at the time. 'You said, to the ambulance officers, that you were either in the process of making a call or had made a call when three men approached you and tried to kill you because you had "seen too much",' she said.

'I don't recall,' Williams answered.

Late in the afternoon, the court called an end to the questioning. The judges conferred, briefly, then announced they would sentence Nemer the following week. In just days, the most controversial case in South Australian history would be settled once and for all.

During that four-day break, a strange thing happened: public perception of the case began to shift. Many of Nemer's staunch opponents found themselves grudgingly impressed by his testimony. He had been penitent and remorseful. Hot-headed, yes, but no more so than any man of his age. Williams, by contrast, suddenly appeared unreliable. His patchy memory and his antagonistic attitude toward Ms Powell led some to wonder what he had to hide. Mr Kourakis would go on to claim the innocent man had been suffering the effects of post-traumatic stress disorder while on the stand. Some accepted that, others did not. The ugly, deeper issues surrounding the case – race and riches – seemed less important all of a sudden. For one weekend, the case was in context; it was about two men and a mistake.

But only for one weekend.

The factions gathered, one more time, in courtroom three on Tuesday, 18 November 2003. It had been 27 months since Nemer fired the shot into Williams's eye. The tension of the previous week continued unabated – the loud-mouthed antagonist was, however, noticeably absent. The main players took up their familiar spots – Nemer near the dock, twiddling his thumbs anxiously; Williams in the back row, silent and sullen-looking – and waited for the decision.

The judges entered, and their continued conflict was immediately obvious. Chief Justice Doyle maintained there was no reason to alter Nemer's original sentence, and all but bowed out of proceedings. It fell to Justice Prior to announce the sentence upon which he and Justice Vanstone had decided. Somewhat appropriately, the incredibly divisive case was to end in a majority decision.

Justice Prior said he and his colleague agreed Nemer had deliberately intended to shoot Williams. There was no warning shot – Nemer, he said, was a liar.

'In our view Mr Nemer's evidence is not credible,' he intoned. 'The suggestion he took the gun from under his father's bed not knowing if it had ammunition or if it was cocked, and that he carried the gun in his pocket in that state is implausible. Nemer's stated reason for approaching the van is flimsy. There was no reason for the respondent to approach the van unless he proposed to discharge his weapon.'

Nemer, once again in a designer suit, smiled nervously and picked at his nails.

'We are satisfied,' Justice Prior concluded, 'beyond a reasonable doubt this offence involved a deliberate firing into the victim's van by Nemer while he was standing close by.' The appropriate penalty, therefore, was far more severe than a suspended sentence and a $100 good behaviour bond. By order of the Court of Criminal Appeal, Paul Habib Nemer was jailed for four years and nine months. He would not be eligible for parole for 21 months. It was a punishment identical to that Justice Vanstone had foreshadowed at the appeal hearing.

As the court sheriff's officers advanced on him, Nemer flashed a quick smile at his family and allowed himself to be led to the cells. As before, some women cried and blew kisses, one yelled, 'We love you, Paul!'. Outside court, the woman told reporters she was 'very proud' of the young man. 'What else would you expect?' she asked angrily. His counsel, meanwhile, made it clear they would lodge papers with the High Court seeking an emergency hearing. Nemer, they said, should not have to spend months in jail when 'serious questions' hung over the legality of the government's actions.

Williams spent the moments after the sentence shaking hands with dozens of people, including Mr Kourakis. He looked overwhelmed. Later, he would thank the public, investigating police, the government's legal team and Premier Rann for 'voicing and acting upon the concerns of the public'. 'It has been the public's interest that has fuelled this case and it is likely the appeal would never have been instigated without this attention,' he said. 'Having been heard, and a just outcome being reached, I feel relieved that this matter is finally over and I am looking forward to the future.'

Mr Rann was uncharacteristically subdued. 'Justice has been done,' he said, leaving the spotlight for Williams.

Nemer was taken, in an unmarked van, from the court to Yatala Labour Prison. He had entered a world far beyond his imagination – the high-security E-division. 'It's a 22-hour lockdown, shared cell arrangement,' he said in a December 2003 statement to the media. 'This was terrifying for me.' He spent the first week of his sentence in that location. His first cellmate was a schizophrenic. 'Every night I was in a cell next to John Bunting, who was convicted of the Snowtown murders,' he said.

Nemer claimed his time in E-division was fraught with danger. 'Because of the extensive media coverage of my case, I was well known by inmates and Correctional Services Officers,' he said. 'There had also been publicity about my family's wealth and, as a consequence, I was warned that I might be at risk. I was terrified about what would happen to me in jail.'

George Nemer went to visit his son. 'I was waiting to see him, and there was this large guy there in the meeting room,' he said in 2009. 'He had tattoos all over his arms. He said to me, "Are you the father of Paul Nemer?". I said "Yes", even though I thought he was going to beat me up. Then he said, "I'm in here but I feel sorry for you, because you got fucked by the government".'

By the end of his fourth week in jail, Nemer felt safer. A move to the lower-security F-division – a facility outside the city, where he could undertake manual labour – no doubt helped. 'In jail, each inmate has a common respect for each other that surpasses that of those who live beyond these walls,' he said in a letter to *The Advertiser* newspaper. 'Most inmates have a decency and show honesty and acts of kindness to other inmates that would rival the friendship of any two people.'

Oddly, he found jail a tonic for the race and class issues that had plagued his prosecution. 'No inmate is "better" than another and no one is treated with difference, no matter their social or economic standing,' he wrote. 'Many of the people I have met in jail are among the most decent and down-to-earth people I have ever had the privilege to converse with. I'm sure I will leave here as a better person as I have seen both sides of life – that of the privileged and that of the less fortunate.'

Nemer had found some measure of peace, but he was not about to make apologies for those he felt had wronged him. 'My case was not dealt with like any other, as the media felt it was necessary to involve my family and their social-economic status,' he noted. 'All I asked for was to be heard as any other person. The government is quick to act on sentences it feels are inadequate.' He was more than prepared, though, to ask for the forgiveness he refused to pass on. 'I have been remorseful for my actions,' he said. 'I am sorry for the pain, both mentally and physically, I have caused the Williams family and friends.'

On 10 December, Ms Powell sought – and won – an expedited hearing before the High Court. The matter was listed for February, meaning counsel would have to fly to Melbourne and try the case before Justice Heydon and Justices Ken Hayne and William Gummow. South Australia's obsession was about to become Victoria's problem – at least for one day.

Adelaide's media also made the trip. They camped out on the steps of 305 William St, Melbourne, early on the morning of 13 February 2004. Their patience was rewarded just before 10 am when Williams arrived. His demeanour had changed drastically since the sentence – he smiled and waved at the cameras, slowing his walk to give the media as much footage as it wanted.

A High Court hearing is intensely fascinating to watch. Each party is given 20 minutes to support their case – already filed, in document form, prior to the hearing – with oral submissions. If a learned judge interrupts their submission or takes them down a long tangent they must answer the call even if it cuts their time in half. On the lectern before each lawyer are mounted two lights and a clock – the green light glows from the start of the 20 minutes, the red light warns there are five minutes left, and the judges are quick to tell counsel when one's time has expired. The notoriety of the Nemer case afforded Ms Powell and Mr Kourakis no special consideration. The matter was but one in a long list, and was not called on until well after 2 pm.

Ms Powell used her 20-minute window well. Eloquently and rapidly, she made three arguments. The government's appeal sprang from an unlawful premise – that it had the right to direct the DPP – and its handling was further marred by 'a pre-judged member of the Full Court'. Justice Vanstone, she said, should have disqualified herself. The fact Nemer received a sentence identical to that which she had suggested, prior to the hearing of evidence, made it all the worse. Oddly, Ms Powell made it through her entire outline without a single interruption from the bench, and with time to spare.

Mr Kourakis rose to present his case, but Justice Hayne waved his hand. 'Mr Solicitor-General, we need not trouble you,' he said casually.

Ms Powell stiffened. Mr Edwardson appeared stunned, while Mr Kourakis smiled. For the gathered media, it was a shock as potent as the original $100 good behaviour bond. The Nemer case had dominated the hearts and minds of South Australia for more than two years, sparking intense debate and exposing uncomfortable truths about Adelaide and its people. Yet the High Court saw it as so trivial, so banal and small-minded, that it could be decided in less than half an hour. Shorn of its political, social, racial and economic context, the case was about no more than a single bullet.

'We are not persuaded that there is any miscarriage of justice in this matter,' Justice Hayne said without conferring with his peers, 'nor that it is in the interests of justice that there be a further appeal. Accordingly, your application is refused.'

It was finally over. Ms Powell, pale and shaken, was led from the court by Mr Edwardson. Visibly distraught, she avoided the media and took refuge in a nearby coffee shop, where she could be seen weeping openly. 'I'm stunned and a bit shell-shocked,' she said later, after regaining her composure.

Williams hailed the decision as a 'relief and a victory'. 'I'm not going to talk about it too much now,' he added, 'but oh yes, I'm relieved.'

Over the phone from Adelaide, Mr Rann offered his congratulations. 'In my view justice has been done today,' he said, repeating his now favourite epithet, 'and I am encouraged by that.'

The Nemer case had an undeniable impact on the administration of justice in South Australia – one that continues to this day. The Rann Government considered it had a mandate, ratified by the High Court, to intervene in court cases and ensure the outcomes were to the liking of its members. For months, victims would walk from the Supreme and District Courts, unsatisfied with the sentences given to their tormentors, and say they would seek an audience with Mr Rann. Law and order became a prime plank of the Labour Party's successful re-election campaign, and was trotted out again in preparation for the 2010 election.

That was not to say the government developed a thicker skin when it came to criticism. In February 2009, a prosecutor appearing in a hit-and-run case criticised laws Mr Rann had brought in to deal with such crimes. He said progress of the case had stalled because of the way the legislation had been written, and commented that many laws drafted by Labour had been 'rushed through, not thought through'. Using its High Court-ratified power, the government directed the prosecutor to return to court one week later and 'unreservedly withdraw' anything he said that was 'critical of those who drafted the provisions'. Copies of the transcript were then emailed to the media by the Attorney-General's office, with a demand that journalists 'ensure' the 'retraction' was printed.

One month after the High Court's ruling, police prosecutors told Adelaide's lawyers they would no longer accept plea bargains. Letters were sent to defence counsel, informing them that all attempts to bargain would be rejected 'due to new post-Nemer policy'. The decision caused a backing-up of cases, slowing the movement of the justice system and stretching the resources of legal aid. Ms Powell quickly weighed in. 'That's unfair to everyone,' she said. 'Clients don't win, victims don't, police and the courts don't. Prosecutors are now being expected to worry about political opinions.'

Mr Rofe did not. Sick of ongoing criticism, resentful of government interference in his work, he resigned. He resurfaced a short time later, working as defence counsel in criminal and civil matters. Often, he worked with Mr Edwardson and Ms Powell. He returned to prosecution work in 2009, freelancing for the department he once ran.

Mr Rann was unambiguous about what he wanted in a new DPP, expressing his desire for an 'Elliot Ness' who would take to the courts with two-fisted toughness. What he got, in February 2005, was Stephen Pallaras, QC. Known for his work in Western Australia, Mr Pallaras had stood at the bar in Hong Kong, San Francisco, Washington, Las Vegas, New York and Tokyo. He appeared, on the surface, to be restrained and quiet. After a short time surveying the landscape, the new boss launched a broadside at the government, vowing his office would not become 'a plaything of the political process'.

'I've only been here two weeks and I've seen more than enough,' he spat during a press conference. 'In fact, in all my experience interstate and overseas, I have never seen anything like this.' The brawl between Mr Pallaras and Mr Rann continues to this day.

Mr Kourakis's efforts were rewarded with an appointment to the Supreme Court bench. In November 2006, it was announced Mr Edwardson would be awarded the prestigious title of QC. In a tumultuous series of events, Mr Rann stepped in personally to block the appointment. 'Being a QC does, and must always, mean more than being able to charge clients thousands of dollars a day,' he said. 'It must be about the highest standards of ethics, not just technical competence. Those letters must stand for something, a certain quality.' The matter was settled when Chief Justice Doyle intervened, refusing to allow anyone to become a QC that year if Mr

Rann stood in Mr Edwardson's path. Mr Rann backed down and Mr Edwardson accepted the honour.

Williams stayed intimately involved with the courts for several months after the High Court decision. He filed a flurry of lawsuits, seeking compensation from those he blamed for his loss of vision. George and Rita Nemer, he claimed, owed him money because they had left the 9mm Browning in an unsecured spot. Paul Nemer, he said, owed him money. He also sought funds from the government's Criminal Injuries Compensation fund and WorkCover. The matters were all settled out of court, quietly, for undisclosed sums. Williams subsequently faded from public view.

On Wednesday 17 August 2005, Paul Nemer was released from Yatala Labour Prison. A chauffeured government car drove him from the facility to his family's Springfield mansion. Immediately, the old prejudices resurfaced. The Public Service Association claimed George Nemer had paid to secure preferential treatment for his son – including a 7 am release time, instead of the usual 10 am – and as much secrecy as possible. The claims were denied. 'It is one of the most false, most ridiculous statements I have heard in my life,' George Nemer said at the time. 'I absolutely deny it.'

Mr Rann was both philosophical and self-congratulatory. 'Nemer has now served his time,' he said. 'But he would not have served any time at all if we had not intervened.'

Nemer did his best to live a quiet life, but his attempts were frustrated at every turn. Photographers, both professional and amateur, hunted for him. They knew a photo of the newly released gunman was an instant front-page story. Whenever there was a shooting in the city, people would joke 'Nemer's at it again'. Then, in April 2003, Nemer received an on-the-spot fine for exceeding the speed limit by

45 kilometres per hour. Reporters seized on the chance to dredge the case up all over again. Wisely, Nemer exercised his right not to face court over the matter and stayed well away from eager eyes.

In late 2008, Paul Habib Nemer left South Australia and moved to the Middle East. His father would not say where. 'He's started his life again,' George Nemer said in 2009. 'He's gone to get a new image, to forget what he has done and to carry on with his studies. He's in a place where no one knows him, and that's how it's going to stay – it only takes one phone call, from someone in Adelaide to someone where he's living, to ruin all he's trying to achieve.'

George Nemer said his son's overseas trip was indefinite. 'Hopefully he can come back to Adelaide one day, when people are ready to accept he has paid for his crime,' he said. 'I'm not declaring him a saint, but there's no point him coming back until people are ready to give him a chance.'

An Undignified Death

Newton and Bone

Small-time drug dealer Gary Kirk Beaumont was no angel. He did not, however, deserve to spend the last 24 hours of his life in prolonged and excruciating agony.

It has long been said there is no dignity in death. Yet few could imagine an end as undignified, as callous and brutal, as Beaumont's. Over the course of a day he was betrayed by an associate, kicked until his liver lacerated, beaten and stabbed between the anus and testicles. He was doused with icy water, dragged through a house and locked in a car boot. He was hung in a bizarre and grotesque simulation of suicide, cut down and finally left to die in his own car.

Cruelly, Beaumont was abandoned just metres from those who could have saved his life – the staff of Adelaide's Queen Elizabeth Hospital. But his killers –Steven John Newton and Rebecca Lee Bone – did not care about Beaumont. Their only concern was for themselves, and their desperate need to avoid jail for murder. Driven by panic, they went to extraordinarily macabre lengths to disguise their involvement. And because of their own stupidity, those evil efforts were doomed to fail from the outset.

◆

For many years, Gary Kirk Beaumont tried to focus his life around his work as an automotive upholsterer. An addiction to amphetamines, however, derailed that goal. While he did not abandon his career, Beaumont found his income insufficient to support his habit. Like many, he turned to petty crime – particularly house theft – to increase his bank balance. When that was not enough, he would sell portions of his own drug stash to associates, or buy larger quantities from his suppliers to split with people he knew.

Late in 2004, a new person entered his circle – a young woman named Meg Hanlon. 'I met him over an internet chat room,' she said in 2007. 'We became best friends instantly and, from there, we began a relationship. We had a special bond – we liked the same things, we had a passion for motorbikes and things like that. He was really good at his trade and I used to help him.' Their first joint restoration was a Mini Moke. 'It was great fun,' Hanlon said. 'Gary had an amazing, mechanically minded brain and it always impressed me that he was able to fix just about anything.'

In February 2005, Hanlon moved into Beaumont's flat at West Beach. 'We shared special moments together, whether it was working on the cars or going down to the beach together,' she said. 'I felt like Gary was my soul mate, and I am sure that he felt the same about me. We had planned to have a life together, and we planned to marry sometime in 2008.'

They endured, like any couple, their share of ups and downs – but not for the usual reasons. 'When I first met Gary, I had just come off of using drugs,' Hanlon said. 'I was using speed, but hadn't used for about four months before meeting him. Gary was using drugs when I met him, but only socially. He was taking speed and ecstasy pills. I started using drugs again socially when I met Gary – and this is no secret. At times it was tumultuous, but it was something that we just couldn't seem to get away from. It took hold of our lives, and this is how we came to know Steven Newton.'

Born in London in 1960, Newton had spent his early years moving between England and Australia. Raised by his father, Newton had little education; his only real schooling came at 14 and lasted just one month. He had trouble socialising and was the target of bullying due to his accent; he fought in numerous street brawls and, eventually, suffered permanent damage to the front lobe of his brain. Newton's best friend – and perhaps his only confidant – was his father.

Newton's history of drug use was extensive. Cannabis, which he began using at 15, served as a gateway to Rohypnol and heroin. Though he had beaten his heroin addiction through a methadone program, his tastes had turned toward methamphetamine – in particular, the street drug known as ice. A voracious user, Newton would consume between three grams and five grams of the drug daily – an expensive lifestyle that forced him to borrow money against his house to afford what he called his 'medication'.

Newton was assessed by forensic neuropsychologist Mark Reid in 2007. 'Newton has used various forms of amphetamines and he told me the effect of this was to put him to sleep,' Dr Reid wrote. 'He said it also "stopped his mind racing and thinking of things". He added that amphetamines tend to make him feel comfortable and relaxed.'

When he was not with his father, Newton spent time in his Birkenhead home with his de facto. Rebecca Lee Bone had lived a happy and secure childhood until the age of nine, when she was the victim of sexual assault. This began a life-long pattern of abuse and victimisation, culminating in her relationship with Newton. A fellow amphetamine user, Bone found herself very much at Newton's mercy.

Forensic psychologist Allen Fugler would examine her in 2008. 'Newton was highly controlling of her social activities . . . he fitted locks to every door in the house to prevent her from leaving,' he wrote. 'He would also regularly remove her clothing for the same purpose. Bone was not permitted to leave the house when not in the company of Newton, and when that did occur he was emotionally abusive toward her.' Newton's behaviour extended toward sexual abuse as well. 'He often held her hostage and would hog tie her before inserting implements into [her body],' Dr Fugler wrote.

In 2006, Newton and Bone met Beaumont and Hanlon through mutual associates. The couples got along well; Newton and Bone became regular customers. For 11 months, Beaumont and Hanlon would travel regularly to Birkenhead to deliver amphetamines. Then, in December, the relationship soured.

'Newton accused Bone of sleeping with Gary, and I accused Gary of sleeping with Bone, because Gary would disappear for about three or four days at a time,' Hanlon said. 'When I accused him, he would just deny it. Every time I tried to bring it up with Gary, he would lose his head over it and tell me not to bring it up or talk about it. Things went bad.'

Toward the end of 2006, Beaumont – always looking for extra cash – stole a heater from a vacant house. He gave it to Newton, who promised to pay $350 when he was able. The money never materialised. 'Gary got pretty angry over it and told me he wanted to get Newton, but I told him that it wasn't worth it and to let it go,' Hanlon said. The others did not share her calm. In the early months of 2007, Bone bombarded Hanlon with a series of harassing text messages, again centred on the alleged affairs. 'She told me she would get me for it,' Hanlon said.

The men argued more violently. 'On June 21, 2007, Gary turned up at home and was fairly frantic, yelling and screaming that Newton was downstairs,' Hanlon said. It was a surprising situation – the couple had a rule that no one was to be told where they lived. 'He said Newton had bitten him on the nose,' Hanlon said. 'I could clearly see the bite mark across the bridge of Gary's nose . . . it was bleeding, and blood was dripping down his nose. I had to get a flannel and wipe the blood from Gary's face.'

The confrontation fizzled out, but the strain between the couples was obvious. 'Newton was always very demanding of Gary and would harass him when it came to getting drugs,' Hanlon said. 'Newton would get angry at Gary very quickly. Gary once told Newton he carried a knife with him and was prepared to use it.' Beaumont had purchased the distinctive weapon – a double-edged, black-handled blade shaped like a bat's wing – during a trip to Queensland in 2006. 'I remember laughing because I couldn't see Gary ever using a knife. I told him that he shouldn't have told Newton about it.'

No matter their disputes, the two couples were inextricably linked by their need for money and drugs. Throughout June 2007, Beaumont met with Newton daily. 'Newton was buying what I thought to be very large amounts,' Hanlon said. 'Gary was sourcing $450 to $500 worth of amphetamines and going half with Newton. I felt really uneasy about it.'

On 24 June, Beaumont received a call on his mobile. 'He was talking to someone for a couple of minutes,' Hanlon said, 'and, when he got off the phone, he told me it was Newton. He said Newton wanted to "get it on", which means he wanted to score some drugs.' They travelled in their car to Birkenhead, intending to sell Newton $200 worth of methamphetamine. As they drove, Beaumont received near-constant text messages from Newton. 'I heard that the messages were about how long we were going to be and about money . . . that Newton had $350 and wanted Gary to answer his phone,' Hanlon said.

As the couple crossed the Birkenhead Bridge, over the Port River, Hanlon pulled onto the side of the road. 'I told Gary I didn't want to meet up with Newton and Bone because, all night long, my gut had been saying I should stay away from them,' she said. 'I was scared of Newton because of his personality and character, and I just wanted to get out of this shit. But then Newton called and asked how long we were going to be, and Gary said two minutes.'

Hanlon drove the couple to Newton's home, but could not push her feelings aside. 'I was really angry with Gary,' she said. 'I wouldn't look at him, and I hardly said a word to him. I hated the fact he would jump whenever Newton told him to. I hated the fact that we were using drugs. I begged him not to go to Newton's house. It didn't feel right and I had a really bad feeling about it because of the incident when Newton bit Gary on the nose.'

Beaumont would not be swayed. He intended to drop the drugs through his usual arrangement: he would call Newton's mobile phone and then hang up, so the addict would meet them in the driveway. Unexpectedly, Newton answered the call and told Beaumont to park in the driveway because 'people who want to buy drugs want to see them first'.

'Gary told me what Newton had told him to do,' Hanlon said, 'and I told him I didn't want to go. I said I'd wait in the car. He was fine with that and gave me a kiss, told me that he loved me and told me to keep the doors locked.' Beaumont slid the flick knife into his pocket. 'I think he showed it to me to reassure me that he would be all right,' Hanlon said. 'He then got out of the car and walked toward Newton's house. He had the drugs in his hand.'

It was the last time Hanlon would see her soul mate alive.

Beaumont had been inside the house for just minutes when long-simmering tensions over money, fidelity and drugs boiled over. Newton and Beaumont exchanged blows while Bone watched; when Beaumont drew his knife, it was knocked out of his hands and used against him. In a vicious assault, Newton forced Beaumont to the ground and laid into him with a series of devastating kicks. Their impact was so forceful they lacerated Beaumont's liver – the first of many life-threatening injuries he would suffer.

Lost in ferocity, Newton inflicted scores of wounds upon Beaumont. An autopsy would later record cuts to his forehead and bruises and abrasions to his eye, lips, ear and jaw. A dumbbell was used to give Beaumont a concussion. The resultant stupor was no mercy, given what was to happen next. Beaumont's trademark blade was used first to slash his face and anus and then, horribly, to stab him in the perineal area – the skin between the anus and testicles. That last blow broke through Beaumont's haze, leaving him writhing on the floor in indescribable agony.

Hanlon, waiting outside, was unaware of her lover's torment. 'About 20 or 30 minutes after Gary left me, I saw Bone approach the car,' she said. 'I was still sitting in the driver's seat and had the doors closed but unlocked. Bone came up to the window, told me she hadn't seen me for some time, and asked me how I was. She then opened the door, leaned into the car and grabbed me by the throat.' Hanlon struggled to no avail. 'She was straight into me. She pushed me down onto the passenger's seat and started to punch me across the face. She punched or hit me about nine times and kept saying I knew what this was for.'

Unable to break free, Hanlon tried to call for help. 'I managed to get my right leg up and put my foot on the horn and sound it,' she said. 'I was also screaming, hoping someone would hear me.' Bone tried to use her hand as a muffle; Hanlon bit her. 'She hit me again and I started to bleed from my face. She kept telling me I can't hide because, wherever I go, she will find me. It was about then I saw Newton walk up to the car.'

In contrast to his de facto, Newton was the portrait of icy calm. 'He really scared me this night, he seemed really smug and calm,' Hanlon said. 'He seemed to strut when he walked. Bone told him I had bitten her on the hand and she hoped I didn't have AIDS. Newton asked me where all the drugs and money were because he "wanted it now". I told him there weren't any drugs in the car.'

Newton, she said, started laughing. 'You should see what I've done to your boyfriend,' he bragged to her. 'I put the dog on him, and then I used that pathetic knife of Gary's on him as well.'

It was a horrid thought. Newton's dog – a 70 kilogram bull-mastiff called Bruno – was a savage beast, kept by its owner in a permanently frenzied state so it would be a better guard dog. It was nothing short of lethal. 'I'd seen the dog on one occasion,' Hanlon said. 'I'd heard it was a big dog that could rip people apart. I had no doubt that, if it was in the car with me, it would kill me.

'Bone told Newton to go get the dog so that they could put it in the car with me,' Hanlon said. 'Then Newton told me to take my clothes off. I had no idea why he said this, but I pictured myself in the car with the dog and no clothes on and got even more scared.'

Fear turned into action. 'Bone took her eyes off me for a minute, so I pushed her in the chest and managed to run away from them,' Hanlon said. Adrenalin soaring, she made it a few streets away before she fell, vomited and passed out from terror. Her unconsciousness, ironically, saved her life – as she lay on the ground, slowly coming to, she noticed Bone driving Beaumont's car up and down the streets. Her attackers were looking for her.

Staying low, Hanlon managed to avoid capture. For two hours, she made her way carefully south toward Henley Beach and the home of a friend. 'I remember trying to ring Gary on his mobile phone but couldn't get through – the message on the phone was saying it was non-contactable,' she said. 'I was soaked from lying in wet grass and hiding. I lay down on my friend's couch and passed out.'

Beaumont's phone was in Newton's possession; he'd switched it off, desperate for time to think. Bone had failed to find Hanlon, and the fear was she had already made contact with the police. Realising they needed to dispose of Beaumont's body, they made their way over to it.

They then discovered that, despite his horrific injuries, Gary Beaumont was still alive.

Newton's composure broke as the reality of their situation sank in. They had tried to kill their drug dealer, and failed. Beaumont's blood was all over their home, soaking into the 14 carpet squares they'd used to decorate the living area. He sent Bone to get Beaumont's car and bring it around the back of their house. While she did that, he took the carpet squares into the back yard – leaving Beaumont on the floor – and hosed them off. As they dried, he and Bone went back inside and dragged Beaumont into the bathroom. Newton all but threw Beaumont into the shower and sprayed him, repeatedly, with ice-cold water.

His goal was not to wash away the copious amounts of blood flowing from the dealer's injuries, but to revive the assaulted man. Naively, Newton believed he and Beaumont could straighten everything out if he could just bring him around. The last thing Newton wanted to do was seek medical attention, or call an ambulance to his home. For one, awkward questions would be asked about Beaumont's present state. For another, the back room of the house was full of cannabis, while the front room contained $200 worth of methamphetamine.

Although he was alive, Beaumont's injuries were too severe for him to fully regain consciousness. Together, Newton and Bone bundled Beaumont into the boot of his own car and locked him in. They drove to Beaumont's home and broke in, stealing many of his and Hanlon's personal items including clothing. Lacking a concrete plan, they began to drive around the metropolitan area. Their hope, now, was that Beaumont would die as he lay in the boot, and they could dump the body at a remote location.

As they drove, a series of moans and gurgling noises could be heard in the boot. Gary Beaumont simply refused to die.

The stress of the situation, combined with the drugs they had ingested, was taking its toll on Newton and Bone. What happened next remains the subject of speculation and argument. Newton would later tell police he and his lover drove Beaumont to a shed at Mallala – a regional centre almost 60 kilometres north of Adelaide. Bone would claim the drive was much shorter – the shed, she claimed, was at another Birkenhead address owned by a friend. Whatever the location, the would-be killers and their victim pulled up alongside a nondescript metal shed and went inside.

Newton had come up with the idea. Producing a length of rope, he suggested they hang Beaumont – who was fading in and out of consciousness – by the neck and make his death look like a suicide. Muscling a solidly built, still-conscious man up toward a roof while fashioning a noose was not the easiest task, but Newton managed somehow. For several minutes, Beaumont swung from the neck and was slowly strangled. Newton and Bone waited for the inevitable . . . but it did not come. Showing remarkable constitution and an ironclad will to live, Beaumont kept breathing.

Their plans, their hopes, were dashed. Finally, they realised the absurdity of their actions. Hanlon had seen them, heard them, listened to their prideful boasts about Beaumont. She had escaped their clutches and was certain to go to the police. No matter what they did, Newton and Bone would forever be the prime suspects in Beaumont's death.

Newton cut Beaumont down, cleaned him up and dressed him in fresh clothes – the items stolen from the West Beach flat. With Bone's help, he dragged Beaumont back into the car boot. The gravely injured man's groans taunted them from the back seat as they drove south.

Meanwhile, at Henley Beach, Hanlon had regained consciousness. It was 3.30 pm. Too afraid to leave her safe haven, she asked her friend to check on Beaumont's flat and see if Gary had returned. The friend came back a short time later, saying the house had been burgled. Realising things had gone horribly wrong, Hanlon dialled triple zero. 'The police met me at my house, as did an ambulance,' Hanlon said. She was taken to the Royal Adelaide Hospital for treatment.

Newton and Bone were bound for a hospital, as well – but not for treatment. Sometime in the afternoon of 25 June, they parked Beaumont's vehicle in the car park of the Queen Elizabeth Hospital. They propped their victim up, as if he were sleeping, and then ran. The car was noticed by several people moving in and out of the hospital, but no one went close enough to check on it until 10.05 pm. By that time, Beaumont had lost his valiant struggle. The combination of the pressure on his neck and the laceration of his liver had killed him.

Had he been found just a few hours earlier, Gary Beaumont would likely have survived.

Detectives from South Australia Police's Major Crime Investigations Branch were assigned the case. When they first spoke to Hanlon at the Royal Adelaide and told her Beaumont had died, the young woman was hysterical. Her first statement to police – enough to get the investigation underway – was a jumbled mix of events from both the night before and the weeks leading up to the murder. Hanlon would eventually be diagnosed with a psychological breakdown from stress, and would spend time recovering in the hospital. She would clarify her account several times, through subsequent statements, as the months wore on.

Neither Newton nor Bone were hard to find. By 26 June, detectives had made telephone contact with Bone and convinced her to turn herself in. Newton was apprehended around the same time by a uniformed police patrol. He was caught speeding in his car and pulled over, voluntarily, to speak with the officers. As soon as they realised who he was, they arrested him.

The couple appeared in the Elizabeth Magistrates Court on 27 June 2007. Bone's application for bail fell on deaf ears – the court felt the alleged crime was simply too serious to warrant any form of release. Ceding to police requests, the court also suppressed publication of the couple's names, images and identities. Major Crime required time to build its case, to gather potential witnesses and to have Hanlon formally identify the alleged killers.

Part of that investigation centred around Bruno, the bull mastiff. The crazed beast was central to Hanlon's account of 24 June. Further, crime scene examiners had found dog hair in the back seat of the stolen Falcon. Detectives began to wonder whether Bruno had been set on Beaumont, as Newton had claimed. The only way to be sure was to take DNA samples from the dog.

It was no easy feat. Bruno was terrifying at the best of times but, by 28 June, he'd not been fed for four days. Detectives met Newton's father at the Birkenhead house and tried to determine the best way of getting a sample. Whenever they approached the backyard, however, Bruno would try to force his head out through the fence and bite off their hands. Extra help was required.

Calls were made and a mobile veterinarian was recruited. He brought along his secret weapon: cat anaesthetic. The detectives were unimpressed until they learned the drug was designed for big cats – lions, tigers and other creatures held in the Adelaide Zoo. While detectives drew Bruno's attention, the vet squirted two doses of the oral sedative into the beast's slavering mouth. It dissolved into the thin membranes surrounding the dog's throat and . . . did nothing at all. Bruno showed no sign of slowing down, nor gave any hint he'd noticed he'd been anaesthetised.

The only way to achieve their goal, the team decided, was to inject the sedative into Bruno's bloodstream. That, of course, meant bringing the animal out from behind the fence and somehow restraining it. Newton's father – who feared Bruno as much as anyone else – managed to loop a choker-chain around the dog's neck, then passed it over to a detective. The officer pulled back on the lead, bracing himself, while his partner and a crime scene examiner lowered Newton's roller door onto Bruno's back. They held it down, pinning the raging dog, while the vet reached around with a hypodermic syringe.

The moment steel touched flesh, Bruno lost his mind. The dog threw his head up and peeled the roller door like a banana skin. Two of the police officers dodged as Bruno made a beeline for the detective holding the choker chain. His life in very real peril, the detective had no choice but to draw his service-issue .357 pistol and fire a single shot into the centre of Bruno's forehead.

Amazingly, the bull-mastiff did not stop. The detective leaped out of the way and Bruno bounded past, onto the street and toward onlookers who had gathered at the sound of gunfire. Officers prepared to fire again, desperate to make sure Bruno did not savage an innocent bystander. Thankfully, the multiple doses of sedative finally kicked in, and the dog sank to its haunches and started panting. A quick check revealed the bullet had hit its mark – so frenzied was Bruno, he had ignored a fatal gunshot wound. The dog was euthanased on the spot, and the DNA samples taken from its carcass.

Neither the public nor the media were made aware of Bruno's fate. Nor did they learn Newton and Bone's names once police had finished their investigations. On 7 February 2008, the couple were ordered to stand trial in the Supreme Court for murder. As happens all too often in South Australia, the magistrate opted to continue the suppression of their identities 'out of an abundance of caution'. There was no basis in law for the decision – no chance of prejudice or of fouling the upcoming trial. Yet, for one more month, Bone and Newton's identities remained part of the seemingly unending list of state secrets that plagues open and transparent justice in the southern capital.

On 12 March 2008, the duo made their first Supreme Court appearance. Representatives of the media argued the time had come for the secrecy surrounding their identities to lapse. Showing greater insight than his colleagues in the lower jurisdictions, Justice John Sulan agreed and the couple were finally made public. Newton was remanded in custody pending trial. Bone had, by this time, secured her release – partially due to talks with the Office of the Director of Public Prosecutions. In exchange for testifying against her lover, the Crown was prepared to downgrade the charge against Bone from murder to assisting an offender. It was a deal her defence counsel considered seriously, and accepted in September.

On 4 November 2008, Newton asked to be re-arraigned on the murder charge. This time he pleaded guilty. Bone was also in attendance, and she pleaded guilty to the downgraded charge of assisting an offender. The case had been passed on to Justice Michael David, who asked prosecution and defence to draft a statement of agreed facts upon which he could pass sentence.

It was a difficult request. Each accused had a different version of the hanging, and wanted their story believed over that of the co-accused. The now-estranged couple deviated on another crucial point as well; the ugly knife wound to Beaumont's perineal area. Newton was adamant he had not used the knife on Beaumont at all – he remembered disarming his dealer, but claimed to have no memory of the blade following that. Bone, seeking the most lenient sentence possible, insisted she had nothing to do with any of the violence that night. Police inquiries shed no light on the matter – forensic experts were unable to determine whether the hanging had taken place at Mallala or Birkenhead. And while officers privately believed Bone had dealt all the knife wounds, they had no way of proving their suspicions.

Newton's counsel arranged for their client to be assessed once more – this time by psychologist Craig Raeside. 'Newton told me he had pleaded guilty to the charge of murdering Gary Beaumont,' he wrote, 'but was somewhat reticent to discuss the matter. Seemingly it upset him, and he would rather not talk about it. He began his account by saying that he felt "quite depressed" about everything that was happening, "the whole thing".'

'Newton understood that Mr Beaumont suffered "a split liver from the fight" but he denied stabbing him,' Dr Raeside wrote. 'He said he drove him to a shed and tried to hang him . . . his motive was to make it look like a suicide. He maintained that he never stabbed Mr Beaumont, and could not explain the reported stab wound to the anus. He wondered if this might have been the result of him kicking Mr Beaumont in the backside.'

Dr Raeside was aware Newton had been consuming amphetamines daily prior to the murder. 'I questioned him about his recollection, and he claimed that he recalled everything clearly,' he wrote. 'He said there was nothing unusual about the quantity he used that day.'

Finally, Dr Raeside wanted to know why Newton had taken so long to confess. 'He was somewhat dismissive, saying, "It's not a good thing to speak about, even now",' he wrote. 'He seemed rather avoidant about discussing the matter in detail with me, whilst accepting his guilt. He concluded the interview saying, "What can I say? I can't say sorry or anything, there's nothing I can do".'

On 28 November 2008, Newton and Bone faced sentencing submissions. Meg Hanlon was called to the bar table to deliver her victim impact statement. Her words made it clear that 18 months had done nothing to ease her pain.

'What happened that night has changed my life forever,' she began, shaking visibly as she spoke. 'My soul mate has gone. He got out of the car to go see Steven Newton and I thought he would be back in the blink of an eye. Instead, that blink of an eye has been one long nightmare. What I have experienced has been beyond what I could have ever imagined. Mostly I feel numb and like there is nothing left, I feel anger and disbelief. I can't even begin, after all this time, to put into words how I feel.'

The fear had stayed with her. 'I feel guilt because I managed to get away from Newton and Bone,' she said. 'When I look back on it, I feel that I would also have been killed if I did not run like I did. I can still hear, in my mind, Newton saying "take your clothes off" and Bone saying "go get the dog". I was so scared.'

Hanlon told the court she had moved house seven times since that night. 'I no longer trust anyone, and have anxiety attacks when I think about what happened to Gary,' she said. 'One of the worst things has been not knowing exactly how Gary died or when he died. I know that terrible things were done to him, things that took away any dignity and that are so terrible that I just can't think about it. Gary was not taken in an accident, but in what seems to me to be a cold and cowardly way. There was every opportunity for him to live if he was given help, but he was deliberately taken from me.'

As Hanlon moved back into the public gallery, an uncomfortable silence filled the courtroom. Justice David had asked to hear an agreed statement of facts, meaning the entirety of the case was about to be laid bare. Hanlon, who had spent more than a year unaware of precisely what Beaumont had endured, was about to find out in the bluntest, harshest method imaginable.

Claire O'Connor, for Newton, took the lectern. Matter-of-factly, she ran through the events of 24 June 2007 in great detail. Every wound, every blow, every moment of violence was related to the court. Hanlon's shaking intensified, and small whimpers escaped her tightly clenched jaw. One of the investigating officers – the same detective who shot Bruno the dog – moved to her side and placed a comforting arm around the grieving woman. It was not enough. As Ms O'Connor continued outlining her client's atrocities, Hanlon stood up and cried out. She ran from the courtroom, followed closely by a victim support officer, and out the building into the sunshine. There, she leaned against the sandstone walls of the Supreme Court and wept hysterically.

Inside, Ms O'Connor continued. She said Newton admitted bashing, dragging and abandoning Beaumont, but the court should not be overly bothered with the assault, she suggested, saying it was unimportant compared to the hanging. 'Newton was in a panicked state, knowing that if he attempted to get treatment for the victim he would be blamed for the injuries that had occurred,' she said. 'At this stage the victim was gurgling . . . he decided to make it look like a suicide. The post-mortem results are consistent with death being caused by the hanging – the victim would have survived the other injuries. Newton now accepts, of course, that every decision he made has led to the death of this man. He now knows he was in the position where, had he sought early and proper medical intervention, the victim would have been able to survive.'

Likewise, she asked the court not to worry itself about the perineal injury. 'The anus stabbing,' she said, 'was only a small injury and did not lead to death,' she said.

Carolyn Lam, prosecuting, disagreed. She said all factors were relevant to sentencing. 'It is the Crown case that this was a brutal killing, motivated by the need for drugs,' she said.

Justice David agreed. 'In my view, rightly or wrongly, the use of a knife on a living being is something about which I have to be concerned,' he said. 'I cannot shy away from it – this is a serious matter. There is a lot of difference between kicking someone to death and stabbing them in the anus with a knife, Ms O'Connor.'

Put on the spot, Ms O'Connor asked for a brief adjournment. She returned 15 minutes later and announced Newton would take the stand and give evidence, under oath, about the brawl.

Released from the dock and allowed to sit at the witness stand, Newton appeared tired and drawn. His eyes darted furtively around the courtroom as he spoke. Under cross-examination, he admitted taking the last of his amphetamine stash half an hour before Beaumont and Hanlon had arrived. 'Gary wanted to borrow some money and I said "no, no, no",' he said. 'He put his hand on my collar and said, "I need this money" and I punched the knife out of his hand. I punched him several times, I kicked him, but I did not stab him. I didn't do the anal wound. I don't know how it got there, but I did not inflict it. I kicked him there, in the anus, but that's all.'

David Stokes, for Bone, spoke next. He sought to downplay his client's involvement in the night's events. 'About the only thing she did do, physically, was put the deceased into the car,' he explained. 'She saw the injury in the genital area and suggested they take the deceased to a hospital, and made this suggestion more than once.'

Bone wanted to offer a different version of the hanging. 'My client came out, because she heard noises, and saw Newton trying to suspend Beaumont from the roof of the shed,' Mr Stokes said. 'Her recollection is that Newton was actually yanking Beaumont up at that stage. She didn't see any movement from Beaumont.'

There was very little Bone could have done to save Beaumont, he said. 'She was completely subject to the will of Steven Newton,' he said. 'She was scared. This is a woman who is vulnerable to domestically violent males and, unfortunately, this is a woman who does not seem to be able to escape from such relationships.'

At the close of the hearing, Justice David revoked Bone's bail. He ordered both she and Newton be held in custody until 18 December, when he would pass sentence.

Hanlon attended the sentencing hearing, but had yet to regain her poise. She arrived at court wearing large, dark sunglasses. She removed them, in the courtroom, to reveal tear-reddened, bloodshot eyes. This time, Major Crime detectives sat with her from the beginning, ready to help her through one more ordeal. Hanlon watched, silently, as Justice David entered the courtroom and pronounced sentence.

'On the pathologist's statement, the cause of death was a combination of ligature strangulation and intra-abdominal haemorrhage due to a laceration of the liver,' he began. 'This is consistent with being punched and kicked severely and continuously. You, Newton, admit to both the beating and the hanging. You also denied inflicting the injuries to Mr Beaumont's anus with a knife. I reject the evidence you gave, and find that you did inflict the injuries. There is no other explanation as to how they came to be.

'The beating you gave Mr Beaumont was violent and callous. Whatever the reason for the initial fight, it is nevertheless clear you continued to kick and beat him when he was in no position to resist. Your motives are unclear, but it is something that has obviously come out of the murky world of the use and sale of hard drugs.

'Following the beating, your behaviour was extremely callous and brutal. Mr Beaumont was put into the boot of a car and driven around for many hours, obviously in a condition close to death. Your behaviour in attempting to hang him, for the sake of obfuscation, was obviously calculating and callous.

'The sentence of this court is that I imprison you for life. Because of the seriousness, the prolonged nature and the violence of this offending, I would set a non-parole period of 20 years.'

In the gallery, Hanlon began to wail. As before, detectives moved to gently restrain her. This time, Hanlon made no effort to break away. She rocked, back and forth, as tears streamed down her face. She did not seem to register when Newton was sent from the dock into the cells, and did not react when he looked at her one final time.

Justice David turned his attention to Bone. It was immediately clear the submissions in her defence had little impact. 'This is serious offending of its kind,' he said. 'Your assistance to Newton was prolonged, and you were present from the time the events started until his body was deposited at the

Queen Elizabeth Hospital – some 24 hours. The sentence of this court is that you serve a term of imprisonment of two years. I set a non-parole period of 15 months. Because of the seriousness of the offending, there is no good reason why that term of imprisonment should be suspended.'

As Bone was led away, Hanlon sobbed. Her grief was not for the killers, of course, but for herself – and for the man she'd loved and lost. Though their relationship had been short and marred by drugs, Hanlon was definite; she would never love anyone as much as she did Gary Beaumont.

'I will never get over what has happened to Gary, and just can't comprehend why it happened and the brutality of what happened,' she said. 'Gary was not an angel, but there was nothing that he had done to deserve what was done to him.'

Rise and Fall of the Artful Dodger

Anthony John Smith

Five paces separated the men. One was a bar worker with a calico bag of money. The other was an armed robber and prison escapee with a loaded gun in his pocket.

In another time and place, Anthony John Smith would have been a folk hero. But at that time – February 2000 – and at that place – Ferguson Avenue, Myrtle Bank – he had a decision to make. In the time it took David Purdue to walk five steps, Smith had to decide whether or not to draw his weapon and add another vicious robbery to his already legendary rap sheet.

'I was just walking down the road and I wasn't going to do anything . . . I was just going along,' Smith later remembered. 'He was walking toward me, he had the money in his hand. I only had about five steps to make a decision about whether I was going to rob him. Mr Purdue was just walking out at the wrong time – for him and for me.'

Dubbed 'The Artful Dodger' by a media grimly obsessed with his prowess, Smith thought himself a modern-day outlaw. He created a false identity, complete with identification documents and a bank account, to case his targets before he robbed them. He lived in five-star luxury, checking into hotels under a series of aliases. He counted his loot – gold bullion, cash and precious jewels – on plush beds and photographed himself lying amongst his spoils. His one and only failure – being caught – was temporary, quickly corrected by a daylight escape that boosted his myth. For 12 months, he had no greater substance than the name on a dozen arrest warrants; it seemed he could strike any target in the city and vanish without a trace. The people of Adelaide were fascinated by the Dodger, but Smith truly believed the hype – and was ready to etch his name in history alongside Jesse James, John Dillinger and Ned Kelly.

◆

Like all outlaws, Smith's story began in unremarkable fashion. He was born on 11 January 1980, minutes before the arrival of his twin sister Rebecca. The family lived in Brompton until the twins were eight years of age, and then moved to Felixstow. Defence lawyer Nick Vadasz would later describe his client's upbringing as 'stable, in some respects, although he spent much of his time being brought up with his grandparents'.

Extended family was very important to Smith's development. Like many people of Aboriginal origin, he benefited from the love and guidance of devoted aunts and uncles. That support, Mr Vadasz explained, was essential. 'In other respects, his young life was extremely dysfunctional,' he said. 'Both parents had serious drug problems – heroin usage, in particular, was endemic – and my client was brought up in a background where criminal offending was very much the norm.'

Years before the Artful Dodger went on his rampage, the citizens of Adelaide had already learned to fear the name Smith. The future outlaw's father, Anthony Thiele Smith, was renowned for staging terrifying armed robberies to feed his drug addictions. 'The father was proud of his achievements and thought it made him a man,' Mr Vadasz said. 'Anthony became confused because he knew it was wrong to offend, but at the same time he wanted to be respected like his father was.'

Beyond the walls of the family home, Smith 'did well without standing out'. He played football for a local team and, oddly, excelled in Latin at Adelaide High School. 'He did particularly well in that [Latin] club,' Mr Vadasz said, 'because he found that, within it, there were no distinctions.' Smith also swam competitively, and it was here he would break out and draw attention to himself. He trained at the prestigious suburb of Payneham, and reached state level, as did his sister Rebecca.

Things started to fall into place for Smith. Swimming, he realised, was a way to command respect without picking up a gun. He could break world records, instead of laws, and become an idol that way. At 14, he was told he was being considered for inclusion in a special squad of Aboriginal children to be trained in backstroke. Encouraged, Smith set himself the goal of qualifying for the Sydney 2000 Olympics and was willing to sacrifice anything to achieve his dream. Unlike many young men of his era – and in direct contrast to his parents – he swore off drugs and alcohol. 'He has no drug problem,' Mr Vadasz proudly told the court, 'and never has had a drug problem. He has no alcohol problem. He is unlikely to ever develop such problems because of what he saw happening around him. And he does not have an early history of violence, unlike many young Aboriginal boys.'

What Smith did have was an infamous, feared, respected father. No matter the success he earned in the pool, his father's notoriety continued to gnaw at him. In 1995, Smith committed an armed robbery – taking him from the starter's block of the Payneham pool to the cellblocks of the Cavan Youth Training Centre. Mr Vadasz would later concede how unusual such an occurrence was. 'He was built up, by his father, to live up to the father's standards of living,' he offered by way of mitigation. 'That early conditioning has remained with him, and explains why a young man with a clear future, intellectual capability and discipline was able to participate in such an offence for his first crime.'

Prison had a sobering effect. Smith completed his Year 10 studies behind bars but was 'too ashamed' to return to high school upon his release. 'He successfully completed Year 11 in a dysfunctional household where heroin abuse was going around,' Mr Vadasz said. 'He had to leave his parents' home when pressure was placed upon him to contribute to the heroin.' Unwilling to return to crime, Smith went to live with his girlfriend, hoping for a clean break. Realising his Olympic dream was dead, Smith found a new aspiration: he would do well enough in Year 12 to qualify for a course in legal studies. Over time, he would train himself to become a prominent criminal defence lawyer, and use his skills to keep his father out of jail. In January 1999, it seemed the dream would become a reality when Smith was accepted into the University of Adelaide.

He didn't make it to orientation week. Like his parents, Smith's girlfriend developed drug problems. She then fell pregnant with his child, forcing him to leave school once and for all and seek work. Given his conviction for armed robbery, eager employers were few and far between. Crime seemed his quickest – and, perhaps, only – solution. 'This is my attitude from when I was a little boy,' Smith said in January 2003. 'Sometimes you have to do things you don't want to do.'

On 7 February 1999, Smith and a 17-year-old accomplice stole a Holden Commodore from a house on Port Road at Hindmarsh, south of Adelaide. They drove it to the Buckingham Arms Hotel at Gilberton, north of the city. Armed with a hammer and a .22 calibre rifle, they tried to break through the glass doors of the hotel's gaming room. Staff members, still inside after closing time, heard loud banging noises and retreated to a secured office by the poker machines. They huddled close to one another as voices from outside demanded they open the doors. Smith, frustrated that the hammer was not breaking through as planned, raised the rifle and took aim. A single bullet shattered the glass and continued on into the office, only just missing worker Melissa Dales. She was ordered out and told to lie, with her workmates, on the floor. 'If you move, I'll shoot you,' Smith snarled, brandishing the weapon. Ms Dales and her colleagues lay frozen, terrified, while Smith and the teenager stole $22,300 from the safe. The robbers then fled through the window.

Ms Dales would never forget the experience, and found her lifestyle crippled in its wake. 'I have trouble going anywhere that has a high risk of hold-ups, or carrying large amounts of cash at work,' she said in 2002. 'I also get upset remembering that the bullet fired from the gun narrowly missed me. I'm incapable of being in the hotel after closing, and feel I will never be fully comfortable there again.'

Her co-worker, Vicki Jaeschke, unwillingly took the horror into her home. 'Being held at gunpoint has affected me in many ways,' she said. 'Smith had no regard for my life, I was so terrified. Now, even television shows provoke violent reactions in me, and returning to work put me under great physical stress. It was almost unbearable. I still wake in the night, thinking Smith is in my room and I am about to be shot.'

For a man who would make his name through daring escapes, Smith was a slow learner. Police found him and the teen, just a few hours after the robbery, hiding in the ceiling of a house one street away from the hotel. Smith claimed he had been on the way to his parents' house, saw the police and panicked, believing he would be blamed 'for whatever crime they were investigating'. The Holden Hill Magistrates Court was unconvinced, and remanded him in custody pending a bail report. Smith was taken to the Adelaide Remand Centre – just a few hundred metres up the road from his high school – to await his next hearing.

It could be argued that, despite the violence, there was still hope for the young man at this point. Whatever prospects remained, however, were dashed once again by Anthony Thiele Smith. One month after his arrest, Smith learned his idol was seriously ill – heroin was finally poised to take his father's life. He appealed, on compassionate grounds, for leave to visit him. Remand Centre management agreed and, at 2 pm on 1 March 1999, Smith was escorted to the Royal Adelaide Hospital. He was flanked, on three sides, by prison guards and an Aboriginal liaison officer. He was handcuffed and dressed in unmistakably prison-issue clothing. And, despite it all, he escaped.

The situation reads, on reflection, like a disaster waiting to happen. Though Smith was handcuffed, his feet were still free. The guards outnumbered him, but were twice his age and no competition for his lithe, athletic frame. They were escorting him through a narrow corridor of buildings and parked cars by walking in single file. None of his chaperons carried mobile phones or portable radios, meaning their cries for help would go unanswered for the precious minutes Smith would need to outpace them. The teenager had been grossly underestimated.

His escape plan – be it deliberate or spontaneous – worked perfectly. As he was being escorted toward the hospital's entrance, Smith broke away from his captors. They gave chase but could not hope to keep up with him. From the hospital, Smith turned right along North Terrace and bolted downhill, along Frome Road. He then turned again, parallel to the River Torrens, and vanished in between the giant trees of Botanic Park. His captors, recognising the hopelessness of their situation, did the only thing they could – they went and found a payphone to call in the greatest prisoner escape in South Australian history.

Reinforcements soon arrived. Officers, detectives and dog squad operatives combed the area and found nothing. Smith, the authorities decided, had already moved on, and so they did as well. It was the worst possible decision they could have made; two hours after Smith had broken away, a man matching his description hailed a taxi and had it take him to the outer suburbs.

'We called the police because the driver thought the man was wearing handcuffs,' a taxi company spokesman explained, later that day. 'He had his hands under his jumper and kept them together the whole time. He did pay, though – he had some cash in his pocket.'

To this day, no satisfactory explanation has been offered for Smith's success. The Royal Adelaide Hospital is situated on the north-east corner of the city – just one street over from the busy Rundle Street shopping precinct. The Botanic Gardens, the Adelaide Zoo and the grounds of the University of Adelaide surround it on three sides. Hundreds of people walk past the hospital during a working day, making use of its cab rank and numerous bus stops. More than four hundred thousand people tour the zoo each year, while in excess of one million people stop to smell the roses in the gardens. Somehow, amongst all those pedestrians, a tall man in a prison jumpsuit managed to run away from prison guards. He evaded an intense police search for two hours and appropriated enough cash to catch a taxi, all without arousing a moment's suspicion. Smith became South Australia's most wanted man and, in that moment, the myth of the Artful Dodger was born.

Police believed the worst was over. Now that Smith was on the run, they could move past their embarrassment and focus on catching him. Telling the media their inquiries 'were continuing', police sought the public's assistance in locating the escapee. 'Smith is 183 cm tall, with athletic build and short dark hair, brown eyes, fair to light brown complexion and a pimply face,' a statement read. Investigators targeted Smith's friends, family and known haunts.

There was, however, one member of the family they did not keep watch on: the escapee's father. It would be their downfall because, just one day after his epic run, Smith returned to the Royal Adelaide Hospital . . . and eluded capture again.

On 2 March, hospital security staff were called to a disturbance on the facility's ground floor. Two men were arguing outside the newsagency kiosk. One of them – who stood 183 centimetres tall, had a light brown complexion and was built like an athlete – quickly turned and fled. They watched the man tear out onto the street and thought nothing more of it. Hours later, a security officer scanned the morning's *Advertiser* newspaper, saw Smith's photo on the front page and realised he had fled for a second time.

'They weren't to know that he was the person who had escaped the day before,' a hospital spokesman, deep in damage control, blustered. 'He was dressed differently and didn't appear to be handcuffed. Maybe he was just testing the waters to see if he would be recognised.' An angry police spokesman announced that pictures of Smith had 'now been distributed' around the hospital.

Smith had, evidently, learned from his past mistakes. Gone were the days of watching opportunities arise before him, only to see them dashed by outside forces. The teenager was now willing and able to confront situations head-on; he had proven he was tougher, faster and smarter than those who wanted his hide. Like his father before him, Smith had become infamous, larger-than-life and respected by his community, albeit for all the wrong reasons. At the age of 19 he had become the sort of man his father would approve of.

Police had yet to correct their biggest failing: underestimating their quarry. In those early days, they did not account for Smith's style, arrogance and sense of the dramatic. They treated him as they would an ordinary criminal, and their investigations into his whereabouts were very ordinary as a result. On 5 March, they returned to the Walkerville house where Smith had hid after the hotel robbery. Their goal, they explained to reporters, was to see if the escapee had returned there to recover the firearm he had used. Detective Superintendent Bob O'Brien, head of investigations in that area, went so far as to speculate Smith's escape was prompted by whatever secrets he had left behind at Walkerville.

His theory held little water – officers in another suburb were testing a rifle that had been handed in by a member of the Aboriginal Sobriety Group. They believed they had Smith's weapon in their possession, and began ballistic and forensic testing to confirm their suspicions. Desperate to cover all bases, police staged a 30-day manhunt and raided dozens of homes.

Sadly, no one thought to focus the search on an area much closer to the hospital. Smith was less than a kilometre away from the scene of his escape. While his friends and family were harassed, and his past movements closely scrutinised, Smith walked 900 metres west of the hospital and checked into a room in the Radisson Playford Hotel. The luxurious hotel had been open for less than 12 months. Smith made the hotel his base of operations for 10 days – from 7 March to 17 March – and paid his $2200 tab in cash.

That money came, unsurprisingly, from his supporters. Friends and family gave Smith about $1000 to fund his outlaw existence, and his new 16-year-old girlfriend joined him at the hotel. But, at $220 a night, their finances were not going to last long. Mindful once again of his father's example, Smith rounded up three friends and began planning his next robbery. Unlike the Buckingham Arms incident, this robbery was to be a masterpiece of careful planning and precise execution. Smith was through with hiding in ceilings, with having the police just seconds behind him. It was time for him to make his own luck.

On 12 March 1999, Smith and two accomplices robbed the ANZ bank at Torrensville. One of the trio was armed with a gun. They smashed their way into the bank's back entrance with a sledgehammer after 5 pm as the bank was closing. Five staff members were still present when Smith entered. Three would need hospitalisation after he left. They were not only menaced with the gun, but attacked with the sledgehammer. 'Open the safe or I'll break your leg,' Smith roared at one. 'Hurry up or I'll shoot you,' he told another. Registers were emptied, as were six safety deposit boxes. The trio left in a stolen Holden Commodore. Smith's accomplices took their share and went their own ways; he returned to the Radisson and his sweetheart.

The robbery, Smith later explained, seemed to make good sense at the time. 'I was on the run, didn't know what I was going to do, so it was for my own resources,' he said in 2003. 'I needed money for what I wanted to do when I was on the run, to survive.' Smith, it seemed, wanted to survive in style – more than $9000 worth of cash, gold bullion and jewellery was taken in the heist.

In a decision that would, later, further cement his mythic status, Smith and his girlfriend decided to celebrate his success with an impromptu photo session. The images, seized by police in 2000, show that Smith was very ready, very early on, to believe his own hype. With his hair newly dyed blond to escape detection, he poses in a white cotton bathrobe, and then shirtless in shorts, on a king-size bed. He shoots the camera, and his girlfriend, a smouldering look – eager to portray himself as a dangerous sex symbol. The most telling shot also features Smith on the bed. This time he wears dark sunglasses, an Adidas baseball cap and tracksuit. An expensive watch is wrapped around his left wrist, while a revolver lays on his outstretched, open right palm. In addition to the gold chains draped around his neck, Smith is surrounded by $184,000 in cash and gold bullion.

'Why take the photos? Ego, I suppose,' he smirked in 2003. 'I don't know, it's just something that happened. Maybe it was ego, maybe it was other reasons.'

Five days after the robbery, Smith and his girlfriend left the Radisson. On 30 March, police discovered where they had been. The Dodger had made it easy for them: he'd left behind two gold rings, studded with rubies and diamonds and taken during the ANZ hold-up, as a token of his affection. In another embarrassment for his department, Detective Chief Inspector Peter Campbell had to admit the fugitive had outmanoeuvred them. 'As far as we are concerned there is no question – he definitely stayed there,' he told reporters. 'It's unusual, and brazen, but who knows what he was thinking.' A hotel spokeswoman, perhaps wisely, declined to comment on their most recent guests.

Detective Chief Inspector Campbell insisted his men 'haven't relented at all' in their search for the fugitive. The people of Adelaide took this vow to heart and sighting Smith, especially in places he had not visited, became a favourite pastime. So, too, was baiting the increasingly desperate police. On April Fools' Day, 1999, officers were called to a domestic dispute at Florian Street, Christie Downs. The occupants shouted a warning that Anthony Smith 'might be inside'. The attending officers withdrew to make way for heavily armed STAR Division officers, who donned their body armour and surrounded the house. A police negotiator was called in to defuse the dangerous situation. Two hours later, a man and a woman – neither of whom was Smith – were convinced to come outside. No charges were filed. Three hours later, city police were called to the Adelaide Railway Station – just across the street from the Radisson Plaza – because Smith was apparently there. Unsurprisingly, the report turned out to be false.

On 28 April, police announced their latest theory: Smith and his girlfriend – who had 'vanished' – were commuting regularly between Adelaide and Melbourne. Detective Senior Constable Harry Worth said the last confirmed sighting of Smith had been the week prior, when he had met up with his girlfriend in Adelaide. 'He has eluded police because of an extensive network of close friends and associates,' he said. 'These people are willing to risk imprisonment themselves to protect Smith.'

Police also linked the Dodger to a robbery outside the Bank SA branch at Plympton on 8 March, during which a woman was shot in the chest. The victim claimed she recognised Smith just before he fired on her. She survived and asked her name be kept secret from the public 'for my own safety'. Yet another warrant was issued for Smith's arrest – for all the good it would do.

In truth, Smith had no urgent need to commit another crime. For one, he had the money from the ANZ robbery. For another, the Australian Federal Government was eager to continue paying him an education benefit. In August, red-faced public servants were forced to admit Centrelink had paid Smith $267.23 a fortnight even after he was arrested for robbing the Buckingham Arms. Not even Smith's highly publicised escape had slowed the wheels of the Aboriginal Study Assistance Scheme, or ABSTUDY. Smith was paid $2100 before the gaffe was discovered. The revelation was a nightmare for Centrelink spokesman Russell Grigg, who joined the long list of public figures unforgettably shamed by Smith. 'Centrelink runs regular checks with Correctional Services and, sometimes, people will be missed by that,' he said. 'At the moment our system is working pretty well, but there are occasional glitches. We are working to improve the processes.' Though a pittance compared to the proceeds of his crimes, the benefits were enough to supplement Smith's lifestyle while allowing him to stay under the radar.

For five months, Smith existed only as a name on a warrant. Alleged sightings continued to occur – most noticeably, a police raid on a Devon Park home in October 1999 – but the Dodger remained out of reach. That didn't stop people from talking about him. The Aboriginal community, in particular, came to worry about its most famous member. The police, they whispered to one another, were tired of being humiliated by Smith. The gloves were off, they warned. Officers had been ordered to shoot Smith on sight, and told they must shoot to kill. The outlaw, the Artful Dodger, was to be the subject of that most feared of bounties: dead or alive.

Word reached Smith and his girlfriend as they migrated from one safe house to another. Now 20, the robber grew very concerned. He had survived, so far, on his legend and the profits of a single robbery – now he was being turned into a target. He decided to move interstate, permanently, and begin life again. In preparation, he obtained a fake New South Wales driver's licence under the name Michael John Harrison. Still yet to learn modesty, Smith donned a long blond wig and square glasses for the photo. He gave his address as National Street, Leichhardt, and his date of birth as 6 February 1978. But that would not be enough to carry him and his love away from the spectre of imminent death. Nor was the loaded gun he now carried with him at all times, enough to guarantee his security.

'Everyone was telling me "You're going to get shot",' he said in 2003. 'If the police knew I had a gun, they're going to have fear in themselves as well – they're only human. I thought that might just give me a chance to get away. The gun was loaded but, if it had no bullets in it, I would have carried it with no bullets in it. I wanted to defend myself and make it less likely that I was going to get shot. It sounds like a silly excuse but that's the reason I had it.'

Smith needed one last score. On 28 January 2000, Michael Harrison paid a visit to the Commonwealth Bank branch in Golden Grove. The polite and courteous 22-year-old provided his driver's licence to a teller and asked to open an account. As the woman went about her work, the man beneath the disguise took careful note of security cameras and screens, possible hiding places and the position of cash drawers. Commonwealth Bank outlets, he knew, all followed a similar design. He could case the branch at Golden Grove and, from his observations, create a near-infallible floor plan to rob any other branch in the state. And Smith's chosen target was on Fullarton Road at Myrtle Bank.

He was not the only man bound for the branch on that day in February. David Purdue, who worked at a nearby hotel, was heading down the footpath in the opposite direction. He had with him a calico bag containing $102 in coins. Thinking of other things, Mr Purdue paid little attention to two teenagers who moved, from the car park, to intercept him.

'He was walking toward me, he had money in his hand and it was enticing to me,' Smith remembered in 2003. 'I had about five steps to make a decision about what to do, and I ended up trying to rob him. My mate had walked past him first, and he's pointed to Mr Purdue. He didn't say 'rob him' or anything like that, but he pointed toward him as he walked past him. 'I didn't want to do it, and I kept saying to myself "Don't do it". Mr Purdue was just walking out at the wrong time – for him and for me.'

Smith confronted Mr Purdue. 'I showed him the gun and said "Hand over the cash", or something like that,' he said. The bar worker was incredulous, unimpressed and convinced the gun was a replica or toy. 'Fuck off,' he replied curtly, and continued on his way, stepping off the footpath. He travelled only a few steps more before Smith drew his gun from his pocket and fired once, hitting Mr Purdue in the back.

'I don't know why I shot him, I can't say why I shot him,' Smith said in 2003. 'It wasn't because he told me to fuck off but it was pretty much after that. The whole thing happened so fast – he's there, bang, I shot him. It happened so fast.'

The sound of the gunshot drew the attention of a nearby motorist. University professor Dr David Brooker was less than two metres away, in his car, and watched in horror as Mr Purdue went down. When Smith grabbed the calico bag and began to run, Dr Brooker gave chase.

'After I shot Mr Purdue I started running, and next thing I can see this car following me,' Smith said in 2003. 'I thought he was a police officer,' Smith said in 2003. 'I know it's wrong now but, at the time, I thought I was going to be shot on sight. I didn't see his face, but I knew it was a male, and I didn't see how old he was. I turned around, pointed the gun and it stopped and turned around. I kept running.'

Smith continued to the corner, but noticed Dr Brooker had resumed his pursuit. 'I got to the corner and that's where I shot at him,' he said. The bullet went through the front passenger-side window. 'Then I approached the car, just to make sure he wasn't going to shoot me. I kept the gun pointed at the car and ran over to it. I thought he was the police and

I wanted to scare him away.' Smith ordered Dr Brooker out of his car and the older man refused. They struggled, and the gun went off. Dr Brooker was wounded in the left side of his chest. 'I didn't know I'd hit him,' Smith said later. 'He jumped out and I took the car – it was automatic.'

Dr Brooker would undergo surgery to remove pieces of shrapnel from his chest. As of 2003, several fragments remained lodged in his body, inoperable. Mr Purdue continues to carry bullet fragments in his lower back, dangerously close to his spine. His personality underwent a radical change in the wake of the shooting; he lost his positive attitude toward his work and suffered a sleep disorder.

Money had been stolen, two men were lying in the street with horrific injuries – the Artful Dodger had returned. Yet this time, by Smith's own admission, things were different. Before, he'd survived on his wits, clever schemes and good turns of fortune. He had terrorised people, taken their money and struck them – even fired a gun during a robbery – but he had never before shot someone. The police had no patience left, referring to Smith as 'desperate' and 'callous'. The senior Smith would have undoubtedly been impressed, and considered it the next stage of his son's maturation into a true man. The younger outlaw, however, felt ill.

'I don't know why I did it and I didn't really have a reason for it,' he lamented in 2003. 'I don't blame them, or anyone else, for the decision I made. I don't know why I shot Mr Purdue. He obviously didn't do what I asked him to, and he didn't give me any money, but I can't say why I shot him. It just happened so fast, and I haven't got an explanation . . . I just made the wrong decision again.'

Smith ditched Dr Brooker's car on the way to his latest hiding spot – 12 Bechervaise Court, Greenwith. The owner,

37-year-old Lyn Marie Harrison, had ties to Smith's girlfriend and, while she had no love for would-be gangsters, was strongly devoted to the young girl. She was also an Aboriginal liaison officer, ready to do all she could to help the troubled in her community. Harrison opened her home to the fugitive couple, and they stayed with her for 15 days. Smith was, once again, hidden from sight. This time, however, he could not hide from his conscience.

'I'd been proud of myself after the ANZ robbery,' he said in 2003. 'But with Mr Purdue, I thought about what I did every single day since it happened. I tried to work out why it happened. I wasn't proud about the things I done anymore. I wished I could change it.' Using Harrison's phone, Smith reached out to legal counsel and explored ways of turning himself in to the police. 'I rang certain people to see what I could do about giving myself up. Other people then rang persons for myself to try and make arrangements. I wanted to give myself up but I wasn't sure whether I should . . . I was in two minds about it. I just had to make sure everything was alright before I went to prison. I tried to make sure that everyone who was important to me was alright.'

While Smith struggled with his decision, an angry police force made it for him. Around noon on 15 February, detectives from the Drug and Organised Crime Investigation Branch received information about Smith's whereabouts. Frustratingly, they had surrounded number 12 just five days earlier, and found no trace of their prey. It was to be the last time the Dodger would humiliate South Australia Police.

By 2.30 pm a 'high-risk arrest operation' had been launched. STAR Group officers invaded the quiet cul-de-sac and moved civilians out of harm's way. 'It's something we never expected to see here,' one evacuated homeowner said.

'It's a bit scary, not just for me but for all the residents because it happened so close to us.' Officers placed telephone calls to other occupants, telling them to stay away from their windows. 'I can't believe it because it is always so quiet here,' said the recipient of one such call. 'There has never been any trouble here. I was pretty scared.'

Bechervaise Court was quickly boxed in – police dogs patrolled both ends of the street while a helicopter circled overhead. One street over – appropriately named Law Court – police set up their command post. A dozen marked and unmarked police cars jostled for space, as did two large communication vans. More than fifty officers then made their move on number 12 and, almost immediately, spotted Smith peering through the front window.

Confirmation of Smith's presence triggered a tense, three-hour standoff. He was not alone inside the house; present, also, were his girlfriend, Harrison and another young woman. Fearing a hostage situation, the officer in charge – Detective Superintendent Rob Maggs – began to negotiate with the Dodger. 'Our aim has always been to arrest Smith in a peaceful way,' he told reporters. 'We had reason to believe Smith was at this location, we put into motion a series of tactics which we had developed should there be a sighting of Smith.'

Finally, after 12 months of mistakes, under-estimation and very public failures, the police were ready to counteract the outlaw's scheming. And, for the first time since he tucked himself into the ceiling of a Walkerville house, Smith had nowhere to run. Every potential escape route led straight down the barrel of a police-issue weapon or, worse, into the jaws of a snarling K9 unit. Realising his year on the run had come to an end, Smith walked out of the house, with his hands on his head, at 5.40 pm. He wore a grey polo t-shirt, white shorts and no shoes. He offered no resistance, even laying down on the ground, while officers handcuffed him.

This time there would be no mistakes; Smith was placed in an unmarked vehicle and driven straight to the City Watch House. He was denied police bail and was remanded in custody to appear in the Adelaide Magistrates Court the next morning. A police search of the house uncovered the photographs taken by the couple back at the Radisson; they were tagged, bagged and added to the evidence pile. Harrison and Smith's girlfriend, meanwhile, were each charged with harbouring an escapee – they, however, were released on bail. In April 2004, Harrison received a suspended one-year sentence for her role in the Dodger's story.

On 16 February 2000, dozens of people and reporters crowded into the public gallery of the Magistrates Court. They found themselves sharing the space with several plain-clothes police officers and eight members of the outlaw's family. Detective Superintendent Maggs's words were still fresh in the gallery's mind; everyone wanted to know what 'tactics' the police had 'developed' in anticipation of capturing Smith. They didn't have to wait long. Smith was led into court at 11.40 am, still wearing the clothes in which he had been arrested. He was accompanied by four armed police officers. Two remained in the dock with him, while two more took up positions within the courtroom. Private security contractors and sheriff's officers guarded the door and the area immediately outside.

Smith was bound at the wrist by handcuffs, and a restraint belt was looped around his waist. His arms were shackled, above the elbows, to the belt. Incarceration seemed to agree with the Dodger – the nerves and guilt of the prior few weeks had faded, and he favoured his supporters with a wry smile. The appearance was short – merely for the setting of dates – and uneventful. Following the hearing, Smith's family approached the media and publicly declared their love. An aunt said all family members would continue to offer their support. 'I was happy to see him, not in the situation he's in, but at least I know he's safe,' she told reporters.

The time had come for Smith to answer for his crimes. After months of committal hearings in the lower jurisdiction, he appeared in the District Court on 15 September 2000, on charges of escaping from custody. He was transported to the Sir Samuel Way building in an unmarked police car, accompanied by three guards. The vehicle was part of a convoy, led by a marked police car and followed by a station wagon. Each car had two more police officers; the station wagon also carried a police dog.

In court, defence lawyer Nick Vadasz sought to turn his client's guilty plea into criticism of the prison system. 'This was an impulsive, unplanned escape,' he argued. 'He was escorted to the hospital to see his father. There was a lot going through his mind – a lot of anxiety, a lot of concern. He was handcuffed at the front . . . for some reason he was not restrained in any other way. He was walking, suddenly he saw an open passage in front of him and he simply ran. It was a temptation that, maybe, should not have been put in his way.'

Lynette Duncan, prosecuting, urged the court not to be swayed. She reminded Judge Robert Lunn that Smith had been in custody less than three weeks before he broke free. He deserved, she said, no less than the maximum seven-year jail term and a 'lengthy' non-parole period. 'This offence of escaping from custody is a serious one,' she said. 'He was being allowed the opportunity to visit his father, and that visit did not go ahead because of the escape. He had been granted permission on compassionate grounds. Mr Smith remained at large for almost a year despite a nationwide manhunt. At no stage did he voluntarily surrender himself to police.'

Sometimes, the decisions of judges are not for mere mortals to understand. Having heard the arguments and weighed the evidence, Judge Lunn ruled in October 2000 that South Australia's most infamous – and, for police, most humiliating – prison escape was worthy of a nine-month minimum term. Further, he chose to backdate commencement of that sentence to the day of Smith's arrest. For engineering a prison escape that allowed him to prey, repeatedly, on the people of Adelaide and directly led to the shooting of two men, the Artful Dodger was ordered to serve less time in prison than he spent on the run. To those who had spent months trying to catch Smith, and for those who fell victim to his gung-ho excess, the sentence was yet another slap in the face.

There was more disappointment to come. Efforts to prosecute Smith over the robberies became bogged down in two years of investigations and negotiations between Mr Vadasz and the Office of the Director of Public Prosecutions. One charge fell, almost immediately, to the wayside. Prosecutor Liesl Chapman felt the Crown could not prove, beyond reasonable doubt, that Smith had shot the woman at Bank SA Plympton in March 1999. The alleged victim was distraught. In late 2002, the woman filed civil action against Smith, saying she had been unable to return to work due to 'extreme emotional distress and fear'. Her claim for unspecified damages was unsuccessful.

In January 2001, Smith showed he didn't need to be on the run to cause problems. He was charged with one count of common assault after he attacked a prison guard. Mr Vadasz was quick to explain the situation. 'For the past 10 or 11 months he has been in solitary, isolated from all prisoners,' he said. 'He has had no contact with his peers, and only limited contact with prison officers. Over that time, he has developed obsessive-compulsive tendencies, specifically an obsession with cleanliness. On that day he was told to go back to his cell by the guard. He over-reacted, much in the terms of the disorder he had acquired, because he had not yet had a shower. He does not suffer from any other psychological disorder, and he is not being specifically treated for this problem at the moment.'

In October 2002, the outlaw pleaded guilty to multiple counts of armed robbery and to shooting Mr Purdue and Dr Brooker with the intent to cause them grievous bodily harm. The case was listed to be heard before Judge Ann Vanstone – a former prosecutor with a tough reputation and a tendency to be blunt. The end seemed near but, once again, Smith moved the goal posts – he announced he wanted to change his plea. He had no intention of harming either man, he insisted, and so was only guilty of the lesser charge of unlawful wounding.

The reason for Smith's sudden legal acumen became clear during a December 2002 hearing in the District Court. 'He's been studying for his crime and justice degree, and his human behaviour and research degree, while he's been in custody,' Mr Vadasz told the court. 'He still has in mind his childhood dream of a career – to be a defence lawyer. He's been advised that's a dream he might want to consider changing, and so he considers he might qualify for psychology. He's been advised he might not be able to practise, however.'

Smith, Mr Vadasz related, had only recently returned to study. 'Following his surrender, my client was immediately taken to G-division,' he said. The maximum security wing of the Yatala Labour Prison north of Adelaide was reserved for the worst of the worst. South Australia's most horrifying criminals – including the 'bodies in barrels' serial killers, John Bunting and Robert Wagner – did and still do call it home. 'Smith was kept in isolation and deprived of most of the very basic facilities given to other prisoners, in particular those in relation to education,' Mr Vadasz continued. 'He was not released from G-division until January of 2001 – he spent 10 or 11 months in solitary.'

Smith's self-education, he said, began upon his arrival in the prison's general population. 'He now spends as much time as he can with his studies. He has scored distinctions or high distinctions in all the subjects he's studied to date. His teachers are confident he will complete one if not both degrees, and once he is released he will make a contribution to society. One teacher has said that, in her eight years working at the prison, Smith is one of the most capable students she has ever come across.'

In January 2003, Smith took the stand in his own defence. It was a tense day in the courtroom. Two sheriff's officers guarded the doors, while another three sat in the public gallery. Two more accompanied Smith to the witness box, while correctional services officers spread themselves throughout the courtroom. Dressed in a smart suit, Smith looked levelly at Judge Vanstone and spoke of his encounters with Mr Purdue and Dr Brooker.

A new element entered his recollections: pressure. Smith claimed he felt obliged to his parents and extended family, and responsible for their financial difficulties. The men with whom he'd committed robberies were no longer his accomplices, they were the people who had pressured him into a life of crime. They had been armed during the robberies, not Smith – he'd never touched a weapon during the ANZ hold-up, and took the rifle from his friend at the Buckingham Arms after it had fired a shot. Smith insisted he was a lonely, fearful man on the run, stealing to survive and hating every minute of it from the beginning – even before he shot Mr Purdue.

Smith also outlined how the incidents had changed his perspective on life. 'I don't blame them, I don't blame anyone, for the decisions I made,' he said. 'I'm not proud of the thing I've done. I wish I could change it, but all I can do is make sure it doesn't happen again. I can do that by getting my education while I'm in prison, and work on my thinking patterns and my views and just everything that is attributable to my behaviour.'

During his two days on the stand, Smith said everything a judge could possibly want to hear. Ms Chapman, in fact, considered his evidence to be too perfect, and went on the attack. 'Look back at the Buckingham Arms robbery,' she said to the court. 'The other man was younger than Smith, who was already an experienced armed robber through his Youth Court offences. He clearly considered himself in charge during that incident. The Crown does not accept he was under any obligation or pressure. We ask Your Honour to find he was the one with the gun that night, that he fired the shot through the office window.'

The ANZ robbery, she continued, was not about family obligation. 'The photos taken at the Radisson show, overwhelmingly, this was about ego, about Smith living it up and showing off to his friends,' she said. 'Again, we ask Your Honour to find he was the one armed with the gun on that day, and any claim to the contrary is another attempt to downplay his role in these affairs. The photos speak for themselves. Smith surrounded himself with the cash, the jewellery and the takings from the ANZ bank with the gun in the palm of his hand. I suggest it is the same gun used in the robbery.'

She urged Judge Vanstone not to accept Smith's version of the events at Myrtle Bank. 'If it's true he only carried the gun for intimidation, then it begs the question: why was it loaded?' she asked. 'He was not there to rob a person on the street but, rather, for the more serious reason of casing the Commonwealth Bank. It could even be the case he was going to rob the bank that day. He was armed, he had someone to help him and they were in the car park around the corner. This was a plan drawn up with the Commonwealth Bank as the focal point.

'With regard to Mr Purdue, Smith was under no pressure to do what he did. No one made him fire that shot. The Crown does not accept he was under pressure to make a split-second decision – he shot Mr Purdue in the back as he was walking away. The only reason Smith did it was because Mr Purdue told him to fuck off, and the only reason Mr Purdue did that was because he didn't think the gun was real.'

Ms Chapman reserved some of her scorn for the shooting of Dr Brooker. 'Smith says he believed Dr Brooker was a police officer,' she all but snarled. 'The fact one is shooting at what one believes is a police officer is not a mitigating factor – it may well be an aggravating factor. The truth is, Smith didn't really care who was driving the car, it could have been anybody. His concern was that he was being followed by a car, and his getaway car was around the corner and he was going to be observed getting into it.

'Defence would have you believe this was a lonely, frightened man on the run, trying to do the right thing. I ask Your Honour not to accept that. This picture of him being scared does not sit well with him walking into the Commonwealth Bank at Golden Grove, in disguise, with a fake ID. That is not a lonely man trying to do the right thing. This is a bold, brazen and calculating armed robber who is prepared to shoot people. The overwhelming weight of evidence proves Anthony John Smith to be a ruthless and egotistical criminal.'

Mr Vadasz disagreed. 'There is no evidence to suggest he is the person who was armed at the ANZ bank,' he said. 'With regards to Myrtle Bank, my learned friend Ms Chapman has raised a number of conjectures about my client. She suggests it was a premeditated, planned event, a scheme to rob the Commonwealth Bank prior to committing the offences involving Mr Purdue and Dr Brooker. Such theories are based on inadequate assumptions. Such theories fail to carry weight. They fail to dislodge the explanations put forward by Mr Smith for his behaviour.' He said nothing before the court proved Smith was casing the Myrtle Bank branch, nor that he had visited the Golden Grove branch in preparation for a robbery. 'Would a person, in preparation for a robbery of a bank, provide that bank with his photo – even a photo that was different to his normal appearance?' he asked.

He said Smith had struggled mightily with his conscience – and his relatives – following the double shooting. 'One part of him told him to follow his current path, some of his family were urging him to surrender himself, others were giving him different advice,' he said. 'There is no evidence to displace the evidence that Smith has given as to his state of mind while on the run.'

Judge Vanstone adjourned the case for a fortnight, saying she wanted time to consider the sentence she would impose. On 13 February 2003 – more than four years after the Buckingham Arms robbery – Smith was brought to the District Court to face his fate. His hands were, once again, shackled to a restraint belt. The suit was gone, replaced with a polo shirt and jeans. He favoured his girlfriend and family, who sat in the public gallery, with a quick smile. He rose when Judge Vanstone entered the court and kept his head bowed, looking penitent. His expression would not remain calm for long.

Her Honour had found, beyond reasonable doubt, that Smith had carried the gun and fired the shot at the Buckingham Arms. 'It is clear from the statements of the witnesses that you entered the gaming room after the shot, carrying the weapon,' she said. 'Plainly, you were concerned that breaking into the gaming room was taking too long.' Nor did she doubt he was the robber armed with the gun during the ANZ heist.

Judge Vanstone made it clear the evidence had convinced her of many things. Smith's own testimony, however, had revealed nothing to her. 'You said your encounters with Mr Purdue and Dr Brooker were spontaneous crimes,' she said. 'When one considers the enormity of the offences committed by you on that day, I see concern for your victims' welfare has not been a feature of your life or your crimes. Your evidence was unpersuasive and cynical. It makes me wonder why you bothered to give evidence at all.'

In the dock, Smith's composure was beginning to break. His head was up, now, and his features flushed. His eyes were fixed, in a deathly glare, on Judge Vanstone – who held his rancour levelly. Unable to intimidate her as he had so many others, unwilling to hear his precious self-delusions attacked with such honesty and venom, Smith began to twitch.

'In the face of all this,' Judge Vanstone continued, 'your prospects seem bleak. One has to remind oneself of your relative youth, given your disturbing criminal history.' She noted his pursuit of education, the work he was putting into his degrees and the good reports of his teachers. 'You wish to work, in the long term, for members of the Aboriginal community,' she said. 'You have gained far greater insight into the negative influences your family background created in you. Plainly, you are a young man with some ability, and that does give hope for the future.'

She opted to give Smith some discount, in sentence, for his relative youth and guilty pleas – late though they were. 'They do not necessarily indicate an acceptance of responsibility,' she said. 'You brazenly kept a room at the Radisson Plaza and took photographs showing off your firearms and your loot. Your violence escalated to the extent that two blameless citizens were shot by you. It grieves me to sentence a man to such a lengthy term, especially a young man, but you brought your fate upon yourself.'

Judge Vanstone paused, and the crowded courtroom fell silent. There was nothing left for Her Honour to do, now, but pronounce sentence. When she did, it was shocking. She ordered Smith serve 12 years for the Buckingham Arms robbery, noting it 'would have been more like 15' if not for his guilty plea. For the ANZ heist, he was to serve seven and a half years – down from ten, again due to his plea. For the litany of crimes committed at Myrtle Bank, Judge Vanstone said a 24-year term would be appropriate but, given Smith's admissions, she would sentence him to 18 years instead. 'That equals a head sentence of 37 and a half years,' she said, 'and that would be a crushing sentence. You will serve time for the Torrensville and Myrtle Bank offences concurrently, but that will be cumulative upon the term for the Buckingham Arms robbery. I therefore impose a head sentence of 30 years.'

Smith's girlfriend, and several members of his family, began weeping. Victims who had attended the hearing, including Mr Purdue, breathed audible sighs of relief. Smith did not immediately react. He knew, from his legal studies, that the matter was far from over. To a criminal, the head sentence is far less important than the non-parole period – the minimum time one must serve before they can plead their case for home detention release. It was this number that interested the Artful Dodger.

'I have asked myself what the minimum term you must serve in jail should be,' Judge Vanstone went on. 'I see nothing particularly outstanding about your prospects of rehabilitation. The appropriate term, therefore, is 18 years.'

Since 1 March 1999, Anthony John Smith had seen himself as the Artful Dodger – a South Australian legend, Adelaide's outlaw son, a folk hero to rival John Dillinger, Jesse James or Ned Kelly. Unlike those towering figures, however, Smith's finale came not in a blaze of glory, nor accompanied by a pithy, iconic final retort. Instead, he threw away every last shred of his delusion – every glimmer of hype he had built around himself – and degenerated into the child he had always been.

'Eighteen years?' he cried, throwing himself at the dock's glass barrier. 'I've got to do 18 years, you fucking slut? Fuck all this, fuck you all!'

For all he had done, Anthony John Smith went to the cells not as a legend but howling, clawing and screaming, his icy calm and mythic image shattered.

He was not alone in his rage. His girlfriend leaped at the police officers who had arrested her beloved, at the victims who had suffered during his crimes. 'I hate you,' she screamed, 'I hate you all!' The girl was dragged out of the courtroom by Smith's family, who were not shy about giving their opinions to the media. 'The sentence was too great,' one woman, who identified herself as the Dodger's aunt, told reporters. 'Other people do worse than he did and they get off scot-free. Some people don't even get what he got for murder. There's two bloody types of law, one for the rich and one for the poor. Aboriginal people get longer sentences, and that's a fact.'

The final word on the matter belonged to the man who had suffered most at his hands. David Purdue walked from the court looking a little shocked, but happy. 'I feel good, very good – I'm all closed, now,' he told reporters. 'Life is back to normal. This has consumed everything for the last three years . . . I'm glad it's over, and I'm glad we all got to see it end. There's some sense of satisfaction, some relief.'

He paused to watch Smith's supporters walk away. 'It's unbelievable about how his family carried on at the end,' he said ruefully. 'Smith stuffed up, what, how many lives? After all the lives he's affected and all the people that have suffered, as far as I'm concerned, he got what he deserved.'

Pleading the Belly

Rebecca Clarke

For someone on trial, there are but two fates: being found guilty of an offence and receiving punishment, or being found not guilty and earning release. There is, under Australian law, no such thing as being found innocent. The justice system does not exonerate one of their alleged actions so much as it allows one back into the community if the prosecution's evidence is lacking.

Rebecca Jane Clarke was determined to find another option. She was not especially bright, nor particularly sympathetic. Yet, during her year-long duel with the South Australian courts, the 22-year-old alcoholic plumbed the depths of case law – be it obscure, ancient or brand new – in her push to be completely absolved of her sins. Her desire to be a social worker for disadvantaged children would not be derailed – not even by a conviction for making lesbian pornography with 14-year-olds. If achieving her dream meant the legal system had to be callously manipulated, so be it.

Such was Clarke's hubris, her self-importance, that the single-minded woman nearly created a legal precedent that, horrifyingly, would have given thousands of paedophiles and rapists a new tool with which they could avoid the jail terms their kind so richly deserved. By pursuing her quest to provide care and support to the young, Clarke was simultaneously guaranteeing that more children would become victims.

◆

The sequence of events resulting in Rebecca Clarke's personal downfall began in July 2005. At that time Clarke was not living in South Australia, but in her hometown of Goulburn, New South Wales. Then 20 years old, she spent her time with either her mother's family or her childhood sweetheart; a man she planned to marry. She worked part-time jobs to support her studies; her life's goal was to become a counsellor for disadvantaged, disabled and traumatised children.

Clarke had yet to meet two people who would have a permanent and negative effect on her life – Renee Jean Malyschko and Daniel Troy Osis, a South Australian couple then aged 22 and 24. Tall and thin, with angular features, Osis's appearance was in sharp contrast to that of his lover, Malyschko, who was short and stocky, with a double chin and lifeless brown hair. Opposites often attract, however, and the couple shared a house in Glenelg North. A hip young suburb, just five minutes from the beach and 20 minutes from Adelaide's nightclub scene, it was a dream location for a young couple looking to have fun. Osis, in particular, needed something to brighten his mood.

'My client had always anticipated he would get into the Royal Australian Air Force,' lawyer Tim Dibden would say in January 2008. 'Unfortunately, he was involved in a car accident while he was working as a pizza boy – he suffered a back injury that meant he would never be able to join the air force.'

Osis found his distraction outside the city's clubs, particularly those along Hindley Street. Stretching from the centre of Adelaide to its westernmost border, Hindley Street is both exciting and dangerous – depending on how far west you have ventured. The strip becomes less mainstream, and more red-light, the further you travel from the shopping nexus of Rundle Mall. McDonald's, vintage bookstores and falafel houses give way to strip clubs, uncountable bars, cheap hotels and several 24-hour sex shops. The area's reputation for weekend violence is such that, in 2010, more than half the South Australian police officers stationed in the area applied for transfers. They were no longer prepared to work in such a hazardous area without substantial increases in pay and extreme decreases in hours.

For a certain segment of the state's youth, Hindley Street has an irresistible appeal. Not all of those drawn, moth-like, to the miniature Sin City are old enough to legally be there. Such was the case with two girls Osis befriended in July 2005.

'Osis's relationship with the girls began when they flagged down a vehicle, being driven by a friend of his, on Hindley Street,' Mr Dibden said in 2008. 'Osis was a passenger, and they jumped in. But he didn't become aware of their ages until August 14 that year.' On that date, Osis was driving and the girls were his passengers. They were headed down Anzac Highway, a four-lane road that connects Adelaide and Glenelg. 'The girls were hanging out of the sunroof of his car and, as a result, they were pulled over by the police,' Mr Dibden said. 'When the police asked for identification, Osis was shocked to find out they were 14 years old. Still, that was of no concern — he had no intention of getting anything out of the girls.'

That would change, but not before Clarke entered the picture. Around the same time as Osis's revelation, she moved from New South Wales to South Australia. She told friends she wanted to be closer to her father, who lived in the town of Strathalbyn in the Adelaide Hills. In truth, the move was prompted by the breakdown of her long-term relationship. Like Osis, Clarke found less-than-exemplary ways of coping with her shattered dreams.

'I started work, spent a week getting to know people, and then got involved with an older man in my office,' Clarke would tell the District Court in June 2007. 'He was 39 and, for a while, it was an on-off thing because he was in another steady relationship. I was drinking a lot — I was drinking every day — and smoking a bit of marijuana. I'd just come home from work and drink a lot of wine and a lot of gin. Sometimes, I'd even get up in the morning and have a drink. I wasn't very happy . . . I felt used by this man, and so I used alcohol to escape.'

She would find solace in another newcomer to the office — Malyschko. 'I'd only known her for a few weeks, maybe a month, but she was the only person I could talk to about the older man situation,' Clarke said. 'We just sort of bonded, and started up a friendship. She was really sympathetic to my situation and I didn't really have any other friends. She was nice to me.'

Clarke was no longer a lonely alcoholic; finally, she had someone to drink with. While the girls spent their Friday nights crawling from one bar to another, Osis entertained his new, young friends. When Malyschko called, wanting to be picked up, he would make the trip into the city and bring her home to join the fun. Malyschko came to know the girls as well as her lover did – by sharing drugs, alcohol and oral sex with them. She and the girls would perform for Osis, who would film the home-made pornography with his video camera and store it on his computer. Often he would take his turn in front of the lens while one of the girls recorded the action.

'There is no doubt these two girls were much older, in terms of their attitudes, than they were chronologically,' lawyer David Stokes said, on Malyschko's behalf, in January 2008. 'When my client first met them, well, one way to put it was that they were playful and flirty toward her. This wasn't limited to Malyschko – these young girls were going out all night, hopping into cars with men they didn't know that were far older.'

Osis and Malyschko were old enough to know better, but the phrase 'common sense' did not appear in their vocabularies. For them, the operative word was 'fun' – and the more alcohol and ecstasy there was on hand, the more fun there was to be had. The girls began skipping school to spend more time with their new older friends, and Malyschko would later admit doing nothing to discourage them. 'My client let this relationship go too far,' Mr Stokes said.

Clarke would play a pivotal role in that. 'The first time I ever went to Renee's house was on a Friday night in September 2005,' she would tell the District Court. 'Renee and I went out for drinks after work, and we were drinking and going from club to club along Hindley Street with some other work colleagues.' They drank gin – Clarke's favourite – and wine, as well as $1 shots of various hard liquor. 'We ordered about 30 of them, and had about 15 each,' Clarke said. 'We drank from 5 pm until about 11 pm.'

Malyschko wanted to go home – and, perhaps sensing another potential sex partner, insisted Clarke join her. 'Renee asked me back to her place but I wanted to stay out and keep drinking, because I really enjoyed drinking,' Clarke said. Eventually she gave in to her friend's requests, and Osis was called for the usual pick-up. They arranged to meet outside the Crazy Horse strip club.

When Osis arrived, Clarke changed her mind. 'There were two girls in the car with him,' she said. 'I'd decided I wanted to go back to the clubs but Renee wanted to go home. "We can't go out," she told me, "because these girls are only 17 and won't be allowed into the clubs".'

It was upon that conversation the subsequent trial would turn. For the next three years, Clarke would loudly and repeatedly insist her knowledge of the girls' ages began and ended with those words from Malyschko. Her treasured drinking buddy and closest confidant, she insisted, had deliberately misled her.

Malyschko would deny those claims just as strongly as Clarke had made them. 'That suggestion is quite vehemently denied by my client,' Mr Stokes growled in January 2008. 'As far as she was concerned, Clarke was only too aware both girls were well under the age of 17.'

That argument was in the future – back in mid 2005, Clarke was far more concerned with alcohol than age. 'Renee promised we'd stop by the bottle shop and get some more drinks if I would go back to her place, and that was what convinced me,' Clarke remembered. 'They actually bought me a whole bottle of gin. That was around midnight, and everything after that is a bit vague.'

Unfortunately for Clarke, the camera never forgets. That night, she became a willing participant in Osis and

Malyschko's Friday night sex games. While Osis rolled the camera, Clarke and Malyschko starred in no less than six short films with the teenagers. During the films – later tendered before the District Court – the naked women can be seen engaging in oral sex acts with the nude girls, teasing one of them with an inflatable toy Coke bottle.

Clarke visited her friend's home on three subsequent occasions but – by her account – had no further sexual contact with the teenagers. Indeed, police found no evidence of such when they raided the Glenelg North address in early 2007. Osis was under investigation for unrelated matters but, when officers viewed a DVD they found in his computer disc tower, their inquiries rapidly turned to matters of child pornography. It was clearly obvious from the first screening, that the girls being drugged, used and violated by Osis, Malyschko and Clarke were below the age of consent – and were, most likely, still children.

Osis was arrested and charged with 18 offences including possessing and producing child pornography, supplying ecstasy to a child and inciting a child to commit an indecent act. Malyschko was picked up next, for the same offences. During interviews, the couple provided Clarke's name to detectives and she was charged with producing child pornography and inciting both children to commit indecent acts. All offences were alleged to have occurred between July 2005 and February 2006.

Osis and Malyschko wasted no time in approaching the Office of the Director of Public Prosecutions for a deal. Through their counsel, they offered to plead guilty to some of the charges against them in return for the remainder being dropped. Clarke was more stubborn; throughout the committal process, in the Adelaide Magistrates Court, she insisted she was innocent of the charges. It was an unusual position for a defendant to take – many say they will plead 'not guilty', but claiming innocence is incredibly rare. The reason for her stance would become apparent over time.

The trio were due to stand trial before District Court Judge Michael Boylan on 4 June 2007. However, prosecutor Geraldine Davison announced a plea bargain had been struck. 'It is my understanding that Osis will plead guilty to seven offences, and those pleas will be accepted in satisfaction of all the allegations against him,' she said. 'Malyschko will plead guilty to five counts.'

She glanced at Clarke, who stood nervously in the dock of the court. 'I'm given to understand Your Honour will still need to hold a trial in relation to Clarke,' she said stiffly. 'There are ongoing discussions, though, so I ask Your Honour not to start the trial until tomorrow.' She said Clarke's counsel would be seeking a trial by judge alone – meaning Judge Boylan would hear the evidence without a jury, and be solely responsible for the verdict.

His Honour, already aware of the DVD he would be required to watch, was satisfied with that course. 'Some of the evidence that needs to be called is such that it's preferable as few people see it as possible,' he said.

Downcast and quiet, Osis and Malyschko entered their pleas with a minimum of fuss. Malyschko flinched slightly when asked to admit she'd driven the girls to perform indecent acts for her amusement. Osis showed no reaction at all and spoke crisply, standing ramrod straight. Judge Boylan ordered their bail would continue and released them; they walked from court into a waiting media crush.

Clarke remained; she was not yet finished with the court. Her counsel, Adam Richards, asked Judge Boylan to impose a suppression order on his client's identity. Prior to that date, he explained, Clarke's privacy had been protected by a South Australian law that forbids public identification of suspected sex offenders until they appear in the District Court. Now that order had fallen away, he needed to justify its replacement with a new media gag.

The state's laws on suppression orders had been re-written just two months earlier by Premier Mike Rann and his Labor government. Concerned that, with in excess of 220 suppression orders made each year, Adelaide was earning the reputation of being 'the secret city', legislators had moved to make the orders more difficult to obtain. Alleged offenders now had to prove identifying them would either prejudice the proper administration of justice – fouling their ability to get a fair trial – or show their children would suffer 'undue hardship' by their naming.

The new laws had been tested, by the District Court, in May 2007. A woman named Traci Lee Kiea Dean had pleaded guilty to criminally neglecting her infant son. Dean, of the low-income suburb of Salisbury Downs, had failed to stop the child eating the methylamphetamine she was cooking in her kitchen. Her lawyers had successfully applied for a suppression order on the grounds Dean's 16-year-old daughter would suffer 'undue hardship' from publicity. The girl, they told Judge Paul Rice, had been teased at school by bullies who called her mother a 'slut' and a 'drug addict', causing her to start fights and eventually be expelled.

Just 72 hours later, Judge Rice lifted the order. He said he agreed with submissions, made by the media, that schoolyard teasing was a normal part of a child's life and not something a court should be concerned with. 'I'm also not convinced the daughter comes under the definition of 'child' in the act,' he said. 'I've no doubt publication of Dean's name would cause some hardship – but I do know it does not amount to undue hardship. The revised act requires special circumstances for suppression, and I do not take the view this is sufficiently serious to warrant the making of an order.'

His bold decision set a precedent that has, in the years since, granted the public far greater access to the stories and decisions of the courts. It also reversed a then-worrying trend that had seen murderers and rapists escape public condemnation by hiding behind their children. It was not, however, enough to stop Clarke on 4 June. She would, throughout her case, remind the world of her belief the legal system should bend to her whims irrespective of the damage caused to the wider community.

Mr Richards told the court his client had a younger brother. He had recently undergone radiotherapy for Hodgkin's lymphoma, and was continuing to struggle with his health. The boy, Mr Richards intoned, would be at significant risk of further illness should he be subjected to scorn and ridicule prompted by his sister's alleged actions. Cancer, he argued, readily qualified as 'special circumstances' under the act and a suppression order was, therefore, warranted.

Caught off-guard by the application, media representatives in the court asked for a five-minute adjournment. Under the revised laws, a court could not impose an order without first seeking the opinion of reporters, and then balancing the community's right to open and transparent justice with the offender's needs. In its submission to the court, made by *The Advertiser*, the media did not oppose Clarke's name being suppressed. Its only request was that Judge Boylan revisit his order at the conclusion of the trial, and revoke it if Clarke were found guilty. His Honour agreed.

And so Clarke left the court as anonymously as she had entered. Showing sympathy for the plight of her brother, the media did not pursue her for photographs or video footage. Yet during the 24 hours between that hearing and the start of Clarke's trial, a new set of facts emerged. The boy battling cancer was actually Clarke's stepbrother and he had a different last name to his accused sister. Before the trial had even begun, Clarke had tipped her hand and showed how manipulative she could be.

Fooling the media is never a good idea; as the old adage holds, reporters always get the last word. Annoyed and frustrated by the deception, crews from all of Adelaide's news outlets waited in force for Clarke on 5 June. From the moment she stepped onto Victoria Square, the young woman became the centre of her own personal media swarm. She was surrounded and chased into the building. Though they could not show her image, reporters intended to make good use of pixelated footage that night.

Clarke sneered at a female reporter, calling her a vulture. The woman replied: 'At least I don't fuck children.'

She had dressed impeccably for court – wide, dark sunglasses, a black blazer and a knee-length business skirt. The professional facade could not hide her nervousness. Clarke fidgeted constantly in the dock as she pleaded not guilty to four counts of producing child pornography and five counts of inciting a child to commit an indecent act. All crimes were said to have occurred between July 2005 and February 2006 at the Glenelg North house. The clear implication was Clarke had met not only with Osis and Malyschko after that first night, but with the girls as well.

Ms Davison told the court there was, really, no need for a trial. 'There is no doubt these acts were committed and that these acts were illegal – they are there, to be seen, in the video footage,' she began. 'There is also no dispute that, at the time these offences were committed by Clarke, the victims were 14 years old. In essence, we are here because Clarke claims she held the belief the girls were older than 16 years when she performed these sex acts with them. She is claiming a defence of honest and reasonable mistake.'

The defence of 'honest and reasonable mistake' is a highly contentious part of the criminal law. Rarely used, it holds that no offence has been committed when a person is totally and honestly unaware their actions have broken the law. It would not work, for example, in a case where a speeding driver kills a pedestrian. There are no grounds upon which that driver could claim to be honestly and reasonably mistaken about the speed limit, or what constitutes safe road use.

In a sex crime case, however, things become murkier. If a defendant could successfully argue their so-called victim looked, dressed and acted far more maturely than another child of their age, could they be reasonably and honestly mistaken? Ms Davison's words sounded alarm bells amongst the more legally minded in the court's public gallery – this was the sort of argument paedophiles and predators would love to use in their own defence.

The veteran prosecutor was having none of it. 'In a nutshell, there is no defence of honest and reasonable mistake,' she said curtly. 'When there is no doubt about the victims' ages, does the accused's state of mind matter? We say the legislation is clear – it says "no". The law exists to protect children, and it exists for that purpose alone. There is no need to have this trial, and to force two young girls to come and give evidence against a legal proposition that simply does not exist. If I'm right about the law, it would be a travesty to hold this trial – because we would merely be going through a charade.'

Mr Richards would not go down without a fight. 'The prosecution is not correct, and the defence does exist,' he replied. 'There is nothing anyone can say about this case that precludes my client using the defence of honest and reasonable mistake. It is available, and it works. And, if Your Honour is against us, then I will take the matter to the Supreme Court.'

No judge enjoys sparking an appeal – especially on the first day of a trial. Hoping to cool inflamed tempers, Judge Boylan said the trial would go ahead as planned, but that he would adjourn for the rest of the day. The evidence would begin on 6 June.

When it did, things had changed once more. Prosecutors had decided to drop seven of the allegations against Clarke. She would face trial, now, on one count each of inciting a child to commit an indecent act and producing child pornography. The focus of the case had narrowed from the entirety of Clarke's friendship with Malyschko and Osis to just the events of that first drunken night. That incident, prosecutors believed, could be proved by the DVD, which would be screened on three television sets mounted in the centre of the courtroom.

Asked how she pleaded to each of the charges, Clarke replied: 'I am not guilty on the basis I believed the girls were 17 years of age.'

Ms Davison began her opening address. 'In September 2005 Clarke, along with Osis and Malyschko, produced material of a pornographic nature,' she said. 'She also incited the child victims to perform acts of simulated and real cunnilingus upon each other, as well as other sex acts depicted on the DVD. Those include the indecent assault of the girls, as well as encouragement to expose their breasts to the camera. As Your Honour will see, it is the DVD itself that proves Clarke had knowledge these girls were children – it can be clearly inferred from her behaviour.'

Her bold submission piqued interest in the courtroom. Given Clarke's consistent denial of the charges – her po-faced claims of ignorance – what was on the DVD? Clarke, by contrast, seemed unconcerned. Her attention was focused on a large, brown paper bag Ms Davison was handing to Judge Boylan's associate. She was tendering its contents – three large dildos of various colours and shapes – as evidence in the trial. Clarke found them so funny that she smirked in the dock.

She had regained her composure by the afternoon, when she was called to give evidence in her own defence. With just the right mix of pathos and self-pity, Clarke recounted the tragic break-up with her childhood love, her spiral into alcoholism and her doomed affair with an older man. She spoke fondly of Malyschko at first, then hardened her attitude as she recounted events closer to that September night.

'Did you know the girls were 14?' Mr Richards asked gently.

'No, I did not,' Clarke said firmly.

'Did anyone tell you they were 14?' he asked.

'No,' she replied.

'Were you aware you were being filmed?'

Clarke hesitated. 'At first I wasn't,' she said at last. 'I knew Osis was standing on the couch but the camera appeared to be sitting on the couch next to him. I didn't realise I was being filmed by it the entire time.'

'Did you realise,' Mr Richards asked, 'that Osis and Malyschko intended to keep the video?'

'No,' Clarke said, looking shocked. 'I never even saw the video.'

Clarke said Malyschko had been 'very vague' about the events of that night during later conversations. Eventually, she had tried to dodge the topic altogether. 'I found out later on, after that evening, about how old the girls were,' Clarke said sadly. 'That was the night before the police came and searched their premises. I'd been planning to go back to Sydney so Renee had invited me over – I hadn't seen her for a really long time. One of the girls was there, and she and Renee had a conversation about that night. The next day, the police came.'

Mr Richards wanted to crystallise his client's evidence and close his case. 'On the night in question, you did not know the girls were 14,' he said aloud. 'Did you question either the girls or Malyschko about the ages of the girls?'

'Not that I can recall,' Clarke said. 'If someone tells you they're 17, you believe them. Judging by where we were, what we were doing and who the girls were with, I just assumed they were the age I was told they were. There was no point in time where I thought that . . . actually, it didn't even enter my head that they would have been the age that they really were.'

Nodding and smiling, Mr Richards sat down. Ms Davison was smiling too – but her grin was humourless. Silently, she took the television remote control from the bar table and started the DVD. Clarke's image appeared on screen; her semi-naked body was tangled around one of the girls. She could be seen reaching out and grabbing the girl's breasts with her hands. 'Your breasts feel like a 10-year-old's,' she moaned lustily.

Ms Davison switched off the screens. 'If the ages of the girls never even entered your head,' she said coolly, 'what did you mean when, on the DVD, you said "Your breasts feel like a ten-year-old's"?'

The colour drained from Clarke's face. 'I was, well, I was just referring to her breasts being small,' she stammered, clearly panicking. 'It didn't have anything to do with the fact I thought she was ten!' Immediately realising her mistake, Clarke tried to correct herself. 'I was just making a comment about small breasts, that's all!'

Ms Davison replied by playing the DVD once again. This time it showed Clarke using the inflatable Coke bottle and encouraging the girls to perform sex acts upon one another. 'I feel like a child molester,' Clarke said to the camera, smiling.

'If the ages of the girls never even entered your head,' Ms Davison repeated, switching off the screens, 'what did you mean when, on the DVD, you said "I feel like a child molester"?'

Clarke's attempt at a reply was a disconnected babble. 'They did have . . . I mean . . . well they were,' she tried and failed to begin. 'I was 21 then, and a 17-year-old to me is a lot younger,' she managed to choke out. 'They were immature, and they looked young!' Again, she quickly corrected herself. 'They looked young because 17 years old, to me, is young!'

Ms Davison asked no more questions, but Clarke would not be silent. 'I was just joking around with Renee,' she pleaded. 'I didn't mean it literally. I just meant they were a lot younger than I was – I never suspected they were that young!'

The damage, however, had been done. Judge Boylan retired to consider his verdict. Due to the District Court's chronic backlog of cases, and a lack of available courtrooms, it would be six months before Clarke was ordered to return to the dock. She arrived at Victoria Square on 6 December 2007, looking completely different than she ever had before. It was not her more relaxed dress sense – a button-up cotton blouse and loose trousers – that caught the eye of the media, nor the gold crucifix that hung around her neck.

It was the fact that Rebecca Jane Clarke was pregnant.

She waddled into court, unaccompanied, to learn her fate. Despite her new fashion sense, she cut quite a distinguished figure as she blithely ignored the cameras and reporters. Mr Richards met her inside and ushered her toward the courtroom. To the world at large, she appeared unconcerned. The facade would not last long.

Judge Boylan entered the court just after 9 am. 'I'm satisfied Clarke honestly and, indeed, reasonably believed the two girls the subject of this offence were 17,' he announced.

Clarke, standing ramrod straight in the dock, beamed. Unfortunately for her, Judge Boylan was not finished.

'However,' he continued, 'I am of the view that does not, as a matter of law, provide a defence to the offences with which she is charged. I therefore find Rebecca Jane Clarke guilty of inciting a child to commit an indecent act, and of producing child pornography.'

Clarke burst into tears, and wept for the remainder of the hearing. She did not appear to notice Judge Boylan setting 31 January 2008, as the date for her sentencing submissions. She barely registered Ms Davison's announcement she would be tendering victim impact statements from both girls – and that the victims themselves may attend court to confront Clarke face to face. Certainly, she paid little heed when Mr Richards leaped to his feet and asked the suppression order continue.

'The people most affected by Your Honour's verdict are my client's father and stepbrother,' he said, ignoring Clarke's victims and their pain. 'It is that 17-year-old who is suffering from Hodgkin's Lymphoma, and he is undergoing intense radiotherapy. They are known to the community in Strathalbyn where they live, and so is Clarke.'

Mr Richards had boned up on his research, particularly Dean's case. 'The law calls for the protection of the welfare of children, and that hardship must be avoided,' he said. 'Someone who is dealing with an aggressive cancer, and is currently waiting for the results of tests, is very different from someone being teased at school.'

The media, again represented by *The Advertiser*, did not disagree. The thrust of its submissions was Clarke had been found guilty, meaning the public's right to know her identity outweighed other concerns. Justice, the media argued, had to be seen to be done, and this could only be accomplished by the public learning the name of the 'lesbian pornographer' whose case had dominated the headlines earlier in the year.

Judge Boylan agreed with the media. 'I will not hold this matter up any longer,' he said. 'While I'm satisfied there might be hardship to Clarke's stepbrother, I'm not satisfied that hardship could be considered undue.'

Clarke was still crying when she left the court. She waddled slowly back to the car park next to the courthouse, clutching her shoulder bag tightly. Like her time in the dock, she seemed to barely notice the media pack surrounding her, asking her questions, getting their first truly usable footage of her. Clarke's story led every news broadcast that night and her photograph was featured in *The Advertiser* the next morning. It was accompanied by photos of Dean and others who had tried – and failed – to hide their identities behind children. Rann government spokesmen called it a victory for their redrafted laws.

On 31 January 2008, Clarke was reunited with Osis and Malyschko. She was, however, lacking representation. Judge Boylan entered court at 9 am to find all three accused, Ms Davison and two lawyers – David Stokes and Tim Dibden – robed and ready to make submissions. Mr Richards was nowhere to be seen. While Judge Boylan seethed, futile attempts were made to contact the missing lawyer. He arrived 45 minutes later, red-faced, breathlessly explaining he thought the submissions were to begin at 10 am.

'Suffice it to say there is no apology sufficient to convey my embarrassment,' he gasped. 'Not only have I held up the court, I have held up my friends at the bar table, the prosecution and the families of the victims. I hope the court can accept my apology.'

Judge Boylan frowned. 'The court does not accept it,' he snapped. 'The court, counsel and many others have been kept waiting for 45 minutes due to your lateness. That's bad enough without the lack of courtrooms and long trial lists this court is facing.'

Mr Richards took his seat quickly. Clarke started crying. She moved away from Osis and Malyschko, who remained impassive and emotionless.

The court first heard a victim impact statement written by one of the girls. She could not bear to face the trio, and so the document was read out by her mother.

'It's taken a long time to pen this,' the statement began, 'because I want all of this to go away. I'm 17 now, and I'm still a child in the eyes of the law. But I'm not really a child anymore – I was robbed of my childhood, robbed of my opportunity to make meaningful relationships, robbed of my ability to trust.

'I don't feel as if I fit in anywhere, because you took away so much of my life. You used me as your form of cheap and disgusting entertainment, a toy you could discard when you had finished playing with it. I cannot possibly think of anything worse for anyone to have to endure, for a lifetime, than what you did to me. I will be living with humiliation every day.

'I feel dirty, disgusting and cheap. You violated me when I was in no position to defend myself, and I can't wipe away the images in my head – what you did to me while I was lying there. I'd thought I was safe in your company but I was actually in danger. I never expected to finish that night as a victim. I'm so sorry for showing such a lack of judgement in my choice of friends, but I never imagined you'd do what you did to me. I'm not a child anymore, but I'm still not mature enough to forgive you.'

The mother took a deep breath, steadied herself, and then read a statement of her own. 'There's no excuse for what you did to my daughter, or to my family,' she said, glaring at the trio in the dock. 'Your utter lack of conscience and decency has not only disgusted me, but has left me horrified and angry. I fear you are all remorseless, and I hope you are brought to justice. It seems that any person – of any age or gender – is capable of violating another.'

Her spot at the bar table was taken by the older sister of the other victim. 'Because of the trauma she has experienced, she can't bring herself to be here today or speak about this,' she explained. 'She was once an outgoing, happy child, and now she is a withdrawn teenager. Her first sexual act was not something to be taped and played back by sick perverts for their amusement.'

David Stokes, for Malyschko, took issue with the statements. He said the victims had 'greatly exaggerated' their trauma. 'These girls were merely swept up by a combination of alcohol, ecstasy and playfulness,' he said. 'In the same way, my client was swept up in the moment. Now, she will have to bear the responsibility of undertaking the acts we have seen on the DVD, and of being an adult facing sentence for an adult crime. There is an acceptance of the wrongness of her behaviour, and she understands she must wear the consequences.'

He asked Judge Boylan to suspend the prison term he would 'inevitably' impose. 'At the very least, these offences warrant a shorter-than-usual non-parole period,' he argued. 'This is an aberration, albeit an unforgivable one, but it won't happen again.'

Tim Dibden, for Osis, could offer little by way of mitigation. 'The psychological report on my client references his indifference and "unawareness" of the seriousness of his offences,' he admitted. 'It says he is in denial, immature, or both. I'd argue that the last of those is, really, the point – that he is immature. Like Malyschko, he too was swept up by alcohol and ecstasy.' His client and Malyschko, he said, had ended their relationship, and Osis was facing bankruptcy proceedings in the Federal Magistrates Court. The best hope for the future, he said, came in the form of a second psychological report that suggested Osis could, through time and counselling, improve himself as a person.

Mr Richards began his submissions with another carefully worded apology – this time on Clarke's behalf. 'My client wishes to express her deep regret to the families of both girls,' he said. 'She understands this must have been truly distressing for the families of the girls involved.' The victims' mother and sister sitting in the back of the court bristled. Mr Richards's choice of words was not lost on them. Clarke clearly felt the girls themselves deserved no sympathy.

Had anyone still questioned Clarke's stance, Mr Richards's next comment removed all doubt. 'At no time did my client realise the ages of these girls,' he repeated. 'She realised they were young, of course, hence her comments on the DVD. But these girls in particular . . . well, physically, the girls in this case are of the ideal held by the media. Look at Audrey Hepburn or Calista Flockhart, or even the Olsen twins. It would be very hard to think, given those celebrities, these girls were under-age.'

It was a truly remarkable submission that earned Judge Boylan's most fierce gaze. His Honour was clearly unimpressed with such an outlandish argument – especially when it caused the families of the victims to cry once again. Yet it was far from the end of Mr Richards's audaciousness.

'Let's not forget, also, that my client is 36 weeks pregnant,' he said, leaving the fact hanging in the air. It was an attempt to plead the belly – an archaic legal tactic dating back to 1387 and the days of capital punishment. In England, women convicted of a serious crime would claim to be pregnant – or hire a man to impregnate them, while in prison – to earn a stay of execution. In most cases, the hangman's noose would be swapped for a life sentence, usually commuted once the woman found 'the love of a good man'. Female pirate Anne Bonny was, according to myth, one of the more famous recipients of the benefit. And while the common law practice had been abolished in 1931, Mr Richards was prepared to invoke it – even by implication – if it would garner more sympathy for his client. She was, after all, a woman with grand plans.

'She has ceased drinking as a result of this,' he went on, 'and been in a situation of virtual house arrest. She no longer knows if she can forge the career she's dreamed of, as a social worker – all because she was disinhibited by alcohol. And after all, my client did not intend to commit this crime. How, then, do we deal with a person that does not know they are committing an offence? A person that is misled – as Clarke was – and had no way of knowing? Were it possible for an offence to be at the very lowest end of the scale of criminality, Your Honour, this would be the case.'

His submissions, coupled with those of Mr Stokes, had left Ms Davison in a foul mood. 'Playfulness,' she all but spat. 'On one level, and to some extent, one can see playfulness in these actions. But this went beyond playfulness into sexual activity in which these girls – these children – are positively encouraged to participate. Playfulness is a justification for the disgusting acts to which these children were encouraged to acquiesce. The plain fact is these girls were children and these offences were serious.

'Notwithstanding the fact Clarke is pregnant, notwithstanding her claims of honest and reasonable mistake, immediate jail time should be served by all three players. Clarke was not, after all, pregnant at the time she was on video with these children. She knew that the trial was pending. Very little can be made of the fact she decided, along the way, to get pregnant while facing the very serious consequences of her very serious behaviour.'

She paused to look at each of the defendants. 'These are very serious offences,' she said again, 'and they are not to be underestimated.'

Judge Boylan said he would consider sentence overnight, and allowed all three defendants to leave on their existing bail conditions. Malyschko and Osis – no longer a couple, but still close friends – left court together, and shared a car ride home. Clarke waddled out alone, tears streaming from behind her dark sunglasses.

It seemed, the next morning, as if she'd not stopped crying. Accompanied by her father, a haggard-looking Clarke arrived at court just before 10.30 am. Osis and Malyschko had been inside for hours after trying – and failing – to beat the media to court. All three were videotaped and photographed for what could very well be the final time. Clarke appeared especially nervous, and constantly rubbed her hands over her swollen stomach. She had tried both brand new and ancient law to keep herself out of prison – now she would learn how successful she had been.

Judge Boylan began his sentencing remarks with Clarke. 'I accept that you were at a low emotional ebb,' he said, 'and, had you not been drinking, I do not doubt you would not have behaved in the manner you did. I have no reason to believe you will offend in this way again, but your offending is nonetheless serious.'

He moved on to Malyschko. 'You had an unremarkable but not especially easy childhood,' he said, 'but also a good work record. You began living with Osis when you were 15. You accept responsibility for your crimes, and acknowledge the seriousness of your behaviour. You do not appear to be at risk of re-offending, and you had had a lot to drink that night.'

He turned to Osis. 'You suffered a setback when your dream of being a pilot ended,' he said, 'but it seems you are now in control of your life. You do not have serious drug or alcohol problems, and you have no history of aberrant sexual behaviour. Your prognosis for the future is good.'

Judge Boylan said the girls 'undoubtedly' enjoyed their friendship with the trio, but should never have been allowed to mix with people so much older than themselves. 'As adults, you had a responsibility to protect these girls from themselves when they were at premises you controlled,' he said. 'You failed to do so, and instead encouraged them to engage in alcohol, drug-taking and sex.'

Clarke visibly shuddered when His Honour turned to her once more. 'I will treat you as if you pleaded guilty,' he said, 'because your defence was a point of law. Had you not admitted to your conduct on the DVD, I would have jailed you for 15 months. Instead, I will impose a sentence of 12 months, with a non-parole period of eight months.'

Clarke went wide-eyed and staggered backwards. She began to breathe heavily, then pant, then hyperventilate. Her schemes had backfired; her dreams had gone up in smoke. Like a caged animal, she looked desperately toward her father in the public gallery. He mouthed soothing comments but they made no impact upon her – she was descending into hysteria.

'However,' Judge Boylan went on, 'because of your prior good record, the fact these offences were out-of-character and you believed – however wrongly – these girls were of age, I find reason exists to suspend your sentence. You will not go to jail if you are prepared instead to sign a two-year good behaviour bond.'

Clarke reacted as if someone had main-lined oxygen into her lungs. She exhaled loudly, collapsing on herself, and bent over double. Unsteady on her feet, she was helped to His Honour's bench by a court sheriff's officer where she shakily signed her release papers. She ran back to her father and fell into his arms.

'Stay out of trouble,' Judge Boylan warned, 'or you will go to jail.'

Malyschko and Osis did not fare as well as their co-accused. Malyschko was jailed for three and a half years, with no chance of parole for two years. Osis was given a four-year term, and ordered to serve at least two years and three months before applying for release. They did not look at each other, nor at the still-weeping Clarke, as they were led away to the cells.

They were, at least, spared one last media scrum. Clarke tried to leave with her head held high, but was unprepared for the savagery of the reporters' questions. Did she think she could be a fit mother with a paedophilia conviction on her record? Should women who make child pornography have to attend parenting courses? Did she really think herself a proper candidate for social work? How would she react if, in 14 years' time, her baby starred in a home-made skin-flick? Battered and distraught, Clarke nonetheless pushed through the masses and disappeared into the parking lot.

She returned, after that, to New South Wales. Clarke was now a known commodity to the people of Goulburn – the local weekly paper ran the story of her conviction on its front page – and to the police force across the border. Shortly after she arrived home, Clarke was served with papers informing her she had been listed on the Australian national register of sex offenders. For the rest of her life, every prospective employer, financial institution, child care service and school would be told what she had done the moment they mentioned her name. She would have to advise the authorities every time she changed address. Clarke had been marked as a deviant – permanently.

Confronted with such news, Clarke did what she always did – tried to find a way out.

Though she never appeared in an Adelaide courtroom again, Clarke kept Mr Richards busy. He appeared before the Court of Criminal Appeal on 4 July 2008, asking for his client's conviction and sentence to be erased. The penalty, he argued, was excessive while the conviction should never have been recorded – because of Clarke's 'honest and reasonable belief'. The latter argument failed to sway Justices Tom Gray, Michael David and Richard White. They were prepared to set aside her jail term – leaving her subject to nothing but the bond – but upheld her sex offender status.

Unsatisfied, Clarke ordered her counsel to go to the High Court. On 13 October, Mr Richards told *The Advertiser* he would run his 'honest and reasonable belief' argument one more time. His confidence had been buoyed by one of the High Court's own rulings – a case known as 'CTM'.

Originating in Coffs Harbour, New South Wales, the case of CTM was also a sexual offence. The appellant – whose identity remains suppressed to this day – was one of three men involved in an October 2004 assault of a sleeping girl. Like Clarke, CTM claimed his actions were prompted by the belief the girl was 16 – the age of consent across the border – and that he would have otherwise abstained from the sort of activity enjoyed by rugby teams across New South Wales. Asked to rule on the case in June 2008, the High Court had concluded the 'honest and reasonable' defence existed, but CTM had failed to properly apply it to his own case. His jail term was to stand – but Mr Richards was sure he could use CTM's tilt to Clarke's benefit. Once again, the strategy had shifted to bleeding-edge legal tactics.

Standing in his way was South Australian Solicitor-General Martin Hinton, QC. The latest appointee to the august office, Mr Hinton had long been regarded as the best prosecutor the state had. His tenacity and mental toughness in court – combined with a witty turn of phrase and a knack for seducing juries – was in direct contrast to his gentle, affable, reserved manner outside court. Even the defence counsel he routinely trounced could not help but enjoy his company when the litigation ended. Following a short tenure as Deputy Director of Public Prosecutions, Mr Hinton moved into the office of the Solicitor-General and almost immediately inherited the Clarke matter.

It was the style of case dear to his heart – raw, untested law. It was also vitally important to the future of criminal justice not only in South Australia, but across the country. One of the most dangerous things in a courtroom is law that is open to interpretation. If a piece of legislation can be twisted, defence counsel will warp and bend it until it best matches the shape they like. In South Australia – where, as of 2009, more than 300 separate child sex cases were ready to go to trial – allowing the 'honest and reasonable' defence would be akin to giving paedophiles a 'get out of jail free' card. Jurors would be asked to judge, for themselves, how old they thought a particular victim was, exposing the children to further anguish and suffering. Sex offenders could walk on a technicality or, worse, those already convicted could win appeals based on 'compelling new evidence'. The scope for miscarriages of justice was frightening – and it would all have been generated by Clarke's refusal to accept responsibility for her actions.

Mr Hinton and Mr Richards crossed swords during the High Court's 13 October 2008 sittings in Adelaide. Having honed his argument through repetition, Mr Richards made excellent use of his 20-minute time limit. He said the problem lay in the construction of South Australia's sex crimes law — specifically, the notion that a crime is committed 'if a person is, or apparently is, under the age of consent'.

'The court can take no comfort from words like "apparently",' Mr Richards said. 'And there can be no way Parliament intended for people who make an honest mistake to face the draconian consequence of prison time. If a person honestly and reasonably believes in a state of affairs, and doing so raises no concern or alarm within them, they are unlikely to make the necessary checks. They will not ask to see a driver's licence, they will base their belief on the appearance and the behaviour of the other person. This law, as written, also catches the person who has been lied to, who honestly believes something is lawful, who has made a mistake.'

He paused for emphasis. 'It cannot have been Parliament's intention that such persons be branded paedophiles for life,' he said sombrely. 'My client, Rebecca Jane Clarke, has been branded a paedophile for life. Her name is on a sex offenders register. That will affect her job prospects, her future, her hopes to be a social worker . . . it is utterly deleterious.'

Mr Hinton, a High Court veteran, was unfazed. 'There is no doubt a conviction for this kind of offence can carry significant, life-long consequences,' he said. 'A sex offence conviction carries with it a stigma that will undoubtedly make life difficult if you are trying to get into a particular type of job or, for example, to get a Green Card to get into the United States. But Parliament, by its drafting of the law, has said that if you are going to engage in this sort of sexual thing, you had better make sure it's not with a child – because you will have no defence. Parliament has, therefore, contemplated all the consequences and, while they are severe, they do not arise the concern of this court.'

The High Court adjourned only briefly. Mr Richards's impassioned defence of Clarke simply could not compete with Mr Hinton's cold, logical reasoning; the court ruled there was error in neither the District Court's ruling nor in the state's laws, and declined to involve itself in the case. More than three years after Clarke had touched her pre-legal co-stars, the case was over.

Rebecca Jane Clarke's opinion on her High Court failure remains unrecorded. Attempts to approach her for comment – by both *The Advertiser* and Goulburn's newspaper – were unsuccessful. Her whereabouts, at present, is unknown . . . except to the members of Australia's police forces. Like her paedophile ilk – predatory men and women who use excuses to justify their sick, sexual excesses – Clarke's name features on the sex offender register. For the authorities charged with protecting children, her location is only ever one mouse-click away.

Much Ado about Wombats

Joseph and Margarete Higham

They had built their refuge far out in the bush, hundreds of kilometres from the people of Adelaide and their prying eyes. It had been designed as a haven, a place where the unwanted could be cared for – loved – by those who truly appreciated them. Those brought in for safekeeping would have the company of their own kind, the dedication of their hosts and protection from those in society who wanted them destroyed.

Joseph and Margarete Higham believed they had founded a sanctuary for stray dogs. Instead, they had created a squalid, living hell of disease, malnourishment and agonisingly slow death. In seeking to care for almost two hundred animals, they had doomed the creatures they loved to baking desert heat, painful parasite bites, dehydration, starvation and mange. One animal in their care was so badly mistreated it had ceased to look like a dog – once a terrier cross, the two-year-old animal was completely bald, and every inch of its skin had turned black with disease. It resembled nothing so much as an alien.

Adelaide's reputation as the centre of bizarre crime dropped to a dubious new level between 2006 and 2007. Because of the Highams, it became the scene of the worst case of animal cruelty in Australian history. The couple Joseph and Margarete Higham chronically abused 190 dogs and six pigs across three rural properties. They went on the run twice, becoming fugitives from justice and sparking national manhunts. They begged for mercy, claiming illness, then ran through the streets of the city to avoid media exposure. And, when they were finally caught, they tried to lay the blame for their cruelty on the shoulders of another – the humble Australian wombat.

◆

The saga of the Highams began in October 2006 in the South Australian town of Sunnydale. Situated 115 kilometres east of Adelaide, the town fell under the watch of the Mid-Murray Council. Its officers had received numerous complaints of dog noise from the locals, and wanted to investigate. Thinking it could do with some outside help, the council made contact with the Royal Society for the Prevention of Cruelty to Animals. Its request for assistance was brought to the attention of Ben Johns, who was the RSPCA's South Australian Operations Manager at the time.

'I'd been in the job for a month,' Johns remembered in 2009. 'Prior to that, I'd been working for the Director of Public Prosecutions in Adelaide, handling criminal cases. I had a degree in zoology from university, and I was enjoying myself in my new role. Looking back, I know I was nowhere near prepared for what was to come.'

Johns decided he and the society's senior inspector, Russell Jarman, would travel to Sunnydale on 9 October. It was a wise choice of partner; Jarman had investigated animal cruelty for 21 years, in both Australia and England. Together, they drove to the scene and met with council staff before entering the Highams' property.

'We drove past the house and things seemed relatively quiet,' Johns said. 'We saw three or four dogs out the front, and a few more dogs hanging around, so Russell and I stopped to look at those. We didn't really know what to expect – we'd just been told there was a lot of noise – but one of the dogs we saw looked a bit dodgy.'

The animal was afflicted with mange – a persistent, contagious skin disease caused by parasitic mites on the skin. The constant biting of the mites causes the sufferer to lose its hair, especially when the dog has a low or impaired immune system.

The mangy mutt was the calm before the storm. 'Around the corner there was a large, barren area,' Jarman said in 2009. 'It was a compound, at least one hundred feet square, surrounded by cyclone fencing. There were a number of vehicles, sheds and caravans inside – as well as a copious amount of dogs. There were eighty dogs, easily, with no shelter and no visible source of water. It was unpleasant, to say the least.'

For Johns, the scene was a complete shock. 'There were these makeshift kennels, if that's what the caravans and vehicles were supposed to be,' he said. 'Everywhere you looked, there were big piles of faeces scattered around. The noise was incredible, just all these dogs barking in unison. You could see, easily, there was a pack mentality amongst the dogs, and they were coming up to the fence growling at us. I remember one trying to scrabble up and over the fence to get at us – and the fence was ten feet high. It was new and confronting for me. I'd not encountered a hoarder at that stage.'

A recognised mental illness, animal hoarding is often linked with obsessive-compulsive disorder. It involves a person keeping a higher-than-usual number of pets in their home. Invariably, the hoarder is unable to take proper care of such a large brood, and the animals suffer acutely.

'The mentality of a hoarder is that they are severe animal lovers,' Johns said. 'They truly believe that, if they do not look after the animals, they will be automatically put down. They view those who take animals away – such as the RSPCA – as people who condemn animals to death.'

During his career, Jarman had dealt with several hoarders. 'I once had a case where a person was keeping 120 cats in their house,' he explained. 'That's the most common form of a hoarder – people who have too many cats. But I had actually encountered a dog hoarder in the UK. That guy had a big, wholesale load of dogs kept in appalling conditions, but that wasn't anything like the degree of what we found at the Higham place.'

To their surprise, the duo saw a man at the centre of the maelstrom. The near-feral dogs were attacking and bullying one another, but following the man as if he were some kind of Pied Piper. He was tall and well-built, clean-shaven with a head of thinning white hair. Joseph Higham was not happy to see the RSPCA officers, but he was not antagonistic toward them. He gave them permission to enter the compound, and spoke with them. 'He gave every indication he was going to be compliant with our requests,' Jarman said.

Johns and Jarman had been caught by surprise. On even a cursory examination, they could see the majority of the dogs needed emergency medical treatment. The animals were either dehydrated, malnourished, or both. Many were emaciated and seemingly all of them suffered from scabbing over the eyes and skin disease. They were hot, stressed and borderline vicious. Yet the officers had come in just one car, and had no way of transporting 80 sick dogs back to Adelaide. A compromise had to be reached, and that meant speaking with Joseph.

The 66-year-old cut a pathetic figure. He walked slowly, almost shuffling, around the property. He spoke constantly of his recurring illnesses, long stints in hospital and physical weakness. Joseph said he was a frail man who did 'everything possible' to care for the dogs he loved. He believed he was doing the animals a huge favour – one old mongrel looking after dozens more.

'We came to an agreement with Joseph,' Jarman said. 'We would come back on October 19 and take 40 more dogs. We honestly thought Joseph was someone we could work with, so we decided to give it a go. He seemed genuinely concerned about the dogs, and we wanted to see what we could all do together.'

The officers took four dogs with them that day. One was chosen because its sluggish, limited movements indicated obvious illness. Two more were in various stages of emaciation and mange. The final choice was the alien-like terrier cross. The poor beast was riddled with mange, leaving it completely bald. It had endured so many mite bites that its skin had blackened and died.

'It would be hard to find another dog, in all the world, that had suffered as much as that poor bugger had,' Jarman said. 'It just sat there, shivering and looking pathetic. We thought it was a puppy, based on its size and shape, but it turned out to be two years old.'

The task of identifying the dogs fell to Jarman, Johns and veterinarian Jillian Hall-Smith. The dogs were taken to the veterinarian's clinic in Angaston – part of the renowned Barossa Valley winery region. Trying to figure out the dogs' ages and breeds was almost impossible. So poor were their conditions, the trio could only guess. Eventually, they determined the otherworldly dog was two while the youngest, they estimated, was just seven weeks old. The eldest dog's hindquarters was so riddled with scar tissue and scabbing that it was impossible to determine its sex.

'It would not have been pleasant to have horrible backbones sticking out and a big pot belly full of worms,' Dr Hall-Smith said in 2008. 'It's distressing for the dog and it's unacceptable for an owner. I can say, being reasonably definite, he would have suffered his whole life.'

'Its body had basically been shutting itself down,' Jarman agreed. 'It was almost impossible to get a needle through its ruined skin. The dog was extremely frail and cold all the time – its best temperature was 34.4 degrees. There was just no way it was going to improve.' On 15 October, the sickly, blackened dog was humanely put down.

Johns contacted Joseph Higham to ensure he would keep their appointment. 'He said he wanted to check with his wife first, and she was in the hospital,' Johns said. 'We didn't see a problem with that. It wasn't like he was going to move – he lived on a massive compound with 90 dogs and pretty significant infrastructure. His capacity to move on, we thought, was pretty limited.'

On 18 October, Jarman received a call from Mid-Murray Council. 'We were told Joseph had disappeared and taken all the dogs with him,' he said. 'He was absolutely nowhere to be found, he'd just upped sticks and gone. It was a bitter disappointment for us, plain and simple.' With Higham gone, the RSPCA had no choice but to declare the seized dogs 'un-owned' and put them down.

'It's a horrible situation for the RSPCA to be in,' Johns said. 'Those animals had some life in them, but it was of an exceedingly poor quality. The decision had to be made.'

Of greater concern was the risk to the rest of the state's animals. 'Joseph was out there somewhere – and we didn't know where – with all those sick animals,' Jarman said. 'Our tests determined the animals we'd seized had forms of mange that were highly contagious. We were worried it would spread.'

With the assistance of police, the RSPCA issued an all-points bulletin calling for information leading to the whereabouts of Joseph Higham. Press releases were faxed to media outlets, and local councils were given flyers describing the man, his vehicle – a red Nissan 'Cabstar' utility – and the dogs. Frustratingly, the release of information achieved nothing. Johns and Jarman could not even discern whether Joseph and Margarete were still in South Australia, and so began to believe they had fled interstate. For a time, inquiries focused – unsuccessfully – on an area just over the New South Wales border.

In February 2007, the RSPCA was contacted by Goyder Regional Council. Its officers had received complaints about a couple living at Sutherlands, two hours north of Adelaide – and 113 kilometres north-east of Sunnydale. The complaints centred around the excessive dog noise coming from a property owned by an elderly man and woman. The couple had been seen driving through the nearest regional centre – called Eudunda – in a red ute.

This time, Johns and Jarman took search warrants and a police escort. Drawing on his background as a prosecutor, Johns made another, more unusual decision – he tipped off the Channel 10 newsroom, and allowed a camera crew to film the raid. 'We used the media, which was a real gamble at the time,' he said. 'It would pay off.'

On 28 February the duo swooped on the Sutherlands property. Channel 10's video of the raid is horrifying. The sanctuary had been reconstructed on hard-packed dirt, as solid as concrete. Hundreds of dogs wander in and out of the frame, snapping and snarling at the camera. Several turn on each other and begin to fight over flyblown bowls of contaminated water or packets of dried out, sun-bleached dog food. Puppies cower from bigger, more aggressive mongrels that swipe at them with their paws. Older, incredibly sick dogs drop and squat, adding more to the massive piles of dung dotting the scene. Intestinal worms can be clearly seen, winding their way through the excrement.

'The environment was very much the same as Sunnydale, other than the fact there was a scattering of trees around the perimeter,' Jarman said. 'There was the same massive fences, this time dividing the area into individual enclosures. It didn't really matter – there were still dogs moving from one area to another, and some running around outside the fence. There were at least 150 dogs there and it was absolute chaos – they were biting us.'

For Johns, it was a carbon copy of Sunnydale. 'To this day, I still don't know how these two somewhat frail oldies were able to move all those dogs, and all that infrastructure, by themselves,' he said. 'These kennels, if that's what you want to call them, were made from heavy-duty, good quality materials. We're talking six, seven-foot high metal panels. It would have taken some really serious effort to move them. Somehow, within a seven-day period, they had been warned by us, found another location, moved out from the first and set up in the second. They'd moved the entire compound – dogs, vehicles, caravans, all of it – by themselves, then dropped off the radar.'

Jarman was in no mood to admire the hoarders' ingenuity. 'It was entirely conceivable, from that first moment, that we were looking at the worst case of animal cruelty in history,' he said. 'What you had was an absolute recipe for disaster. In a single location you had hundreds of dogs running wild, inbreeding, an utter lack of food and water, dehydration, starvation, illness and rampant mange. It was the perfect cocktail for an absolute bloody mess.'

Joseph Higham was not among the dogs this time. Instead, the investigators found his wife, Margarete, in a nearby house. She was a tall, lean woman who swept her long, grey hair into a tight bun on the back of her head. Even in the midst of such heat and suffering, the 73-year-old was well dressed in slacks and a stylish top. Like her husband, she insisted the animals were being well cared for. She can be seen, on Channel 10's recording, presenting Jarman with a can of antiseptic, fly-repellent spray. One can, she claims, is enough for the 150 dogs on site. She then points out a single tab of mange treatment – not much bigger than a bar of soap – had been left out near the feed to help the animals recover from their infections.

'Eventually she gave up arguing with us, probably because the police were there,' Jarman said. 'We got some compliance out of her, and we started going through the dogs as best we could. Their condition, in general, was poor to very poor.

Seven dogs required immediate care, and a large number of those were puppies.'

Margarete was not willing to let the dogs go. 'The weird thing was, she had names for every last one of the dogs,' Jarman said. 'You could argue she was making them up on the spot, and pulling names out of the ether, but she was remarkably consistent with her choices. She was almost offended we would take any of them.'

That, Jarman said, is the essence of a hoarder. 'It's kind of indirect mistreatment and suffering. These people don't intend to cause these animals harm, and they don't set out to hurt their dogs. They are simply unable to manage the situations they create for themselves, and that leads to the grossest of suffering for these poor animals.'

With police encouragement, Margarete agreed to surrender seven dogs to Johns and Jarman. Among them were three of her favourites – two cross-bred kelpies and a Blue Heeler, who she called Frog, Wrinkle and Scar. The others, all female, were too sick and diseased for their ages or breeds to be determined with any clarity. Within hours, all the dogs save for Frog, Wrinkle and Scar had been humanely destroyed due to their incredibly poor health. The survivors were transferred to the RSPCA's headquarters at Lonsdale, south of Adelaide, supposedly for rehabilitation.

'Their behaviour was so bad, so feral, that there was no way they could ever become pets,' Johns said. 'No matter how you worked with it, or encouraged it to trust humans, you couldn't give a dog from that sort of environment to a family. It's lived in a pack, become used to fighting for food and water – how would it react if a child innocently took food from its bowl, or pulled its tail? These dogs had no future, and we knew it, but we still had to look after them.

We were going to prosecute the Highams for animal cruelty, and those three dogs were our case.'

On 2 March, Johns and Jarman made a second trip to Sutherlands. Taking no chances, they had organised backup. Police were again in attendance, as were Goyder council officers deputised for the afternoon. A fleet of vehicles had been organised so the RSPCA could rescue as many dogs as possible. The couple's masks of frailty had slipped; the authorities were now wise to their con. 'We knew, by that second occasion, these people were far more cunning and industrious than we had thought,' Johns said.

The joint effort seized 113 dogs – each one decimated by disease or mange – from the compound. Of those taken, 82 were puppies. In a heartbreaking moment, Johns and Jarman had to leave a further 50 dogs behind. South Australian law, in operation at the time, banned the RSPCA from taking animals that showed 'no outward sign of illness'.

That afternoon, the RSPCA examined each dog to determine its fate. The night that followed was one the organisation would never forget.

'We put out a bowl of food, and three of the puppies savaged one another to get to it,' Jarman remembered. 'When you've got that mentality, at such a young age, you can't rehabilitate the animal. That's the stark reality we were facing, and there was nothing we could do except put them down.

'We had no room to keep them – in the whole of South Australia, the RSPCA has the capacity to care for 160 dogs. That includes strays, breeders and dogs involved in prosecutions. We would have had to hold 120 barmy, stressed, ill dogs for upwards of 12 months – longer, depending on any trial – and, as operations manager, I just couldn't authorise that. I couldn't tie up so many of our resources.'

Officers destroyed 64 dogs that night. 'We were all there, working late, and it felt like some kind of production-line slaughter,' Johns said. 'We wanted to rescue these dogs and, instead, we ended up putting down a lot of dogs in a short space of time. People were in tears – and we're talking about people who had worked for the RSPCA for years. There is nothing comparable to that experience – no other time when people are asked to make such wholesale decisions about life and death. Nothing.'

The rest of the animals were put down over subsequent days. Eleven survivors were treated, approved for release and given to good homes. Within a month, all had been returned to the RSPCA due to their uncontrollable natures. They had to be destroyed. Of all the dogs taken from the Highams, only Scar, Wrinkle and Frog were still alive – and they were confined to a segregated kennel area in Lonsdale. Their viciousness was so great that they could not mingle with the rest of the animals.

Jarman made one more trip to Sutherlands. He was not surprised in the slightest to find the Highams and the remaining dogs were gone.

On 19 April 2007, Joseph and Margarete Higham were charged in their absence with 11 counts of ill-treating an animal. If convicted they faced – in addition to fines and possible jail terms – a lifetime ban on owning a pet.

Andrew Charlton, for the RSPCA, urged the Adelaide Magistrates Court to expedite the case to trial. His client, he said, held 'grave concerns' for the welfare of the missing dogs. The Highams, refusing to give their new address to the court, asked for an adjournment so they could seek legal advice. As is the norm for cases with unrepresented defendants, the court ruled in the couple's favour and put the case off for a month.

It was time for the Highams to play their game in a new way. If they were to slip the noose and keep their dogs, they had to expand the nature of their cunning. They would not hide from the justice system, per se – they would exploit its loopholes, run wild within its margins, and conspire to have the case delayed time after time. The fact they had barely enough money to hire a lawyer would turn out to be one of their greatest boons in befuddling the RSPCA's prosecution.

Little was achieved at the 18 May hearing – just as the Highams intended. The RSPCA came armed with 120 pages of evidence it intended to tender against the couple. Newly hired defence lawyer Donald Bentley – who appeared in the place of his clients – promptly informed the court such 'voluminous' information would need to be 'considered carefully' before the Highams could enter pleas to the charges. Again the case was put off for one month.

By 27 July, Mr Charlton's patience had frayed. He was angry with the Highams who had, once again, failed to attend court. 'This case has been hanging around since April, and there's a major problem,' he said. 'That problem is there were dogs still at the property, and we now have information there are some 100 dogs there now. We've offered to enter plea negotiations with the defendants but their counsel has declined – so this matter should be resolved today. The photos we can provide should alone be enough to prove them guilty of at least some of the charges.'

Mr Bentley was unfazed. 'There are no dogs on the site anymore,' he said coolly, 'and my clients will be pleading not guilty to all charges. Further, after today I am on leave during August, and I would prefer to handle this matter myself than brief other counsel.'

Magistrate Bill Ackland put the matter off until September. Mr Charlton was desperate for forward motion. 'Is there nothing earlier?' he asked as the court rose. 'I know defence has insisted there are no animals in his clients' possession, but there was a minimum of 70 the last time the RSPCA was on site. We do not accept the Highams have somehow disposed of them. Most of them are, probably, still suffering the same problems as the ones we've seized.'

Though Magistrate Ackland was sympathetic, his hands were tied. 'That's the earliest date, I'm told, we have available,' he said as he left the bench. 'By the way – the defendants will need to be here, in court, on the next occasion. I want to speak to them myself.'

Trapped by the Highams' manoeuvring, the RSPCA again turned to the media to plead its case. 'We're really concerned at how this is dragging on,' spokeswoman Aimee McKay said outside court. 'We're baffled by the pleas of not guilty, given the evidence against the Highams is overwhelming. On top of that, we're concerned these people still have at least 70 dogs, and find their claims they have re-homed the animals to be quite unbelievable. There is, we feel, no doubt that these animals continue to suffer in the hands of people who have mistreated them before.'

Magistrate Ackland had demanded the Highams appear before him. That order fell on deaf ears. Mr Bentley returned to court on 12 September, a solo act once more. The magistrate – who had taken time to view the RSPCA's evidence, prior to the hearing – was unhappy. 'I've looked at photographs of 11 dogs this morning,' he said, 'and they have been self-evidently neglected. Were I you, counsel,

I would urge your clients to reconsider their pleas of not guilty before the trial.'

Mr Bentley was resolute. 'We have eight witnesses, ready to testify that each and every one of those animals was well-treated and cared for,' he said.

Openly sceptical, Magistrate Ackland nonetheless ordered the matter be listed for trial on 18 December 2007. He further ordered the parties attend a status hearing a month earlier, to ensure the matter would run smoothly and all evidence would be ready. No one spoke aloud of the obvious concern – that the Highams would never appear in court, be it for a trial or otherwise.

Unsurprisingly, the Highams were absent on 19 November. Strangely, so was Mr Bentley. In his place stood a lawyer named Ursula Matson. She introduced herself to a very confused Mr Charlton with a smile, saying he 'shouldn't worry' about the change in counsel. It was not going to matter for long.

'The good news is I've managed to obtain my clients' instructions on this matter,' she told Magistrate Alfio Grasso, the man in charge of status conferences. 'My instructions are to obtain a veterinarian's report given that, from the prosecution perspective, there is very little room to negotiate.' She paused. 'The bad news is, with the trial a few weeks away, the Highams have been unable to fulfil their contractual obligations to my firm. Our fees are, really, just not feasible for them. In those circumstances, I cannot undertake to provide representation for them at all.'

It was a tactical masterstroke, a gambit designed to achieve two goals at once. First, it presented the Highams as hard-working Aussie battlers, doing their level best to follow the procedures of a system they didn't understand using money they did not have. That was the sort of act that won the hearts of magistrates. Secondly, by hiring lawyers they knew they could never afford in the long term, the Highams had guaranteed another lengthy adjournment. No magistrate, after all, wants to put elderly, unrepresented defendants through the grind of a trial without exhausting alternatives. All of that, together, served a third goal – keeping the dogs in the Highams' possession. Their ultimate aim would be fulfilled by the simplest of plots.

Or so they thought.

Ms Matson apologised to both the court and a visibly distressed Mr Charlton. The Highams, she stressed, were applying for Legal Aid. Should they be successful, she and her firm would return to court as soon as possible, ready to try the case. In the meantime, she asked that she be allowed to withdraw as the solicitor of record . . . and have the 18 December trial date vacated.

Mr Charlton leaped to his feet to object, but was silenced by a wave of Magistrate Grasso's hand. 'Leave is granted for you to withdraw from the file,' he told Ms Matson. 'As to your second application, that is refused. This matter has waited long enough, and I therefore decline to cancel the trial beginning 18 December. We will go ahead as planned – whether or not the Highams have representation.'

The couple had, after seven long months, been at last outmanoeuvred. Without a lawyer to act as a buffer, they had no choice but to front court and try to con Magistrate Grasso face to face. That confrontation occurred on 10 December 2007. For only the second time, Joseph and Margarete appeared in court in person – but they did not arrive together.

Margarete was first at the courthouse. She wore a prim white blouse and a long, flowing floral skirt. Her hair was wrapped up in a silk scarf, and she used a yellow parasol to shield herself from the sun – and from the media cameras that tracked her across Victoria Square. Margarete had supporters, as well. A wizened, elderly man tried to use his cane to shoo reporters away, while a younger, black-haired woman shrieked indignantly at all who crossed her path. Jarman, who attended the hearing, would later tell the media the duo were 'repeat customers' – persons who had been prosecuted, numerous times, by the RSPCA for animal cruelty. They had, apparently, formed a support group for 'persecuted breeders'.

Joseph, who came from the opposite direction, used the calamity surrounding his wife to avoid detection completely. He slipped inside, unnoticed, and met with his conspirators in the lobby. As they chatted, Joseph stood ramrod straight, towering over his wife and peers. Then, as they moved toward the elevators, a strange transformation occurred. Joseph seemed to grow older with every step he took – his feet would shake, and his shoulders would hunch further forward. By the time he exited the elevator, one could be forgiven for thinking he was the older of the Highams, not his wife.

The couple and their friends entered the court to find a new adversary waiting. Mr Charlton was still in the room but, now, his role was to brief senior counsel. The RSPCA had hired noted defence lawyer Blair Tremaine to handle the case. It seemed an odd choice – but only to those who did not know the advocate. Beyond Victoria Square, Mr Tremaine's passion was horses. He had volunteered to handle an animal cruelty case – involving a stable that had failed to care for the hooves and teeth of its horses – the year before, and won. Mr Tremaine loved animals and knew how criminals thought. His experience was to prove invaluable.

'I understand my instructing solicitor,' he began, gesturing to Mr Charlton, 'has had numerous, extensive discussions with the Highams. The matter is, therefore, ready to proceed next week as planned, and we have 18 witnesses ready to give evidence.'

Joseph and Margarete were caught on the back foot. Leaving her husband coughing and spluttering in the public gallery, Margarete walked to the bar table. Hers was a plea for mercy. 'I wrote to the RSPCA because I felt that the court would prefer this to be settled without a trial. Their letter back stated, rather rudely, that if we wanted to avoid a trial we should plead guilty,' she said, screwing up her face in disgust. 'We can't do that, Your Honour.'

Magistrate Grasso understood the situation perfectly. 'Well then, we proceed to trial,' he said brightly, flipping open his diary to tick the following Monday. 'Will you be having a lawyer present?'

Joseph coughed loudly once again, then moaned slightly. His friends made a fuss of tending to him – the woman patted his hand. 'We're asking for an adjournment because of my husband's health,' Margarete went on, pointing to her beloved. 'On November 22, he was rushed – by ambulance, after having a blackout – to the Royal Adelaide Hospital. He spent seven days in care, Your Honour – seven days! He only recently came out, and we still haven't found out what the blackout was due to.' She clasped her hands over her heart. 'His own doctor has sent him for a brain scan,' she said, her voice quivering plaintively. 'I feel he just can't go through a trial so soon. He's had a second blackout since!'

Mr Tremaine interrupted. 'Your Honour, this prosecution covers two raids on two properties, and the lives of hundreds of dogs,' he said. 'I oppose any adjournment. We've not seen any medical report relating to any so-called blackout, nor any evidence supporting what's been led from the bar table.'

That sent Margarete scurrying back to the gallery. She took her handbag from one of the chairs and fished out a crumpled piece of green paper. It was about half the size of a piece of typing paper. She tried to hand it directly to Magistrate Grasso but was stopped by a wary sheriff's officer; the item was taken from her and passed to His Honour.

'This document,' Magistrate Grasso said after a moment, 'tells me Mr Higham was in hospital, went in an ambulance, had an x-ray and has a follow-up appointment. It does not, in any way, indicate he's unfit to face court. There is nothing on this piece of paper to tell me he cannot attend a trial.' He raised his hand before Mr Tremaine could speak. 'However, I will allow both defendants time to get a medical report from Mr Higham's doctor.'

'We're waiting for the results of the brain scan,' Margarete offered.

'I'm not,' Magistrate Grasso said firmly. 'None of us can afford to wait that long. You'll come back before me in three days' time, first thing in the morning. If you have no evidence, you can expect to be standing trial next week.'

The Highams and their posse left the court in foul moods. Margarete stormed down the steps first, using her canary-coloured parasol to push through the television cameras. When they zoomed in on her face, she opened the umbrella and covered herself. She made such a production of her departure – all colour, movement and confrontation – that, once again, her husband had time to sneak out and head east, along Angas Street.

This time, however, Joseph's escape did not go unnoticed. One television crew and a newspaper photographer caught sight of him and gave chase. They stayed about ten metres behind to begin with, getting as much footage as they could without tipping their hand. Finally, Joseph paused near a small community theatre to take a breath, turned around to check on his wife ... and saw the pursuit. His reaction was totally unexpected.

He ran.

Joseph Higham – 66 years old, too ill to be facing prosecution, sufferer of mystery blackouts – sprinted away from the cameras like an Olympian. He easily outpaced three men young enough to be his children and dashed 300 metres toward Pulteney Street. Even without their heavy equipment, the media men would have been hard-pressed to keep up with Joseph. They did their best, but could not beat him to the doors of a Mitsubishi spare parts dealership. The alleged dog hoarder barrelled inside and slammed the door behind him. Unable, legally, to film on private property, the media gave up the chase.

One photo from that day, however, became famous in the city's newsrooms. It shows Joseph in full stride, gripping the brim of his hat with his left hand while his right flies out behind him. The shot was instantly dubbed – and, to this day, remains known as – 'The Running Man'.

It was the single greatest mistake the Highams could have made. The footage ran not only on the local television news, but on interstate broadcasts as well. The next day, the headline in *The Advertiser* read: 'Too ill for trial, but fit enough to run away'. The RSPCA called a press conference to highlight the vast divide between the Higham's claims and the reality of the situation. The couple's desperately constructed pretext had crumbled because Joseph had panicked. No one – especially Magistrate Grasso – would believe the old man was poorly

when he could outrun three men less than half his age. A
new deception was required – but, unexpectedly, truth was
their salvation.

Bombarded by public outrage, Margarete fell severely ill.
Her doctors said she needed rest and medication. Joseph
successfully parlayed his concern for his wife into the much-
needed medical certificate that declared him unfit to stand
trial. Armed with a doctor's note, excusing him from the
criminal justice system for two months, he returned to court
on 13 December.

'I most certainly do not consent to an adjournment of
this trial,' Mr Tremaine blustered. Like Mr Charlton before
him, his patience was at an end. 'And if Your Honour is
disposed to grant the application, then we ask another trial
date be set right now. Some of these charges date back over
a year – animals have been suffering, in this defendant's
care, since 2006.'

There was another, more pressing concern. 'The last
time the RSPCA attended the Sutherlands property, there
were less than 100 dogs there,' Mr Tremaine said. 'We have
information the defendants have since taken possession of a
further 100 dogs. If both defendants are unwell, and require
rest and medication, the animals still in their care could
suffer further.'

Magistrate Grasso's displeasure was obvious. The
Highams had overstepped their bounds once again. Had
they simply cried illness, he might have been disposed to
give them a break. Presented, however, with clear evidence
of the same pattern of alleged offending that comprised the
charges, he became annoyed.

'You have got a whole lot of dogs in your possession?' he
asked Joseph, who had attended court alone.

'Yes,' he replied.

'Then you're going to have to get rid of them,' Magistrate Grasso snapped. 'I'm going to have to remand both you and your wife on strict bail. Among the conditions of those bail agreements will be a restriction on the number of dogs you are allowed to own, and I think two each would be fair.'

Joseph's face flushed red. His chest puffed up with self-importance. 'Under what legislation of this state is it said that a man can only have two dogs?' he demanded.

'I'm making it a condition of your release from this courtroom,' Magistrate Grasso fired back. 'And you will do it, or you will be remanded in custody right now.'

Joseph demurred somewhat, becoming passive once more. 'My wife is not here, and she just can't come in today to sign bail papers,' he pleaded.

'Then she will have to come in very soon,' Magistrate Grasso replied. 'She has 48 hours.'

The Highams had run out of tricks. Joseph left the court with his head bowed and made only a token attempt to dodge the cameras. He had been humbled in court, forced to sign away his dogs, and locked into a new trial date – 7 April 2008. His movements controlled by a bail agreement, he risked additional criminal charges – not to mention arrest – if he strayed. Like the dogs he had kept, Joseph Higham was penned in. And so he did the only thing he could do; the same thing as the rabid dogs in his care had done when the RSPCA arrived.

He scaled the fence.

'To be honest, we expected them to run again,' Johns said in 2009. 'We conducted a check of the property and they were gone – people, dogs, the lot. The truth is, we had no way of stopping them from running off. There was no way we could put permanent surveillance on them, and we had no right to barge in and take the rest of the animals away.'

Though the Highams had breached the conditions of their bail, the court took no action against them. Like the RSPCA, the Magistrates Court has only limited resources. It fell back on its standard operating procedure: give the accused until their next court date to resurface and, if they failed to do so, contemplate action at that stage. Johns and Jarman, however, had other plans.

'We went right out and put the word out,' Jarman said. 'We got in touch with every single RSPCA office in the country and gave them descriptions of Joseph, of Margarete, of the ute and of the dogs. We were pretty sure they'd gone over the border and into Victoria, but we weren't taking chances. We got a huge response from so many people, with a lot of possible sightings, but nothing panned out.'

Joseph and Margarete Higham failed to answer their bail on 17 March 2008. The court immediately issued a warrant for their arrest. Police took note of the information gathered by the RSPCA over the intervening three months and began inquiries of their own. They, too, met with no success. On 7 April, Magistrate Cathy Deland – the third adjudicator to handle the case – granted Mr Tremaine's application to try the Highams in their absence, and the prosecution began in earnest.

With no one to contest his submissions, Mr Tremaine's case took less than a fortnight. Jarman gave evidence. Magistrate Deland watched, her face puckered with distaste, as the prosecution screened Channel 10's footage of the raid and tendered photos of the dogs who had died. Dr Hall-Smith took the stand and spoke about the blackened, alien, mange-ridden dog taken from Sunnydale.

'It looked like it had been malnourished its whole life,' she said, visibly distressed. 'It was in a completely unacceptable condition. You could tell, from that, it was going to be a very worm-infested dog . . . it had a very distended abdomen. It had a corneal ulcer and a heavy burden of mange. It would have been unimaginably itchy – the sort of dog that would have just torn itself apart from scratching. It had underdeveloped, soft, stumpy legs and never really stood up. You could tell this was a life-long thing. It certainly had not reached the full potential nature had given it.'

For the first time, images of the dog were released to the public. The photos ran in newspapers nation-wide with the headline 'Couple blamed for this horror escape justice'. News reports focused on two things: the sheer horror of the cruelty, and the fact the Highams were still on the run.

At the end of the prosecution case, Magistrate Deland retired to consider her verdict. On 31 April, she found Joseph and Margarete Higham guilty of all 11 counts of animal cruelty. She cancelled the earlier warrant issued for their arrest and replaced it with a second, more serious warrant. The couple were now convicted criminals and were to be brought in as soon as possible.

Now backed by the full might of the police, the RSPCA moved quickly. On 1 May, officers raided a property at Loxton, 252 kilometres east of Adelaide. The joint task force found no sign of the couple, but noted the site's proximity to the Victorian border. Johns and Jarman were intrigued. Aside from distance, why would the Highams make for Victoria and not, say, Queensland or New South Wales?

The duo teamed with their interstate counterparts to crosscheck their animal cruelty files. What they uncovered was, sadly, no surprise. Joseph and Margarete Higham were avoiding much of the east coast because they had convictions there, as well. Indeed, the couple had committed 123 offences in New South Wales and Queensland under a series of aliases.

Joseph's criminal history dated back to 1993. He had convictions under the name 'John Joseph Manning' for assaulting police, breaching bail, passing valueless cheques and fraud. In 2005, Tamworth Magistrates Court had recorded multiple convictions for aggravated animal cruelty and imposed a 12-year jail term. That term had been suspended on condition of a 12-month good behaviour bond, which he had still been serving at the time of the Sunnydale offences.

Margarete, too, had been penalised for those same crimes with an identical sentence. She had been convicted under her maiden name – Economos – and further ordered not to buy, keep or have possession of any more animals. Finally, she was told to pay the local RSPCA $45,000 compensation for their cleaning up of the mess she had made. Suddenly, the couple's desperation to hold on to their dogs made perfect sense. They had fled New South Wales because of the ban, and tried to start again in South Australia.

'As a result of the convictions, the response we got that time was huge,' Jarman said. 'Every major RSPCA office was notified, and would check in regularly with us. But, in the end, it was pure luck we found them.'

About a week after the verdict, officers from Victoria Police's dog squad surrounded a property near Caserton, about 70 kilometres east of Mount Gambier. The strike force believed that, behind the padlocked gates, they would find a large cannabis crop. Their canine units, however, reacted not to the smell of drugs but to the scent of wild dogs running loose on the property. To their horror, the officers – well versed in animal husbandry – saw hundreds of malnourished, emaciated, dehydrated dogs snapping ravenously at one another. They also saw a woman huddling up against some caravans at the back of the property, desperately trying to avoid notice. She was tall, thin and had long grey hair wound up in a bun on the back of her head.

'The dog squad contacted us to say that they were pretty sure they'd found the Highams,' Jarman said. 'But they were unsure because they seemed to have so many dogs again. The truth was the animals had been breeding – or, more accurately, in-breeding. And then there would have been the dogs they'd picked up along the way. They'd read those "free to a good home" advertisements in the paper. By the time the police contacted us, the Highams were back up to 120 dogs again. It was amazing.'

Johns had a decision to make. 'At that point, I just wanted this to be over and done with – I wanted to get those dogs away from the Highams once and for all,' he said. 'That said, we had no guarantee the people seen by the police were the Highams. There were serious doubts as to whether we could afford to fly Russell Jarman to Victoria; we wondered whether we should leave it for the Victorians to handle. But if it was them, and we weren't there to finish our own case, we'd look like idiots.'

Deciding to risk it, Johns ordered Jarman onto a plane. The inspector could not have been happier. 'The desire to catch these buggers was a big part of the smile on my face,' he said. 'I got to Caserton on Friday 16 May, and was met by a police officer, two RSPCA inspectors and a council officer. We marched right up to the property and, as we approached, you could see all these dogs everywhere. It was absolutely consistent with inbreeding, and some were the mangy dogs

I'd seen before. I knew, right then, that was it – that it was damn well the right place.

'As we got right up close, a woman came out with a beanie pulled down over her head. That was one of my favourite moments in the entire prosecution – when I looked at that woman, turned to the police officer and said, "That's Margarete Higham."'

Being a member of South Australia's RSPCA, Jarman had no jurisdiction at Caserton. It did not bother him in the least. He got to stand to one side, happy and satisfied, as the locals arrested Margarete and began to disassemble the hellish sanctuary. They seized 120 dogs and, oddly, six fully grown pigs the Highams had collected in their travels. There was, however, no sign of Joseph anywhere.

'Margarete was acting all cagey, which was to be expected given she'd been arrested this time,' Jarman said. 'When she was asked about Joseph, she claimed he'd gone away from the site and not come back. She had no idea where he was, she insisted. She also kept saying he'd not taken any of the vehicles with him which, of course, made absolutely no sense at all.'

Police tossed the caravans and living quarters for clues. For all her skills disappearing with dogs, Margarete had no idea of how to hide evidence. 'They went through the beds and all the pieces of paper in the place, and found one that had an address written on it,' Jarman said. 'It was for a backpacker's hostel in Carrington Street, back in Adelaide. That place was one street over from the Adelaide Magistrates Court – almost directly behind it, actually. The bugger was hiding in plain sight.'

Jarman quickly called Johns, who in turn contacted South Australia Police. A unit was dispatched to Carrington Street and, minutes later, Joseph Higham was arrested without incident. He was marched across the road to the cells beneath the courthouse. Margarete, meanwhile, made a brief appearance in the Mount Gambier Magistrates Court before being extradited to Adelaide. Both were refused bail, given their history of fleeing from authorities, and remanded to face Magistrate Deland on 26 May.

Their time in prison, though only short, was not kind to the Highams. Margarete entered the dock first looking dishevelled and worn – far from the co-ordinated, primly dressed lady who had fronted the court months earlier. Joseph sported a full, bushy white beard and appeared bewildered, looking wild-eyed from his security escort to Mr Tremaine, who stood at the bar table, and back again. The only sign of his old self came as Magistrate Deland walked into the courtroom – Joseph turned to his wife, winked and smiled.

'You and each of you were found guilty, in your absence, of 11 counts of animal cruelty,' Magistrate Deland began. 'It's now my task to sort out why these offences occurred, and then pass sentence upon you both.'

She quizzed them on their criminal history, including the suspended sentences they had breached. Joseph, determined to continue playing the bumbling fool, claimed he could not remember and, anyway, he didn't have his reading glasses and so could not peruse the court file. Margarete, appearing defeated, took the opposite tack. Humbly and quietly, she admitted to everything in her antecedent report.

That galvanised her husband into action. He demanded – and was granted – a chance to speak 'about the circumstances' leading up to the Sunnydale raid. His rambling, yet eloquent, five-minute speech gave an insight into the fevered workings of his mind.

'Your Honour, when the public hears a word like "cruelty", they have visions of people hitting dogs and picking on them,' he said. 'In our case, these 11 charges result from the keeping of dogs on 400 acres of property absolutely filled with wombats. That was the first sign of the end – the wombats. When we took our dogs to the vet, because they were sick, the vet said wombats transmit mange and diseases to other animals. The wombats are to blame for our dogs being sick.'

The courtroom fell into utter silence. Joseph was staring at Ms Deland with fervour in his eyes. Mr Tremaine and the RSPCA team looked boggled.

'The vet recommended a chemical wash,' Joseph continued, 'and we were treating the dogs with that, but it was so strong that I put myself in hospital. I got poisoned by it, Your Honour! We tried other things, and that's when the RSPCA came.' He shot Mr Tremaine a filthy glare. 'As far as they're concerned, if a dog doesn't look 100 per cent all the time, then you're ill-treating it,' he sneered. 'And that's where this all started from.'

He paused to smile at his wife again. 'The only thing we're probably guilty of is having more animals than we could really look after,' he said. 'And let me tell you, these dogs got better treatment from us than they would have anyone else – and that includes the RSPCA! We had 200 dogs and we've only been found guilty of 11 charges. When you think about it, that's not too bad – is it?'

He sat back down. Before anyone could answer his question, Margarete rose. 'I just want to say that we've always tried our best to look after animals,' she said, blinking tears from her eyes. 'But the mange, from the wombats, it was just so catching, so damaging to the dogs. That's why we moved to Sutherlands – not because of the court case, but to give the dogs a better home! We needed seven months, that was all, to get the infections under control. This would have all been sorted out, then.'

She, too, scowled at Mr Tremaine. 'Instead, we were raided more times than anyone else in Australia,' she spat. 'It's always the pensioners that suffer – the people who really love animals. Not like the RSPCA. They won't take old dogs, no one takes old dogs, but we were caring for dogs that were 15, even 17 years old. If a dog of that age went to the RSPCA, I know it wouldn't even get near a program that would let it get near the public and into a good home. I'm not compelled to have dogs – I'm not, no matter what anyone says – I just find it difficult when there's nowhere else for them to go.'

Margarete's tears flowed easily. 'Then, right before Christmas, we were told we had to give away all our dogs but four,' she blubbered. 'We drove around and around, to all the shelters and refuges, and were told they just couldn't take so many dogs at that time of year. The only option we had was to kill them, or to run away. And that's why we took them away.'

She sat down. Magistrate Deland waited a beat. 'With respect to each of you, I'm going to order psychological assessments be done,' she said. The couple were remanded in custody until 27 June.

The media had a field day. 'Infectious wombats to blame, claim dog hoarders' screamed *The Advertiser*'s headline. Channel 10 re-ran footage of the Sutherlands raid, making sure to point out the lack of wombats in front of the camera. Channel 7 make good use of Joseph's 'running man' stint, while the *AdelaideNow* website put the story on top of its news list. The thumbnail image chosen to illustrate Joseph's claims was a close-up of a snarling wombat baring its teeth.

Johns and Jarman simply took it in their stride. 'We'd never heard of infectious wombats before,' Johns said. 'We had no clue where they'd come up with that.'

The 27 June hearing did not go ahead as planned. Victoria's RSPCA had decided to file animal cruelty charges over the condition of the dogs seized from Caserton. The Highams flagged their intention to apply for bail, and said they had hired lawyers Anthony Allen and Kathryn Waite to represent them. Retaining Mr Allen was an interesting choice. He had only recently moved from prosecution to defence – and, in his former position, had opposed Mr Tremaine many times. Now their roles had reversed.

The matter came on again on 3 July. Magistrate Deland had, by that time, viewed home detention bail reports compiled by the Department of Correction Services. According to that body, both Joseph and Margarete Higham were suitable candidates for bail. It seemed a ridiculous conclusion, given their numerous disappearances and continued flouting of warrants. Sadly, bail is incredibly easy to get in South Australia's courts. In a state where more than 80 per cent of offenders charged with murder are released on home detention bail conditions, dog hoarders face little opposition.

Not that Mr Tremaine did not try. 'A further 85 counts of animal cruelty have been filed against these people in Victoria,' he said. 'That's 85 more reasons for them to abscond. There's only a few states left where they've not been, where they've not treated animals horribly, but they could still go there.'

Magistrate Deland was, nonetheless, swayed by the reports. The couple were bailed to a Glen Osmond house, owned by a friend, on condition they would forfeit $2000 each if they ran. They would also be subject to 24-hour electronic monitoring. Under that system, the Highams would wear tracking bracelets around their ankles and could never be any more than a few hundred metres from a telephone. The bracelet would constantly transmit a signal to the authorities via the telephone and, should the signal stop, the Highams would be tracked down and arrested.

Under South Australian law, prosecuting authorities can ask the Supreme Court to review the grant of bail. Defendants must be held in custody until that hearing, which must occur within 72 hours. Mr Tremaine sought to invoke that right but was cut off by Mr Allen.

'The real question here is whether the RSPCA has any standing as a prosecuting authority,' he smiled. 'The police can request a bail review, as can the Crown. But, under the legislation, there is no authority for local governments or outside agencies to take up the Supreme Court's time.'

Magistrate Deland agreed, and the Highams were freed. They did not leave court through the front door – they were, instead, taken back to the City Watch House and released from there. The RSPCA, however, would not be silenced.

'These people pose a high risk of re-offending, and there is no way they are going to abide by the terms of their bail,' spokeswoman Aimee McKay said outside court. 'It's fair to say this has been very, very frustrating for us. It's dragging on, and we want to see it end as soon as possible.'

Her words all but invited disaster. On 24 July, Joseph Higham was rushed to hospital because of heart complications. He underwent an emergency triple bypass. Magistrate Deland had no choice but to cancel the scheduled August hearing and put off sentencing until the convicted dog hoarder was well enough to face court again.

In the meantime, the psychological reports were compiled. Dr Craig Raeside had unfettered access to Joseph Higham while he recovered, and was able to speak to the elusive man at length. He learned the 66-year-old was the son of a police officer, and had completed the first year of a university law degree as a young man. He had, however, made his living in both the building and real estate industries instead, and had been married to Margarete for 35 years.

Joseph had been, Dr Raeside wrote, of normal mental health until November 2007. 'The mental breakdown was out of the blue, and lasted for about three weeks,' his report says. 'Since that time he has not been well, but he has not been taking any medication for depression or psychological illness.' That decline, he found, coincided with the increasing number of dogs in his possession. 'He and his wife were very much the same, in that they were fond of dogs,' Dr Raeside wrote. 'They began collecting strays aged between 15 and 20 years, and those that were abandoned as puppies.'

He had reacted badly to the RSPCA raids. 'He experienced considerable trauma when the dogs that he believed "were otherwise healthy" were taken, believing that to be outrageous and extremely distressing,' he wrote. 'He felt himself the victim of an RSPCA "beat-up", that he was being accused of selling dogs to the local Chinese restaurant.'

Joseph had failed to cope with the court process, also. 'He consciously disobeyed the court's orders and did not get rid of his dogs,' the report says. 'He felt his life had been shattered, and believed it was outrageous he was banned from keeping more dogs. It is of note he was more concerned about the animals that had been "taken away, never to return" than he was about being found guilty in his absence. Nonetheless he feels victimised, saying he was "kept doubled-up" in a

4 metre by 3 metre cell while in custody when an "RSPCA cage is 5 metres by 3 metres". He continues to maintain his innocence of the charges.'

Dr Raeside had also visited Margarete. The youngest of two sisters from Port Lincoln, Margarete had devoted her life to two passions – animals and piano-playing. As a young woman, she had studied with Adelaide's prestigious Conservatory of Music, and her skills had taken her overseas for a number of performances. Eventually, her love of animals pushed her promising future aside.

'She began to accumulate dogs that other people had left behind,' Dr Raeside wrote. 'She and her husband re-arranged their lives so that they could "care" for the animals. He worked during the day, she worked at night, someone was always with the dogs. She "saw there was a great need out there for someone to do something" about unwanted dogs.' Margarete believed herself to be a crusader – and Dr Raeside could find no deeper reason for that. 'There is no psycho-logical explanation for her behaviour,' he wrote, clearing her of the hoarding disorder. She was sane – strange, but sane.

The court reconvened on 17 October 2008. Joseph Higham was still too ill to attend; Magistrate Deland ordered sentencing submissions go ahead as planned. Mr Tremaine had been doing his research in the interim.

'The first matter I want to raise is the suggestion the mange, in this matter, came from wombats,' he said. 'The evidence I have is that wombats are not a source of mange. It's not a disease they get, nor that their bodies support. I ask Your Honour to pay no regard to that submission.'

Ms Waite, for Joseph, agreed. 'It's been made much ado of, this wombat thing,' she conceded. 'It's really no more than my client noticing the dogs were losing their hair, visiting a vet for advice, mentioning the foxes and wombats on the property and the vet mentioning a connection between wombats and mange. It's less a circumstance of mitigation and more an example of the ad-hoc advice my client had taken, from vets, over the years.

'The simple fact is, whenever Joseph Higham came across a dog, he could not say "no" to taking it if it seemed the dog would otherwise be put down. As a result, he and his animals got into so much trouble that it would take a team of people to deal with the many and varied sorts of problems these dogs had. He, being elderly, was just trying his very best to keep up with the situation.'

She said Joseph's feelings about the case 'go beyond remorse'. 'There is nothing he thinks about more than the effect this case has had on the dogs,' she said. 'It is unimaginably hard for him, now, realising many of these dogs – some he has raised from pups – were put down as a result of his actions, because of the ways he was trying to help them. He is most concerned about an order banning him from owning dogs again, as he feels he will lose the will to live without animal companionship. Such a penalty is an extreme punishment for a man like him.'

Mr Allen asked the court to release Margarete Higham without further penalty. She had, he ventured, suffered enough already. 'Her time on remand was spent in protective custody,' he explained. 'That was a result of the publicity surrounding the case, and the reactions of the other female inmates to the nature of the charges.' Dog lovers, it seemed, were prolific behind prison walls. 'She was therefore incarcerated with women who had been charged with far more serious crimes, such as murder. It was devastating for a woman of her age to be forced into such company, and I'm sure Your Honour can imagine how that has affected my client. That was, in all senses, a very real penalty.'

Margarete Higham was sentenced three days later. She stood in the dock alone because her husband had, yet again, breached his bail and refused to attend court. Ms Waite claimed he feared 'a cardiac episode' should he have to face the media; Magistrate Deland made it clear she cared little for Joseph's concerns and ordered he surrender himself by 2.15 pm the next day or risk a further arrest. Her no-nonsense demeanour brought a smile to the faces of Mr Tremaine and the RSPCA team – after so very long, an end to the Higham saga was finally in sight.

It was not, however, the ending they had expected. For all that she had done – all the suffering she had caused – Margarete Higham was given a suspended two-month jail term. She was further ordered to reimburse the $18,000 the RSPCA had spent dealing with the dogs.

The victory could not have been more hollow. 'We definitely wanted to see her receive an immediate jail sentence, given the gravity of what she'd done,' Johns said. 'Dr Raeside's report concluded that she was fine, mentally, so there was no excuse for her actions. And we knew there was no way we would ever see a cent of that $18,000. You only had to look at the footage of the raids to see these were people who had no assets, no money, nothing more than their clothes and their dogs. It was a relief the case was almost over, yes, but it wasn't what we wanted.'

Joseph Higham appeared, without incident, the next day. He submitted meekly to sentencing, wringing a green beanie in his hand as Magistrate Deland spoke. Margarete watched from the public gallery, and smiled slightly as her husband received a penalty identical to hers. Any hope Johns or Jarman had of their long, hard work resulting in jail time evaporated.

'Sitting there in court, looking at them, I knew that we'd be seeing them again – that they would offend again,' Jarman remembered. 'I had absolutely nothing to back that up, no evidence to base it on, but I just knew. I really, really suspected that, sooner or later, we'd be at their door again. They'd learned nothing from it all.'

His suspicions were confirmed almost immediately. There is, on the ground floor of the Adelaide Magistrates Court, an office staffed by Justices of the Peace. These volunteers, who work long shifts for small financial considerations, must witness and sign any suspended sentence before a criminal is allowed to leave the building. The queue is always long, and the media knows to wait outside the building for some time – often hours – in order to get shots of the newly sentenced offender. Joseph and Margarete were last seen, just after 3 pm on 21 October, waiting in line to have his sentence witnessed. When sheriff's officers closed the building at 5 pm, the Highams had not left. A search was conducted, with officers going through every toilet and witness room, but there was no sign of the dog hoarders. They had, somehow, slipped away. Vanished, as was their style.

Another 24 hours would pass before an internal Courts Administration Authority investigation determined what had happened. 'A volunteer Justice of the Peace let Mr and Mrs Higham out of the Adelaide Magistrates Court by a side door,' a red-faced media spokesman announced. 'The JP, who is not a Courts Administration Authority staff member, has been spoken to and told that this was inappropriate and a breach of protocol. The Royal Association of Justices has been contacted and they will formally advise their members they are not authorised to let anyone in or out of secured areas within court precincts.'

Sheriff's officers, furious at being disrespected and publicly embarrassed, provided a few more details. They had heard Joseph Higham complaining of media harassment and downplaying his offending, telling the JP it was 'just a few sick dogs'. The JP, who was roughly the same age as Joseph, must have agreed it was 'always the pensioners who suffer', and taken pity on his peers. He was noticeably absent from the Magistrates Court thereafter.

The RSPCA, meanwhile, was finding positives where it could. 'It was great they were held in custody, even for a little while,' Johns said. 'No one ever goes to jail for animal cruelty, unfortunately, so at least that happened. At the end of the day, though, no jail penalty can ever match up to the horrible things they let happen to those animals. You could have jailed them, immediately, for four times as long as the sentences they got and it still wouldn't have been enough'

There was also a very sad task to be performed. Frog, Wrinkle and Scar were still in the organisation's kennels at Lonsdale. With the prosecution concluded, and no hope of rehabilitating the trio, Jarman and his team had but one choice.

'The girls who work in the shelter had really tried hard with them,' he said. 'But right to the end of it, once the case was over, we knew they were never going to be candidates for re-homing. After all the poor dogs had been through, after justice had been served, and after we'd all come to know and love the dogs, we still had to make the decision to put them down. That's the real consequence of what Joseph and Margarete Higham did. They ruined their dogs forever.'

The Delusional Assassin

Jean Eric Gassy

A mong the law books scattered across the South Australian
Supreme Court bar table stood a thick, bound volume,
seemingly out of place – the psychiatrist's 'bible', *DSM-IV.*
Prosecutor Peter Brebner, QC, had set the book – the guide
to recognising and diagnosing mental illnesses – alongside
his well-thumbed legal tomes, ready for trial. It was an
unusual weapon for a case against an alleged murderer.
Unusual, yet fitting – for few killers are as complicated in
their bloodthirstiness as Dr Jean Eric Gassy.

In the space of eight years, the keenly intelligent man
transformed from respected psychiatrist to obsessive, delusional assassin. Consumed by bitterness, stung by slights both
real and imagined, a man once concerned with healing trained
himself into a stalker and a vengeance-driven murderer.

◆

Dr Margaret Tobin was South Australia's director of Mental
Health Services. A larger-than-life woman, she was part of
a family of highly intelligent professionals. Dr Tobin was a
devoted gardener with a love of native plants, a fondness for

the warbling of magpies and a hobby of collecting brooches. Happily married to Don Scott, the couple had endured much together including the death of Mr Scott's mother. 'We came back from the funeral in Melbourne and went shopping for several hours, buying lots of brightly coloured things,' he would later remember. 'Margaret turned to me and said, "Now we can settle and get on with our lives".'

They had begun to plan renovations to their house, their love deepening every day. 'At night, when we were watching television, she would put her head against me and under my arm and say, "I just fit, don't I?",' Mr Scott said. 'I was probably the most spoiled man in Australia, if not the world.'

On 14 October 2002, Dr Tobin was lunching with her friends and colleagues. One of the most caring and insightful psychiatrists in the field, she was a woman genuinely concerned with the mental health of not only her patients, but also her staff. They were her friends, she felt, and their wellbeing was just as important as that of their charges. Passionate and unafraid to ruffle feathers, Dr Tobin had been making waves since her posting to the role.

At 2.28 pm, she and her co-workers left the Symposium Café, in Gay's Arcade off Rundle Mall, and made their way back to her office – located on the eighth floor of the Citi-Centre Building on nearby Hindmarsh Square. Chatting amiably, not one member of the group noticed a dark-skinned man with a beard and long hair loitering in the foyer. Nor did they realise he followed them, just a few steps behind, into an elevator. Dr Tobin continued to speak with her friends as the lift ascended, bidding them goodbye when they exited on the seventh floor.

What happened next – in the space of seconds between the seventh and eighth floors – may never be known. For a short span, Dr Tobin was alone in a sealed elevator with Jean Eric Gassy, a heavily armed man who meant to kill her because of their mutual past.

The elevator doors opened on the eighth floor and Dr Tobin stepped into a government-issue reception area. As she did, the dark-skinned man drew a semi-automatic 9mm Glock pistol and fired three shots. The results were instantly devastating, puncturing Dr Tobin's arm, lung, liver, stomach, chest, bowel and diaphragm. Even so, the assassin fired a fourth shot into her body either as it fell, or after she had hit the ground. In the chaos that followed, ambulance officers were called, peers and colleagues gathered around their fallen boss and a media crew was ushered out of the building. There was no sign of the gunman – later, it would be guessed he slipped into a stairwell, ran to the ground floor and fled the scene.

It was a near-perfect execution – no clear witness identification, no trail, no physical evidence. Gruesomely, it was carried out on the same day that the 'bodies in the barrels' trial began in the South Australian Supreme Court – sirens from the ambulances headed to the Citi-Centre Building could be heard at the courthouse, across the other side of Adelaide.

The worst news, however, would not be known until after Gassy's arrest. Dr Tobin was but the first in Gassy's list of intended victims – one chronicled on several sheets of paper and a used railway ticket. Had he not been caught – had his own delusions and ego not tripped him, causing him to fall into the hands of the police who had painstakingly conducted their case, it is likely six more respected medical professionals would have died.

Psychiatry, the profession governed by *DSM-IV*, was the thread that linked all of Gassy's actions. Studies of the mind – and those who carry them out – were used to motivate, discover, capture, try and sentence the disgraced doctor. In turn, Gassy himself would claim psychiatry was being used to discredit and vilify him and even bring about his death in prison through medical negligence.

In the early 1990s, Dr Tobin was appointed to a senior role in St George's Hospital, Sydney, where Gassy worked. He welcomed the change in management, at least at first. He confided this to one of his patients, a woman who would later give evidence in his trial. 'He said that he felt she (Dr Tobin) would be an ally against the problems he was having with the nursing staff,' she told the jury. At the same time, Dr Tobin had taken notice of Gassy – and reports of his increasingly erratic behaviour – and made efforts to resolve the situation. This compassion, so characteristic of the woman, would literally be the death of her. Gassy came to believe his boss was, as he told a patient, 'out to get' him.

'During this period he also raised with me he thought his office had been bugged,' the patient testified. '(He said) he had got his office debugged and had got someone to go through his office and see if there was a bug planted.' During one session, he asked to look through her bag. 'I had a haversack with me . . . and he queried me about what was in my bag. I made a comment back to him, laughing (about) why he was so concerned about what was in my bag . . . then it came up possibly that this session was being taped by Margaret Tobin.'

Gassy – who counted handgun shooting among his hobbies – took extended sick leave in 1993, citing 'burn-out'. Dr Tobin then drafted a letter to the New South Wales Medical Board: 'I am writing to express my concern that a staff member of my division, Dr Gassy, has had a prolonged period of sick leave,' it said in part. 'In view of the fact psychiatric reasons are cited, I would like to be assured Dr Gassy will be fit to (perform) the full range of duties when he returns to work. If the board can become involved . . . I would be most grateful.'

That letter sparked a sequence of events that led to Gassy's deregistration as a psychiatrist . . . as well as a nine-year vendetta. Mr Brebner would tell the jury Gassy's 'resentment and anger' toward Dr Tobin 'endured, escalated and intensified' as his career slipped away. When he was ordered to undergo evaluation, he told his patient Dr Tobin 'had won'.

A psychiatrist named Dr Jonathan Phillips examined Gassy in 1993, concluding his new charge was not suffering from a delusional psychological condition. A year later, Dr John Woodforde challenged that diagnosis at the request of the New South Wales Medical Board. 'It was thought that he may be ill and, as part of the board's assessment, they wanted me to provide an opinion,' he testified during the trial. His initial diagnosis was a 'persecutory delusional disorder' – the most common type of mental disturbance in which the sufferer believes he has been targeted by others for harm – rendering Gassy unfit to practise. 'I noted in my report (that) his grasp of reality was tenuous and he is probably deluded, and he denied that was the case,' Dr Woodforde said. '(It said that) at the present time, it's not possible to say if, or when, Dr Gassy will be fit to resume the practice of medicine.

Gassy remained 'irrational, mistrustful and probably delusional' during a re-examination three months later. Dr Woodforde said he noted, in his second report, Gassy's claims he left St George's Hospital 'because of concerns with Dr

Tobin and other staff. (It says) he believes it is not in his best interests to work there . . . in order to put Dr Tobin out of the picture. This was so she would not have any opportunity to express an opinion regarding his future employment.'

St George, in Gassy's opinion, was 'anti-psychiatry'. '(He) perceived there to be an administrative attitude of allowing the role of psychiatry at the hospital to wither on the vine,' Dr Woodforde said. '(He) believed the staff had an attitude that (Gassy's) interest in patients was related to their attractiveness. (He) could not give any evidence to support those beliefs of innuendo, rumours and actions of others.' In 1995, Dr Phillips backed up his colleague after a second examination, supporting the positive diagnosis before the board's Professional Standards Committee.

Gassy's hatred was growing – not only for Dr Tobin, but also for anyone who crossed his path. Sometime after their consultations, Dr Phillips and Dr Woodforde became targets. So, too, did a member of the NSW Medical Board's Impaired Registrants Panel that, between 1994 and 1997, conducted inquiries that led to his de-registration as a psychiatrist. He began to keep a list of 'persons of interest', of those who had come between him and his chosen profession. Late in 1997, he spoke with Robert Stand, a man he had known for 23 years. 'He was in a trial process, I believe it was for deregistration,' Mr Stand testified. 'He mentioned a lady and said that she was giving him trouble at his trial (and) she was trying to influence the outcome.'

Adrift without his career, Gassy's mental state worsened. He became convinced he had contracted HIV, and sought treatment from a Sydney-based professional. 'He believed he was suffering from HIV and had been treating himself,' Mr Brebner told the jury. 'The doctor found he was not (infected) and told him, but Gassy was unconvinced by his opinion.' Gassy sought out Dr Stephen Addlestein, a specialist immunologist, whose diagnosis was also not to his liking. Not only did he tell Gassy he was not infected, he refused his demands for prescription drugs. Trusting his own medical background, Gassy 'self-diagnosed' the condition, deciding the denial of drugs was part of a larger conspiracy within the medical profession to ensure his death. He also added Dr Addlestein to his 'persons of interest' list.

His hatred gave him new purpose. Gassy spent increasing periods of time at the firing range, honing his marksmanship skills. He studied books on criminology and forensics, learning how evidence could be disguised and ballistics tests fooled. He browsed a website, the jury would later hear, detailing 'the science of firearms identification as it relates to the investigation of a crime'. Around this time he found work as a security guard and became familiar with his employer's preferred weapon – a Glock pistol loaded with Speer Gold Dot ammunition. The Glock, Gassy learned, was perfect for 'anti-personnel use'.

It was around this time Gassy's 'persons of interest' list began to expand. The document covered multiple pages with intimate details of the lives of his targets. Doctors Phillips and Addlestein were there, as was the head of the Professional Standards Committee – Dr Kathleen Willhelm – and Dr Peter Arnold, the presiding member of the Impaired Registrants Panel. Also included was Dr David Burke, who had worked with both Gassy and Dr Tobin at St George's Hospital. During the trial, Mr Brebner would claim Gassy believed the two doctors had conspired against him.

The 'persons of interest' list noted changes in appearance, new jobs and security systems used at places of employment.

Photographs accompanied several of the names – over time, some were swapped out for newer images as they became available. Gassy took to keeping a shortened version of the list on a used railway ticket in his wallet. Mr Brebner told the jury it contained abbreviated mentions of doctors Arnold, Woodforde and Phillips, as well as their addresses. A section torn from the ticket, he claimed, would likely have contained similar details about Dr Tobin.

Early in 2002, Gassy suffered a bout of prolonged illness. In the prosecution case, it was this sickness that changed the disgraced doctor's behaviour from unhealthy obsession to bloody vengeance. Fearing he would die before having a chance to balance the scales, Gassy began to prepare himself for the murder of the first target from his list – the woman he believed had sparked his downfall.

To kill Dr Tobin, he needed to be close to her. Justifiably proud of his marksmanship, Gassy still needed to be within the Glock's range to use it. Leaving nothing to chance, he made sure he had plenty of spare parts for the weapon, even if that meant risking public exposure to collect them. Shortly before the murder, Gassy collected a package of Glock slides – the top piece of the gun – from Australian Customs officer Violet Palmer. Giving evidence, Ms Palmer said she and Gassy has spoken briefly that day. 'We had a conversation at the front counter, had a couple of jokes, because he thought (the slide) was a piece of art,' she said. The mood turned less jovial, however, when Gassy 'hung around' in the office's waiting area to look at the lethal implement.

Gassy made a first, abortive attempt to kill Dr Tobin five months before his success in Adelaide. He learned, through the psychiatric newsletters he continued to read, that the object of his ire would be leading a workshop in Brisbane.

Dr Tobin was to be one of the main guests at the 2002 conference of the Royal Australian and New Zealand College of Psychiatry. Hiring a car under the alias Chris King, Gassy travelled to Brisbane, stopping along the way to order more parts for his Glock. It was a decision that would eventually help cause his downfall – although he used an alias, Gassy provided the gun shop owner with his real firearms licence. Then he moved on to the Brisbane Convention Centre.

It was to be a spectacular failure. Audio-visual technician Paul Ceron saw Gassy looking at a board displaying information about the conference and its events. 'He looked a little out of place . . . fairly scruffy, messy hair and unshaven,' Mr Ceron would testify. Standing out as he did amongst the ranks of well-groomed medical specialists, Gassy also drew the attention of sound technician Robert Champion. Mr Champion was taking a cigarette break on the plaza outside the centre when he heard a very familiar sound – that of a gun falling onto concrete. 'I recognised the noise from a sound I'd heard in our company's sound library,' he would later tell the jury. 'I've worked on a movie which had a lot of guns being dropped. (Across the plaza) I saw a gentleman crouch down, stand back up and . . . tuck something back into his trousers. He stood up very quickly . . . we made eye contact, which unnerved me a little bit, so I turned away from him.' Well and truly discovered, Gassy fled, his vengeance delayed temporarily.

That was not the case in Adelaide on 14 October. Indeed, Gassy's murderous actions were so successful they seemed to be, at first blush, the perfect 'hit'. Looking below the surface, the delusional doctor had made many mistakes – errors that allowed a 30-person task force to comb three states and gather evidence to secure his conviction. Veteran SA Major

Crime detectives Sergeant Mick Standing and Senior Sergeant Lyn Strange led the operation, and within hours of the murder were compiling lists of suspects and early leads. One of the more unusual possibilities – which went on to capture media and public attention – was that the killer might have been of Aboriginal descent, given his complexion and hair.

An identikit was prepared, based solely on that loose description, but it was enough to start the ball rolling. Watching television in Brisbane, Robert Champion saw in the identikit the man he had confronted on the plaza, and placed a call to South Australia Police. In turn, officers learned the licence plate number of the car Gassy had been driving at the time – which he had thought to pay for with cash, but had used his real driver's licence to secure. As one lead followed another, the driver's licence allowed police to check the New South Wales firearms register, where they learned of Gassy's dual 9mm Glocks and, eventually, of his connection to Dr Tobin through the deregistration process. Interviews were hastily arranged with former colleagues of both parties and, just one week after the murder, Gassy had become the prime suspect.

The 'false start' in Brisbane, and the visit to the firearms store, gave detectives a pattern to follow. Believing Gassy would have acted similarly leading up to the Adelaide incident, they again checked with hire car companies and uncovered a dark grey Nissan Pulsar that, forensic experts would determine, contained gunshot residue. The decision was made to formally question Gassy and, on 29 October, detectives executed a search warrant on his Oyster Bay residence. They found the Glocks, the spare slides and a large quantity of Speer Gold Dot ammunition. Not only was it the bullet of choice for Gassy's instructor, but also the same type of munition that had killed Dr Tobin. Finally, the 'persons of interest' list was taken, but even it did not provide officers with enough evidence to charge Gassy.

That would come later, thanks to a trip to Balranald in central New South Wales. A man calling himself David Pais had stayed there on the night of 12 October. Certain they had found the midway point of Gassy's route, detectives publicly appealed for information on a Mr Pais or a grey Nissan and, within 30 minutes, had a positive call. The owner of the Lindy Lodge Motel in Woodville, just outside Adelaide, had rented a room to Mr Pais the night before Dr Tobin was murdered – and identified Mr Pais as Gassy, based on photographs. It was all detectives needed for an arrest and, during a special sitting of the Adelaide Magistrates Court on 9 November, they were given permission to arrest Gassy for murder. At 3 pm on the same day, Sydney's Homicide Squad took the delusional doctor into custody.

The legalities began on 11 November 2002, at Sydney's Central Local Court, when Gassy's lawyer – destined to be the first of many – warned that custody for his client would be a 'death sentence'. With no access in jail to anti-HIV drugs, and the 'fact' Gassy needed an operation to remove a tumour from his tongue, it was argued anything less than release on bail would be highly dangerous. The impassioned pleas fell on deaf ears, and that first lawyer left the case.

At the same time, detectives narrowed their search in an effort to lock down their case. Gassy, they learned, had returned to the Lindy Lodge Motel after the murder and then travelled to the Arndale Shopping Centre, west of the Adelaide CBD, where he had a haircut and a shave. The would-be master of disguise had left too clear a trail. The final piece of evidence police would need was found in a rubbish dump at Renmark, in the Riverland. Having visited dozens of shops, hotels and motels, detectives found a surveillance tape showing Gassy throwing something in a petrol station rubbish bin on 14 October. State Emergency Service volunteers and police searched the local rubbish tip and found several receipts from hotels in Balranald and Brisbane – one of which was located right next door to the Brisbane Convention Centre.

Gassy made his first brief appearance in the Adelaide Magistrates Court on 13 November 2002, having been extradited from Sydney. He did not apply for bail – meaning the allegations against him did not have to be detailed, and so the public remained in the dark about the case. Secrecy was to dominate proceedings right up to the midpoint of the trial. The second suppression order – gagging any mention of pre-trial legal argument and banning the publication of photos of Gassy – was handed down in April 2003.

One month later, the prosecution expressed concerns that Gassy was doing all he could to delay his inevitable Supreme Court trial. They had good reason to be concerned. By the time he came to trial, Gassy would have hired and fired no less than seven lawyers, including some of Adelaide's most prominent counsel. The former psychiatrist felt luminaries such as Stephen Ey and Kevin Borick had treated him unfairly.

Mr Ey's appearances for Gassy were the most notable – minutes after being sacked, he leaped to his feet to help his former client argue against a media application to publish information about the case. He acted, Mr Ey said, as 'a friend of the court' – drawing much ire from senior members of the media contingent. Despite heated argument, Mr Ey won the application for his erstwhile employer and walked away.

Six months after her client's arrest, Julia Davey – Gassy's fifth lawyer in six months – argued she had not received sufficient information to make full submissions. Ian Press – Mr Brebner's predecessor as prosecutor – warned that if Gassy kept changing lawyers 'the committal process could be indefinite'.

Finally, more than 10 months after Dr Tobin's murder, Gassy pleaded not guilty and was committed to stand trial before newly minted Supreme Court appointee Ann Vanstone. A former Crown prosecutor and District Court judge, Justice Vanstone had a reputation of being both canny and clinical, possessed of a good rapport with jurors and near-unending patience for the complexities of legal argument. Her skills stood her in good stead for the trial that was to come.

Having sacked his sixth lawyer, Gassy said he was fed up and announced plans to represent himself in court. This lasted until the arrival of Sydney lawyer Roger de Robillard who, in May 2003, announced he had been retained, by Gassy's parents, to act for their son.

It was the beginning of several days of cut-and-thrust between Mr de Robillard and Justice Vanstone, who soon expressed her concerns about the new face in her courtroom. At first doubts were raised over his ability to act in a South Australian trial given jurisdictional issues. Justice Vanstone wanted to know if his practising certificate allowed him to take part in a South Australian proceeding. Mr de Robillard wanted to know if the court would allow him to open the defence case while letting Gassy cross-examine the witnesses himself.

Next, there was a secret from the past that Mr de Robillard decided to share with the court. 'I used to act for the government of Vanuatu as their counsel,' he said in pre-trial argument, which was suppressed from publication at the time. 'I had difficulty with certain Australian diplomats in Vanuatu because they resented the fact I was giving independent advice to the government. As a result of that problem, which went on for a couple of years, I was in fact then imprisoned for contempt of court.'

Mr de Robillard said his conviction had been overturned on appeal. He'd served five weeks in jail before being released. '(Then) I fell behind in the lodgement of my tax returns because my practice was disrupted for about two years,' he said. As a result, Mr de Robillard said he underwent regular checks with his accountant to ensure he was eligible to practise law.

One week after the revelation, Gassy was without counsel – Mr de Robillard announcing there was 'nothing further' he could do to help. 'Having a barrister such as myself is simply causing his parents unnecessary expense,' he told Justice Vanstone as he departed the bar table one last time.

Alone again, Gassy claimed he was the victim of a conspiracy among Australian psychiatrists. He said it was 'impossible to remove the label' once someone was diagnosed as delusional. 'No one would be prepared to stick their neck out and categorically say that I did not suffer from any disorder given the fact that senior psychiatrists have said that I do,' he informed the court. 'It's a small world, my case would be well known within the psychiatry community now'.

These claims prompted the inclusion of *DSM-IV* at the bar table – Mr Brebner's prosecution strategy needing to encompass his adversary's illness as well as his guilt. During his opening address on 8 July 2004, Mr Brebner laid out a scenario in which Gassy, driven by the delusional belief Dr Tobin had conspired to initiate his deregistration, used a false identity to travel to Adelaide and kill her. Gassy's decision to act, more than eight years after the fact, was prompted by another delusional belief – that he was dying of HIV – for which there was no supporting medical evidence.

Gassy did not wait to begin his counter-case, planting the seeds of his defence in one of his earliest cross-examinations. Facing witness Beth Kotze – another Sydney psychiatrist – from the dock of the court, he asked if Dr Tobin was a lesbian. Stunned silence followed the question, broken when Justice Vanstone ordered Gassy to explain himself. His response was both simple and radical – Dr Tobin, he said, may well have been shot by someone from an 'underground world' of lesbians and 'same-sex persons'.

'The defence case is that that's the reason that the police have not caught the real shooter,' Gassy told the court. 'As the victim was not a declared same-sex person, it's an underground world (and) the real killer or real shooter may have been a part of that world.' Dr Kotze, a long-time friend of Dr Tobin, disagreed strongly. 'To the best of my knowledge, she was not a lesbian . . . (I say that) on the basis of my observations of Dr Tobin with her husband, my observations of her with other men and the ordinary verbal intimacies we shared, as friends, about our marriages.'

Beginning his defence case proper, Gassy gave the jury an insight into his reasons for firing so many lawyers. 'I am not delusional,' he emphasised. 'My level of function is incompatible with the presence of any major psychiatric disorder. One of the reasons I am representing myself is because I hope to demonstrate I am mentally competent.' At times, his defence strategy was straight from a textbook – literally. Gassy referred to Dr Tobin as 'the victim' and, when asked why, said it came from a book he had read on trial techniques. '(The book) suggests you should not personalise the opposition,' he said.

The prosecution case, he said, was about 'mistaken identity' and 'the violation of the rule of law'. Further, his incarceration and the continued refusals to provide him with HIV medication were attempts by South Australian medical practitioners 'in positions of power' to kill him. 'I have been deliberately deprived of anti-HIV treatment in a pre-emptive strike following a presumption of guilt,' he said. 'This is no less than an attempt at execution before the jury verdict in a country without the death penalty (and) a gross abuse of state power. They (the medical elite) see my incarceration as a pre-emptive strike to remove a potential threat.'

He urged the jury to consider two things. The first was that he 'obviously' had contracted HIV, given skin, vision and respiratory problems he had suffered. The second was Dr Tobin's sexuality. She was, he said a 'closet lesbian and a leader of the sisterhood. The real killer is either from the underground lesbian world or someone seriously threatened by the changes she instituted in the mental health system in South Australia'.

Giving credit to the deceased, Gassy said Dr Tobin was 'observant and perceptive'. Given their prior dealings, she would have recognised him had he been the shooter, and would have mentioned him to those who tried to help her as she died. 'The actual shooter was waiting in the conference room on level eight,' he said. '(The shooter) escaped by the fire escape stairs.' He had little respect for this alternative culprit, saying the grouping of shots on her body pointed to an amateur, not a skilled marksman such as himself.

In any event, he said, Dr Tobin played only a 'peripheral' role in his professional ruin. He admitted the names and addresses written on the railway ticket were references to doctors involved in the deregistration process. It was information compiled, he said, as a 'practice run' for a career as a private investigator. Asked by Mr Brebner to identify a near-illegible scrawl on the ticket, Gassy said he could not. 'Since I've had this exhibit, I've been trying to figure it out (and) nothing seems to fit,' he said. 'It seems to have two Rs.' Mr Brebner suggested the word – or name – began with an M, but Gassy disagreed.

He also disagreed with the prosecution's suggestions of motive. 'I was not happy about what (the persons on the list) had done . . . (but to call it) resentment is a bit strong,' he said. As for Dr Tobin, he said he had never been unhappy with her 'to the same extent as the other people' named in the prosecution case. He claimed to hold no belief she had been working 'behind the scenes' to have him deregistered and removed from St George's Hospital. 'I would not have thought she had the ability to do that, given she had been in Sydney only a year,' he said.

Under intense cross-examination, he agreed keeping the list – which had 'seemed like a good idea' – could implicate him in Dr Tobin's murder but maintained it had no specific purpose other than naming those involved in his deregistration. 'I thought somehow if I had more information about the (deregistration) process, that somehow it might be useful,' he said, adding he did not believe there was a conspiracy against him. 'I would not use that word and I don't see the need to use any particular word,' he said.

Gassy had explanations for every facet of the prosecution case. The hire car mileage attributed to the Brisbane and Adelaide trips was recorded by driving around Sydney practising 'surveillance techniques'. His absence from his apartment at pivotal times was due to holidays in remote locations, places where no one knew him and where he could not be contacted. Newspaper clippings and internet printouts about Dr Tobin's murder were in his apartment due to general interest – he'd known the victim, after all. 'It is hardly surprising, given that both the victim and (I) were both psychiatrists and being murdered is an occupational hazard,' he would go on to say.

Mr Brebner dismissed it all, and used his own closing address to encourage the jury to do the same. He said the accused murderer's theories were products of his 'own imagination' and could not be supported by evidence. '(Gassy) is obviously intelligent and resourceful . . . you might well consider (the murder) is what you would expect to see if he had taken every precaution he could think of,' he said. 'The reason so much (evidence) was found . . . was because he had thought, after a fortnight had passed . . . he had, in fact, got clean away with it and saw no need to destroy any more evidence.'

Claims about Dr Tobin's sexuality were equally imaginary, he said, as no one had made threats against her during her time in Adelaide. 'Might the killer have been possibly connected with this so-called underground lesbian world, despite the fact that the evidence makes it plain Dr Tobin did not have any such preferences whatsoever?' he asked the jury. 'The only suggestion that she was a closet lesbian seems to be a product of (Gassy's) own imagination.'

Mr Brebner said Gassy was 'predisposed' to anger and resentment because of his delusional disorder, and had maintained 'a disturbing interest' in those he blamed for his personal, professional and financial ruin. 'Do you think,' he asked the jury in conclusion, 'the only reasonable and rational explanation for the combination of factors, as disclosed by the evidence, is that it was in fact (Gassy) who fired the fatal shots?'

Gassy was not finished. 'According to the prosecutor, the shooter had waited eight and a half years for his moment,' he told the jury. 'Surely, someone motivated by revenge would have wanted the victim to know who was killing her and why. The shooting has the hallmarks of a killing in which the shooter had little emotional investment.' The list and the railway ticket, he said, were inconclusive. 'Even if you decide (the list) had a non-innocent purpose, it's a long way from obtaining information about a person . . . to conspiring to kill them.'

His argument had some impact. The jury of eight men and four women – required under South Australian law to return a unanimous verdict – began its deliberations on 22 September 2004. At 2.40 pm, the jurors asked Her Honour for an explanation of 'reasonable doubt'. It was a question that unsettled members of Dr Tobin's family, who had been present throughout the trial, as well as the officers who had conducted the investigation. They felt little better when, at 4.10 pm, the jury announced it 'did not believe' it could come to a decision.

With the spectre of a retrial looming, Justice Vanstone urged the jurors to resume their deliberations. 'Of course I respect your position, but in the terms of the scale of this case, the number of witnesses heard and the time it has taken, your deliberations have not been prolonged,' she assured them. Reminding them of the oath they swore to give a true verdict, she said careful considerations of individual opinions might prove the key to reaching a decision. 'A calm and objective discussion of the evidence often leads to a better understanding of the differences of opinion you may have,' she said. '(Discussion) may convince you that your original opinion was wrong.'

On the third day of deliberations – 14 hours into their discussions – the jury again turned to Justice Vanstone for advice. They sent her a note, via sheriff's officers, at 11.10 am on 23 September asking how they might 'move forward'. Word of the note prompted those gathered outside courtroom two of the Sir Samuel Way Building – Dr Tobin's friends and family, police, media and Gassy's father – to quickly take their seats. It was the first time the jury had been heard from since 5 pm the previous day.

Justice Vanstone's 28-minute direction to the jurors was carefully worded – and, though no one knew it at the time, would eventually become yet another weapon in the delusional assassin's arsenal. 'Sometimes, when one reaches a difficult position and cannot move on, it's good to go back to the beginning,' she said. 'I'm not suggesting you would start the whole process again but, rather, why not take stock right back from the beginning?' Dividing the evidence into a number of categories, she asked them to consider each in turn and weigh up the arguments for and against the prosecution. They needed to satisfy themselves, she said, that Gassy had been in Adelaide at the time of the murder and had the motive to kill. 'Of course, I do not know where your difficulty is but, if you go through that process, you can ask yourselves, "Are we in agreement to this point?"' she said. 'If you are not, you need to isolate the exact point where your views diverge and focus on that point.'

Twenty minutes later, the jury returned with a unanimous verdict of guilty. The condemnation of his peers provoked little reaction from Gassy. Nor did it change his mind about legal self-defence. Offered the chance to speak to a lawyer before making sentencing submissions, Gassy declined. 'I will not be seeking any legal advice, Your Honour,' he said. When Mr Brebner collected his books from the bar table, *DSM-IV* was one of the last tomes he slotted into his case.

It was the moment Don Scott, Dr Tobin's husband, had been waiting for. After 11 weeks, 163 witnesses and $1 million in taxpayer funds, the jury reached its decision on what would have been his wife's 54th birthday. 'Gassy had gone to a lot of trouble for this crime . . . he had travelled through three states and had a lot of hate, cowardice and envy,' Mr Scott said after the verdict. 'I try not to feel anything towards him now . . . as Margaret would have said, we all just have to get on with it.' He said he and his mother-in-law, Jean, were grateful for the hard work and 'humanity' of the Major Crime detectives who had secured Gassy's conviction. 'Margaret's death was a terrible loss to the family, and we will continue to miss her,' he said.

Her example, together with his own admitted 'stubbornness', would provide him the strength to conquer his grieving. 'She would always say to me 'just do the usual thing, think about it and you will come through – so I did,' he said. Memories, too, kept him warm. 'She would come home sometimes on a Friday night with her eyes nearly closed . . . I used to feed her, pour red wine into her and put her to bed. About 1.30 pm the next day she would come out, her eyes wired, and say, "What are we doing today?". She was like a re-energised child.'

The verdict freed Mr Scott from a personal superstition. 'For some reason, I got it into my head that if I started mucking with things on the house, something would go wrong with the trial,' he said of the long-postponed renovation. The couple's goal had been to turn their suburban Adelaide home into an oasis of native vegetation, finished off with Dr Tobin's signature touch – a pot or ornament in every corner of the garden. 'Now I can get back to it. Like Margaret would've said: "You have nothing holding you back, get on with it".'

Thanks to the vagaries of the South Australian legal system, Gassy was not immediately sentenced. Justice Vanstone declined to impose the mandatory life sentence until she had heard submissions – which did not occur for several weeks. Given his moment, Mr Brebner wasted no time and minced no words. Gassy's prospects for rehabilitation, he said, were 'non existent', and he would pose a grave risk to those people on his list for the rest of his life.

When Justice Vanstone did finally sentence the killer, imposing a 34-year non-parole period, she echoed the prosecutor's words. It was likely, she said, that he would die in jail but that was a consequence of his 'cool, calculated and clever' assassination. 'Not only do you have no contrition for what you have done, but you see the task as unfinished,' she said. 'There is no question in my mind that (those on the list) have been in danger in the last eight years leading to your arrest. As well, I am satisfied that in your time in custody, new persons have been added to your list of targets. As long as you live, you will be profoundly dangerous.'

She refused to buy into the ongoing debate about Gassy's mental competency. 'I am sure your personality is flawed (but) there is absolutely no doubt in my mind that, at the time you committed this crime, you were mentally competent,' she said. 'It seems to me that this killing must rank in the worst category of murder.'

Jailed, Gassy turned his attention to new targets. Justice Vanstone became his new fixation – she had taken an 'overactive role' in his trial, he claimed, and made no less than 27 errors. Taking his case to the Court of Criminal Appeal, Gassy claimed the presiding judge 'prompted' Mr Brebner during his arguments and refused defence requests to re-examine key witnesses. The direction to the jury that ended the 14-hour deadlock, meanwhile, was unfair. 'It presented only the prosecution's case and even suggested to the jury that it should disregard important parts of the defence,' he claimed in documents filed with the court. Following a long series of appeal hearings, the Full Court of the Court of Criminal Appeal unanimously rejected Gassy's claims just before Christmas 2005.

It was perfectly timed, in Mr Scott's opinion. 'Dr Gassy's taken a lot away from me, but he's also given me three presents,' he said at the time. 'He got caught, he got convicted and now he's failed in his appeal. This is a really fantastic Christmas present.'

Undaunted, Gassy turned once again to old business. The life inmate of Yatala Labour Prison launched a civil lawsuit against the Department of Correctional Services. They were trying to kill him, he claimed, by refusing to provide him with anti-HIV medication. The suit attracted little fanfare and was dealt with quite quickly – which was just as well, given its true purpose. Once again, Gassy had fooled the establishment. Those guarding him had not been his true targets after all. The lawsuit had provided him with the time he needed – and, most importantly, unrestricted computer access – to follow through with his real goal, and seek special leave to appeal against his conviction and sentence in the High Court of Australia.

The august body visits the southern capital but twice a year, and hears constitutional cases in a magnificent, custom-built courtroom on the fifth floor of the Federal Court building. The bi-annual sitting is, for lawyers and journalists, the 'world series' of legality. Barristers and solicitors clear their calendars for that week in order to watch their peers crash and burn.

Widespread was the shock when, in August 2007, Gassy appeared amongst the special leave applicants in the High Court's Adelaide sittings. Given his love of conspiracy theories and long, rambling speeches on irrelevant topics, how would the assassin fare in such stringently controlled conditions? Another, more frightening, question was courtroom security. Adelaide's Federal Court building has but one cell, deep underground, and its elevator services only a single courtroom. Word quickly spread that the judges had refused to squeeze themselves into that smaller court for Gassy's hearing, and had ordered he be brought to their specialist chamber once his matter was called. The distance between the elevator doors and the court's bar table was 40 metres. Crossing it would take Gassy past four more elevators, a staircase and an open-air atrium. He would also encounter dozens of civilians, both in the public walkways and the court registry office – each and every one a potential hostage.

For the correctional services officers who had custody of Gassy, and the South Australia police officers tasked with guarding the public, a nightmare had begun. How could they safely move one of the most dangerous men in the country through a minefield of possible catastrophes while ensuring he lacked opportunity to escape or harm someone? In the lead-up to the hearing date, rumours tore through the legal community like wildfire. Gassy, one story claimed, would be shackled at the wrists, waist and ankles, with all of his extremities connected to one another. He would be wearing a collar, claimed another, with loops through which guards could direct him with foot-long control rods. There would be five guards – no, eight; possibly 12 – who would surround him like a killer in an action movie, then walk him backwards to the court to retard his movement. He would be blinkered so he could not see the public. Most worrying of all was the claim Gassy's keepers were banned from carrying firearms or any other form of projectile weaponry. The fear, according to rumour, was that Gassy's marksmanship was so terrifyingly accurate, he could snag a gun from a guard and kill as many as three bystanders before anyone could bring him down. Such concerns made no difference to the Australian Federal Police, who unapologetically announced their officers – who would assume responsibility for Gassy within the courtroom itself – would all be armed.

The 70 people attending the hearing held their breath when, just before lunch, Gassy was brought onto the public walkway. His every moment was shadowed by five guards from Yatala Labour Prison's maximum-security G-division – men who had been dealing with the assassin, every day, since his arrest. He was handcuffed, but not under any other form of restraint. For a man supposedly dying from HIV-related illnesses, Gassy looked remarkably fit. He had gained weight since his sentencing, and his now-long dark hair was pulled back in a thick ponytail. He wore a dark suit with a white shirt and glanced, casually, around the atrium as he walked. One could be forgiven for thinking he was memorising people in the crowd – or, more disturbingly, looking for familiar faces. If that were the case, Gassy was to go back to his cell disappointed; neither Mr Scott nor any members of Dr Tobin's family attended the hearing.

Gassy's escorts brought him to the doors of the High Court's chamber and handed him over to the AFP. Three officers guarded the inside of the door; two remained outside it, in the atrium. Another flanked Gassy as he moved toward the bar table and remained by his side. Several others positioned themselves at locations within the public gallery, joining the correctional services officers who knew the assassin only too well. Gassy took his seat and looked to his right where, just 5 metres away, sat his nemesis. Though Peter Brebner was widely tipped to be the next judge of the District Court – a rumour that, months later, would turn out to be correct – he was not about to pass on the assassin's brief just yet. Having scored his conviction, and then batted down his petition to the Full Court of the Supreme Court, Mr Brebner was looking to take the hat-trick in the High Court before he ascended to the bench himself. Cool and professional as always, the prosecutor did not blink when an AFP officer leaned forward and unlocked Gassy's handcuffs – but many in the gallery did, and an audible gasp rippled through those assembled.

The judges of the High Court entered and informed Gassy he had 20 minutes to speak. 'We've read your written outline, and you may speak on any topic you wish,' they said. 'You can do whatever you want with your 20 minutes.'

Gassy took them at their word, launching into another masterclass of paranoid delusion. 'I wish to start with the initial police search of the home of the applicant's mother,' he began, once again referring to himself in the third person. 'The trial judge went to extreme lengths to hide the illegality of the issuing and execution of the warrant. She interfered in the cross-examination of witnesses, she prevented defence counsel from pursuing lines of inquiry to do with the search and execution of the warrants. Judicial bias was evident throughout the proceedings, as the judge sought to cover up gross misconduct, and unsafe and unsatisfactory verdicts.'

His goal rapidly became clear. Knowing the High Court could only grant him a retrial, Gassy sought to attack the evidence that had secured his conviction. He wanted everything police had learned, from the moment they had tracked the journey made by 'David Pais', erased. And, as befitted his extremist mentality, he was willing to go to great lengths to blacken the reputation of the Major Crime Investigations Branch by labelling them 'totalitarian'.

'Mrs Gassy was unlawfully stopped as she drove away from her home,' he claimed. 'She was not in breach of any law and she was not suspected of any offence. The applicant's mother was coerced, and prevented from speaking with the applicant. Police used the mother as a human shield between themselves and the applicant, and permission to investigate the premises was obtained by implied coercion. It is a feature of a totalitarian society that police would use a family member to extract information, it is not a feature of our society.' The actions of police, he argued, were completely unnecessary. 'Who in their right mind would stand in the way of armed police officers, executing a warrant, after what happened to Ted Bundy?' he asked, name-checking the infamous US serial killer who had a history of clashing with arresting officers. 'Had the police not acted illegally and improperly, evidence might not have been obtained – that is the real evil here,' he said.

Gassy had many complaints. He gave a long list of reasons why his beloved Glocks – his 'works of art' – should have been excluded from evidence at trial. 'There is no match between the barrels of the applicant's Glocks and the bullets found at the murder scene,' he said. 'These are matters of ballistics, of shot-to-shot variation. These sorts of tests are esoteric, and are not even mentioned in television shows like *CSI*.' Allowing such evidence to be tendered was, apparently, just one of dozens of 'completely disingenuous rulings' made by Justice Vanstone. The nature of the others, however, would remain a mystery to those sitting in the gallery because Gassy's rail against the South Australia Police had devoured all of his 20 minutes. He was told, gently but firmly, that his submissions had ended and he needed to sit back down.

Gassy was completely prepared to blame Judge Vanstone for his suffering. Shockingly, so was the High Court. Mr Brebner was asked, by the panel, not to address his own written submissions but, instead, to discuss Her Honour's final direction to the jury. 'It does not raise any point of principle,' Mr Brebner replied smoothly, earning a sour glare from Gassy. 'It's desirable for trial judges to help juries along if they can. Such things are not a question for this court unless there is a real risk of a miscarriage of justice, and there is not here. Her Honour was at pains to remind the jury to return to the evidence and arguments. Her Honour was merely implying that, if the prosecution case fell at any hurdles, that would be the end of the matter. She was suggesting a process, not a result.'

Given a chance to respond, Gassy opted instead to talk about his target shooting prowess and those fateful few seconds inside the elevator. 'Tobin did not identify her killer,' he said, still loathe to personalise the enemy. 'She was the applicant's immediate superior for six months between 1993 and 1994, and was intimately familiar with his appearance. She would have known, had her killer been the applicant, and she would have said so before she died. Also, it's inconceivable that a killer bent on revenge, who had been waiting eight-and-a-half years for his moment, would not have identified himself to her.'

The bench announced it would take a short adjournment to discuss the case. It was yet another surprise in a day full of them – and would not be the last. Gassy was allowed to remain at the bar table, without handcuffs, during the break. The 70-strong gallery sat nervously, unwilling to single themselves out for attention by moving. Likely, the assassin would have paid them no mind; he was content to stare at the front of the courtroom. When the court reconvened, the judges had a double-edged decision. Gassy's claims of improper police conduct were dismissed out of hand; the hard work of Major Crime detectives would remain admissible were there a retrial, as would the complete transcript of the first trial. As to the question of special leave, the judges had a novel answer. The appropriateness or otherwise of Justice Vanstone's final direction would be immediately referred to the seven-member Full Bench of the High Court for determination. Gassy had won another round.

Emboldened, Gassy went on the offensive. At a high-security status hearing in October 2007, he introduced his secret weapon. Somehow, he had obtained a letter written by one of the jurors in his trial. That person had complained, to the Sheriff of South Australia's courts, that he or she had been 'pressured' to return a guilty verdict following Justice Vanstone's speech. Gassy claimed more jurors could have felt the same way due to the 'unbalancing' effect of Her Honour's 'interference'. Mr Brebner said the letter constituted fresh evidence and could not reasonably be included in the special leave argument. Justice Kenneth Hayne, who had convened the preliminary hearing, said it was another matter for the Full Bench to determine.

Gassy went before the Full Bench in December 2007, this time against a new opponent – then-Solicitor General of South Australia Chris Kourakis, SC. His position on the situation was markedly different than that of Mr Brebner. 'We concede Justice Vanstone did not properly put the defence case in her final directions to the jury,' he told the court. 'However, the situation remains that there was no substantial miscarriage of justice.'

Justice William Gummow was not prepared to accept that submission, given the convenient timing of the guilty verdict. 'What we do know is that the jury were having difficulties, they were deliberating for some time and then, after this, the clouds lifted,' he said. He and the rest of the bench reserved their decision to a date to be set.

Pundits thought it would come by January. They were wrong. On 14 March 2008, the Full Bench of the High Court awarded Jean Eric Gassy a retrial for the murder of Dr Margaret Tobin. In a majority decision, the court ruled Justice Vanstone had made a 'serious error', resulting in a 'substantial miscarriage of justice'. She had swayed the jury's deliberations with her final direction, the court said, causing them to return a guilty verdict. The ruling was a slap in the face not only for Her Honour, but also for the Full Court of the Supreme Court – whose own decision on Gassy's case had now been overturned by a higher authority.

It also shattered the peace Don Scott had regained only recently. Still, the widower battled to take it in his stride and turned, once again, to his beloved wife for inspiration. 'This is like being kicked in the guts,' he said. 'Shock and disappointment were my first feelings, but not with the system as such. I still want people to have the chance at a fair trial because that was part of what drove Margaret – that you had rights in the community.' His brother-in-law, Damien, also weighed in. 'Because of the appeal, Gassy has been lingering there in the background but, to a large extent, most of us have managed to put it aside,' he said. 'We're disappointed, but not surprised.'

Tuesday, 27 May 2008 was an important day in the Gassy saga. It officially began his second Supreme Court prosecution, complete with a brand-new plea of not guilty. It also marked the final time the assassin would cross swords with Mr Brebner, whose move to the District Court bench was imminent. Finally, Mr Scott returned to the courtroom after staying away from the High Court proceedings. The matter was too real now – the spectre of an acquittal too haunting – for him to be anywhere but the Sir Samuel Way building.

Told, by Mr Brebner, that more than 160 witnesses were likely to be called for the prosecution, Justice Trish Kelly called for speed. 'From the court's point of view, this matter should proceed in August,' she said. However, she would not be hearing the trial. It was put on the docket of Justice Kevin Duggan – a long-serving judicial officer of infinite patience, friendly demeanour and military precision – but would not kick off in 2008. Thanks to a series of pre-trial hearings and legal manoeuvring by Gassy – all of which occurred behind closed doors in secret 'directions hearings' – the trial was delayed until 17 February 2009.

This time, the prosecution was run in tandem by Emily Telfer and Jim Pearce, QC. The first five minutes of Ms Telfer's opening address made it clear Gassy's second trial was to be a carbon copy of the first – a déjà vu of delusional thought. With the High Court having backed the work of SAPOL detectives, there was no need to stray from the script. Best of all, the prosecution could call up the transcript of the first trial at any time and confront Gassy with his own words. Should the assassin seek to deviate, even slightly, from his fantastical claims of isolated camping trips and long, surveillance-practising drives around Sydney, he would be tripped up. And Gassy knew it; like the prosecution, the defence case was a mirror image of that which came before. The underground lesbian world was still responsible for the murder, Gassy was still an expert pistol shooter who would never have grouped his bullets so poorly, Dr Tobin still would have surely identified him before she breathed her last.

For 47 days, nine men and three woman heard every shred of evidence both for and against Gassy's guilt. They reviewed the evidence of both their trial and its predecessor, scanned thousands of pages of transcript, hefted the Glocks and considered evidence taken from rubbish dumps, apartment buildings and Gassy's own wallet. On 6 May 2009, they knocked on the door of courtroom eight and said they had a unanimous verdict. They had been deliberating for just three and a half hours.

Gassy, still sporting the extra weight, was not allowed to sit at the bar table this time. He was kept in the dock, guarded by two sheriff's officers. Two more manned the door while Gassy's correctional services keepers – the same men who had chaperoned him at the High Court – sat tensely in the back row of the gallery. As always, Gassy attracted a crowd. Aside from the media, a school class on excursion filled the rows, as did a number of young lawyers and associates for other judges. Gassy's long-suffering parents sat to the left of the court, just one row from Mr Scott. The assassin's mother began weeping as her son was brought in; he favoured her with a smile but succeeded only in increasing her grief. She was comforted by her husband but to no avail, and finally put her head between her legs and cried. The jury had not even entered yet.

For a moment so fraught with tension, it was almost comically anti-climactic. Justice Duggan confirmed, with the jury foreperson, that a unanimous verdict had been reached. Though the nine men and four women had deliberated for less than a quarter of the marathon their peers had endured, they were of one mind when it came to Jean Eric Gassy. And that one mind said 'guilty'.

Mr Scott flushed red and began shaking, tears streaming down his cheeks. Gassy, by contrast, showed no reaction at all. He folded his hands behind his back and fixed a baleful stare on the jury foreperson – which was returned with steel. No one in this jury, it was clear, would be complaining of pressure. Unlike the wake of his first trial, Gassy did not watch each individual juror leave the box as they were dismissed. Instead he nodded to his parents and went back to his cell, seemingly to prepare sentencing submissions.

It was a very different Gassy who next appeared in court. On 1 June 2009, it seemed as if his fire had gone out. His submissions as to sentence were brief, and amounted to little more than a final, weak denial of suffering any delusional disorder.

Mr Pearce was more than willing to fill in the time. He dubbed Gassy a 'remorseless killer' who had committed 'cold-blooded, premeditated murder' and had non-existent prospects of rehabilitation. Echoing Justice Vanstone's original sentence, he too declared the assassin would remain a risk to his intended targets unless and until he succumbed to psychiatric help. 'It isn't a case of them being overly nervous,' he explained. 'It is a case of these people basing their fears on their professional understanding. The people on Gassy's hit list are entitled to live the rest of their lives without fear. Any non-parole period Your Honour sees fit to impose should reflect the fact that these decent, hardworking people will otherwise live their lives in fear.'

Justice Duggan also received victim impact statements from Dr Tobin's family. Her sister, Mary, said her 'career-focused' sibling had fought all her life for a better mental health system. 'Sadly, her courage to take action resulted in the loss of her own life,' she said. 'We are relieved that, with this verdict, justice has been achieved.' Mr Scott said his wife's death had 'left a void which will never be filled . . . a gaping hole' and a 'greater burden of loss'. 'I continue to miss her love, sense of fun and intelligence,' he said.

Gassy's half-decade run in South Australia's courts climaxed on 5 June 2009. Before a packed gallery, Justice Duggan imposed the mandatory life sentence for murder. In determining a non-parole period, His Honour said Gassy 'harboured a grudge' against Dr Tobin over his deregistration, and 'continued to deny' both his guilt and diagnosis as suffering from a delusional, paranoid mental illness. 'Nevertheless, you obviously knew what you were doing, you acted deliberately and you gave a great deal of thought on how to carry out the offence,' he said. The appropriate punishment for such a scheme, he decided, was 30 years – four years less than the term imposed by Justice Vanstone. Justice Duggan said legislative changes, related to proportionality in sentencing and passed by Parliament in 2007, made such a difference necessary. Nonetheless, Gassy would remain in prison until at least November 2032, when he would be 75 years old.

The reduction was of no consequence to Dr Tobin's loved ones. 'It's great news and we are all really relieved,' her brother, Damien, said on behalf of the family.

Mr Scott, too, found himself exorcised of long-held demons. His 2004 vow that he would 'try' not to feel anything toward his wife's killer could finally be honoured. 'I don't feel anything toward Gassy,' he said outside court, his face a picture of determination. 'He took my best friend from me. He made it difficult for the people who have been around me, because no one's been able to have all of me because I could not give all of myself.

'I know Margaret would have told me to finally do what I've been supposed to do all along – get amongst it again and live my life. That's what she always did, and life is just too short to do things any other way than her way. I feel great – really, really good. It's done, it's dusted, and shortly I will go and have a quiet drink. Finally, I feel I can give of myself, I can feel comfortable with and in myself, because I feel nothing toward Gassy.'

Twice-beaten, finally bowed, the delusional assassin finally sank into the depths of the prison system and disappeared. But Gassy's mania has always been fuelled by ego – a slight against his person, no matter how minor, must be avenged. So it was that, on 3 August, the former psychiatrist returned to the court. Having quietly accepted both the jury's verdict and Justice Duggan's sentence, Gassy now wanted permission to file appeal papers. The beaten man of May and June had gone; the wild-eyed, aggressive Gassy of years past had returned. He wasted no time in detailing the forces that had galvanised his transformation.

'On July 22, a rope was planted in my cell,' he announced. 'I was then taken from my cell to G-division – which is a punishment unit – and I am still there now.'

He made two requests of Justice Michael David. The first was that his application for permission to appeal be adjourned. The second was that His Honour intervene in the operation of the prison system and order Gassy be permitted access to his cell, his law books and his copious volumes of documentary material so that he could quickly prepare his latest rail against those who sought to cage him. Justice David unsurprisingly refused, noting his utter lack of jurisdiction over Yatala Labour Prison.

Gassy left court unsatisfied, a sour look etched on his face. The 'conspiracy' against him continued . . . and no doubt, within the twisted confines of his mind, always will.

Punishment of a God

Rajini Narayan

Acrid, foul-smelling smoke billowed from the townhouse and blanketed the neighbourhood. Residents, roused from their sleep, filled the quiet suburban street. Horrified, they watched as flames rose from an upstairs window and licked at the pre-dawn sky. An ambulance was quick to arrive, and paramedics stretchered a badly burned man away for treatment. Shocked and wanting answers, neighbours searched out the man's wife. When asked what had happened to her husband, Rajini Narayan answered in a faltering, haunted voice.

'My husband loves another woman,' she said. 'He hugs her. I'm a jealous wife – his penis should belong to me. I just wanted to burn his penis so it belongs to me and no one else.' Narayan looked back toward the fire. 'It's just his penis I wanted to burn,' she said quietly. 'I didn't mean this to happen.'

From that moment in December 2008, Rajini Narayan seemed destined to join the infamous ranks of Adelaide's bizarre criminal set. She eventually did – but not for the reasons anyone imagined. What looked at first to be Australia's own Lorena Bobbitt was a deeper, more twisted tale of infidelity, psychological domination, domestic abuse and religious fervour. Over the next three years the case canvassed fortune-telling, secret Bible readings and a centuries-old Hindu love story – and ended in controversy.

•

Narayan was born in Lautoka, Fiji, in August 1964. She was the only child of a strict Indian family whose devotion to the Hindu faith was absolute. Narayan grew up praying to many different gods and reading from sacred texts including the Ramayana. Its seven volumes chronicle the journey of the deity Rama and its message is one of faithfulness despite harsh circumstances. Rama is depicted as the ideal man and perfect human. The text also details his great love affair with the Lady Sita. Like her holy husband, Sita is held up as an example for all Hindus. She is the standard setter for wifely and womanly virtues.

One particular story about the couple had a profound impact on a young Narayan. 'It says how King Ravana kidnapped Sita,' she said in 2010. 'Lord Rama goes and kills King Ravana and gets his wife back.' But Rama will not look at her, and Sita asks for a pyre so she might end her life. 'He then makes a fire and makes his wife walk over that fire,' Narayan said.

Sita emerges unharmed – a sign she was pure despite her ordeal. Rama rushes to embrace her. He reveals he never doubted her fidelity but knew it had to be proven before the eyes of the world so she would be accepted as his queen.

From the moment she read that tale Narayan aspired to be like Sita – and to have a husband like Rama. When she was twenty-two, her parents arranged for her to wed a man named Satish. The couple had wed in April 1986, and their ceremony was very traditional. Satish walked around a ceremonial fire pit to mark his new bride with a red *sindoor* dot, signifying his ownership of her.

'In India, we say "it's up to the woman",' Narayan said in October 2010. 'If there's anything wrong with the husband, it's the wife's loving devotion that will change it. Marriage is like a mortar and pestle – one is useless without the other.' Unlike Western weddings, Hindu marriages last beyond death. 'We believe in seven lifetimes or reincarnations,' she explained. 'We say that you will be married to that man for the next seven lifetimes, so you do your best. You are there to please him, honour him, respect him. That's just what an Indian wife should do.' Wives were also expected to keep their own counsel. 'If anything happens it should stay within your house, within the four walls of your bedroom, and nobody should know,' she said.

Satish Narayan was a fiercely intelligent man who designed military systems. His work took the couple around Australia. They had three children – Jessica, Daniel and Chantelle – and eventually settled in a townhouse on Cleland Avenue, Unley. Just eight minutes from the city, it is one of South Australia's more prestigious suburbs – and an indication of Satish's success. He had taken a contract with Raytheon Australia, and was working on a combat system for Royal Australian Navy warships. Despite his hefty salary, Satish insisted his wife continue to work and support the family. She did so, never questioning his edict. Their life looked to be quiet and idyllic – right up until 4 am, 7 December 2008.

Narayan was arrested outside her burning home. She was charged with causing grievous bodily harm to Satish, endangering the lives of their children, and arson. Remanded in custody, Narayan made no immediate application for bail. Her lawyers instead sought the expertise of eminent forensic psychiatrist Dr Craig Raeside. His three confidential reports were presented to the Adelaide Magistrates Court on 5 January 2009. Based on these reports defence counsel asked that their client be released. Lucy Boord, prosecuting, opposed the request. The game, she said, had changed.

'The alleged victim, Satish Narayan, died on December 27,' she told the court. 'He died in hospital several weeks after the incident. The accused is now charged with murder.' Her motive, Ms Boord said, was vengeance. 'The victim was asleep in his bed,' she said of the crime. 'The accused had just learned he had been having an affair. She came into the bedroom and doused his genital area with petrol and set it alight.' That fire had spread to the rest of the property, she said, because an agonised Satish had 'knocked over' a bottle of methylated spirits. The townhouse had sustained more than $1 million in damage.

Ms Boord classed Narayan's comments to the neighbours as 'admissions' of guilt and deliberate action. 'She poses a substantial risk to the community given this flagrant offending,' she said, warning Narayan might also be a danger to herself. 'Witnesses heard the accused making references to using a police officer's gun on herself,' she said. 'She also made references as to whether she "should be alive or not".'

Magistrate Bill Ackland was deeply concerned. 'I would feel more comfortable if another psychiatric assessment were to happen,' he said. 'I would ask that that take place before we go any further with this bail application.' He put the matter off for four days.

The case was an instant sensation with the general public. Like Lorena Bobbitt before her, Narayan became the inspiration for dozens of poor-taste jokes. She was the 'penis-burning wife', according to the headlines – the terror of men everywhere. Her notoriety quickly spread overseas. Representatives for US television personality Dr Phil McGraw contacted *The Advertiser* newspaper. They wanted contact details for Narayan's counsel, hoping they could secure her for an upcoming episode of their show. The topic, they said, was 'cheating husbands' and 'wives who strike back'. Although *The Advertiser* declined to assist Dr Phil, the celebrity counsellor made contact with Narayan's solicitors. Understandably, they refused to take part in the show.

When they returned to court on 9 January, Narayan's lawyers were nonetheless emboldened. Dr Raeside's opinion, they said, was unchanged – but so was Ms Boord's view. 'We are still very concerned about whether she understands or comprehends how her actions have landed her in this particular situation,' she said. 'And we're still very concerned about the accused herself, given the nature and premeditation of the offending.'

Magistrate Ackland agreed the 'gravity' of the charges was self-evident 'but the statutory presumption in favour of bail remains.' He released Narayan on a $15,000 guarantee, ordering she surrender her passport, wear an electronic monitoring bracelet at all times and undergo continued psychiatric analysis. He declined to order her adult daughter, Jessica, serve as a guarantor. 'There's an inevitable tension between the loyalties of a child and the responsibilities of a guarantor,' he observed.

While Narayan signed release papers, Adelaide's media gathered outside the court. Aside from a grainy, split-second image of Narayan at the scene, there were no images of the alleged killer to be had. Narayan was not about to provide any. She ran from court to a waiting car, using a piece of paper to shield her face.

Narayan's next court appearance, on 17 April 2009, was much more sedate. Dressed in a simple sari, she walked into and out of court without incident. She made no effort to avoid the media and appeared calm, even serene. The hearing was short. Magistrate Ackland ordered she enter pleas to the charges in June. The case looked to be on schedule.

Privately, prosecutors were vexed. Satish's body had been examined by the state's top forensic experts, all of whom had come to the same inescapable conclusion: the only unburned portion of the dead man's body was his genital region. The evidence simply did not match Narayan's account of events, nor did it parse with the case prosecutors were building against her. Several theories were bandied about before one gained traction. One expert suggested the accelerant had splashed onto, and away from, the victim's genitals before it was set alight. He hypothesised some sort of 'flame halo' had existed, however briefly, around Satish's manhood. That, he posited, would explain the conflicting evidence.

Top barrister Lindy Powell, QC, was not convinced. Narayan's solicitors had retained her services in case of a trial. Having perused the prosecution's brief of evidence, Ms Powell insisted on seeking a second expert opinion. That report set the renowned litigator on a different track. Extensive, confidential discussions were had – first with Narayan, then prosecutors. The June hearing came and went without pleas, and the case disappeared from the cause lists for nine months.

When it re-emerged in January 2010, its complexion had shifted. Prosecutor Karen Ingleton told the court there were 'one or two bits and pieces' still outstanding. 'We've been provided with some defence documents today, and they may form the basis of a guilty plea,' she said. 'I haven't seen them, read them or considered them yet. It's appropriate the prosecution be given time to consider these documents and determine whether a plea is likely to be accepted. If not, then the matter can be committed for trial on the next occasion.'

The possibility of a plea bargain set tongues wagging in the court precinct. What had Ms Powell uncovered that would leave prosecutors willing to accept manslaughter instead of murder? Answers were not immediately forthcoming. The files of the Adelaide Magistrates Court's registry are not for public viewing. The media cannot access affidavits, nor briefs of evidence lodged for the court's consideration. This is done, of course, to protect the proper administration of justice. No one's interests are served if potential jurors get wind of details months before they are asked to determine a person's guilt or innocence. As a consequence, however, speculation becomes rife. So it was with the Narayan case as journalists and lawyers alike wondered what new twist would emerge.

Narayan faced the Supreme Court of South Australia for the first time on 12 April 2010. She pleaded not guilty to one count of murder and one count of arson causing more than $30,000 damage. The endangering life counts had been dropped, and the proposed plea bargain had failed to materialise. Justice John Sulan remanded Narayan on continuing bail until a directions hearing one month later. Once again, the case disappeared from the lists as prosecutors and defence counsel wrangled with the evidence in a series of closed-court hearings. Narayan did her best to stay out of the public spotlight. She was seen just once, shopping for shoes in a suburban mall, and then not again until the morning of her trial.

On 27 September 2010, Narayan made her way through a media scrum for the start of her trial. She was dressed entirely in white and accompanied by a large group of supporters, including her own mother. They filled one half of the court room's public gallery. Some of the well-wishers were of

Indian descent; others were white or Sudanese. They were not the kind of support group one would expect a devout Hindu housewife to gather around her. Stranger still was their demeanour. As they waited for the trial to begin, they spoke openly about the power that comes from faith in Jesus Christ. The other half of the gallery was uniformly Indian – Satish's relatives had flown in from around the world to observe the case.

Narayan sat quietly in the dock as a jury of eight women and four men was empanelled. She kept her back to the public gallery and covered her face with one hand as if ashamed of her situation. Just before 11 am, prosecutor Tim Preston began his opening address.

'In the early morning of December 7, 2008, a fire started in a townhouse on Cleland Avenue, Unley,' Mr Preston said. 'That fire was started by the accused. She, her husband and their children escaped the premises before the fire took serious hold. As the fire raged, neighbours congregated in the street. The accused said to them "I did it, it was not an accident". She said she had started the fire, that she had found out her husband was having an affair, and that she had wanted to burn her husband's penis. She told them she had got some methylated spirits, poured it on her husband and lit it – and that it had "gotten out of control".'

Mr Preston regarded the jury carefully. 'Satish Narayan suffered burns to 75 per cent of his body. The burns were most severe on his back.' He paused to make sure jurors were listening. 'His penis was not burned.'

The fire, he continued, was spread not by methylated spirits but by petrol. Investigators had found a 5 litre can of it in the townhouse's undamaged laundry, and a small beaker of fuel in the master bedroom. The ignition device, he said, was not immediately evident, and was located only after Narayan was questioned. Like everything else about the case, the weapon was odd – it was a candle that had been given to her by a psychic.

'On December 5, two days before the fire, the accused consulted with a tarot card reader on Goodwood Road,' Mr Preston continued. 'She told the tarot reader that she had found, amongst the mail sent to her home, a letter addressed to a woman who was a friend of her husband. It was a replacement Visa card issued in that woman's name. The accused told the tarot reader she had been wanting to cut down her working hours but her husband did not want her to do so. She told the tarot reader she now realised she had been working to pay for the other woman.'

Narayan, he said, was arrested immediately after the fire. 'She had in her possession an email and the Visa card issued to the other woman,' he said. 'The email was a poem with the accompanying lines: "Hi honey, this is special, it applies so much to my sweetheart, love from your baby".' Mr Preston held up a copy of the email. 'This amounts to evidence of a motive, on the part of the accused, to at the very least inflict grievous bodily harm upon the deceased.'

It was a case of murder, Mr Preston insisted. Wounded emotionally by her husband's infidelity and betrayal, Narayan had deliberately set out to retaliate by injuring him physically. 'It might be suggested, on behalf of the accused, that the affair gives rise to some provocation by the deceased,' he said, glancing toward Ms Powell. 'Behaviour of such a kind that might cause an ordinary person to lose his or her self-control. In my submission to you, provocation does not arise here. If the accused believed her husband was having an affair that provides motive for murder and nothing else.'

Ms Powell chose to open to the jury immediately, rather than wait until the end of the prosecution case. She had a clear view of the matter at hand, and wanted jurors to share it from the outset. 'What occurred was undoubtedly a tragedy,' she said solemnly. 'It was a tragedy for Rajini Narayan because, despite more than 20 years of domination, of emotional and physical abuse by her husband, Rajini Narayan more than loved her husband – she idolised him.'

It was as if the air had been sucked out of the court-room. Even seasoned reporters stopped, pens hovering over their notebooks, at Ms Powell's words. Domestic abuse is never a welcome topic. The barrister's first thrust had its desired effect; everyone, especially the jurors, felt acutely uncomfortable.

'This is not a case of a long, abusive relationship where the resentment of an abused wife simmers and grows until she can bear it no more,' Ms Powell continued. 'This is not a case where the wife decides that she does not have to put up with being dominated and abused any longer, and with all that built-up resentment she strikes back.' She shook her head. 'This case is not like that at all.'

'This is a case where a woman loved and idolised her husband so deeply and profoundly that she accepted and tolerated his beatings and abuse. A case where, despite her attempts to keep that secret and try to be what she thought was the perfect wife, she discovered her worst fears were true. Fears that had arisen when she found that Visa card, fears that she was in real danger of losing the man she loved – her god – to another woman.'

Ms Powell allowed that to sink in. 'And how did she discover that affair, ladies and gentlemen? She discovered it because her husband gave her the passwords to his computer.

You might well infer that he meant for her to discover the affair because it was his intention to leave but he was too frightened, too cowardly, to confront her himself. You might well infer that he took the coward's way out.'

Narayan was overcome by the revelation, Ms Powell said, and lost her ability to think and act rationally. 'She became consumed with the idea that she wanted to burn the tip of her husband's penis,' she said, placing heavy emphasis on that last word. 'She had that idea – as illogical as it may seem to you and me – not because she wanted to hurt him, not because she wanted to punish him, not out of revenge or hatred. She had that idea because, in her confusion, she genuinely believed that by doing it she would keep him as a husband. She thought she could stop him from leaving her and going to the other woman, and that would somehow make him love her again and be hers for all time.' Ms Powell locked eyes with the jury. 'But, ladies and gentlemen, events did not go the way that Rajini Narayan expected them to.'

She said Narayan had sat at her husband's computer for an hour and a half before pouring out a beaker of petrol in the laundry. 'She also grabbed a lit candle, the same one that the psychic had given her two days before the fire,' Ms Powell said. 'She went upstairs, to her husband, with the highly-confused notion that she would burn the tip of his penis and that would somehow make him stay with her. She told her husband "I've seen your emails, you say that you love her. I'm going to burn your penis and I'm going to tell your family what you have done". But Satish Narayan reacted in a way that Rajini Narayan never expected. He looked at her as she stood there then rolled over in bed, turning his back to her and saying "no you won't, you fat dumb bitch".'

Ms Powell said that rebuke, in the wake of betrayal and abuse, was too much for Narayan. 'She had been prepared to stand up to him for the first time in her life,' she said. 'He dismissed her, he insulted her, and he treated this huge step that she had taken as a non-event, not worthy of being taken seriously. And in that split-second, Rajini Narayan threw petrol from the beaker and the lit candle onto her husband's back. In that split-second, she lost control.'

The South Australian public had waited 21 months to learn the truth about the 'penis-burning wife'. Instead of being salacious it was sad, complicated and entirely unpalatable. Battle lines had been drawn, and the community split down the middle. Many remained staunch in their belief Narayan had committed an inexcusable crime regardless of Satish's actions. A growing number, however, saw her as the victim and him as the instigator; a cruel and brutal coward who deserved his incendiary fate. Ms Powell had successfully portrayed the dead man as the villain and begun her campaign to beatify her client, to make Narayan appear more sympathetic.

For legal-watchers, the respective openings explained the many pre-trial delays experienced by the case. Satish's injuries were not the result of any unprecedented forensic anomaly or 'flame halo'. Narayan's initial account of the incident did not match the evidence because it was not true. Ms Powell's further inquiries had brought the new version of events to light – an account provided to prosecutors back in January 2010. She may have failed to secure a plea bargain, but Ms Powell had succeeded in defining the prosecution case. She had not only sketched the battlefield, but framed the rules of engagement.

On 6 October 2010, Narayan took the stand in her own defence. There was no room in the cramped witness box to turn her back to the public gallery. She did her best not to look at her in-laws while admitting Satish's abuse began just three months into their marriage.

'My grandma used to live with us,' she said. 'Whenever my husband was angry with me she would say "all you have to do is put some water in your mouth and not swallow". That meant you couldn't talk back. I didn't use the water but I did try to be quiet and respectful toward him, and keep my mouth shut. Right from the start, I was trying to behave in the manner that was expected of me.'

It was not enough. 'He would be angry and tell me I was not the perfect wife, daughter-in-law or sister-in-law, and tell me I needed to work on that and polish myself up to his standard,' she said. 'Once I corrected him about something and he started hitting me, saying it would "teach me a lesson" to not correct him and "not talk too loudly". I felt it was criticism to improve me, to help me become the perfect wife I wanted to be.' The style of abuse varied. 'Usually it was an open-hand (slap) or a push on the chest. Over time he started getting more violent, and then you might get a few kicks in your stomach. He'd tell me "you only try to improve the person you love" when he was beating me up.'

Ms Powell asked if Narayan had ever fought back. 'You don't fight your god,' she replied, as if the question were nonsense. 'You respect him, you honour him, you do everything to please him. I did not like to be beaten, but I told myself I had to be better and try harder.' Narayan said she deserved the harsh treatment. 'I did, because I wasn't the perfect wife,' she insisted. 'My husband was the perfect husband. I idolised him. He was the only male in my life after my father died, and he was all I had. He told me I wasn't the perfect wife, so that's what I believed.'

Her devotion went only so far. In 1990, Satish beat her so hard that he drew blood. Narayan went to the police to obtain a restraining order. Satish convinced her to drop the application, promising he would attend marriage counselling with her. He only went twice, but ceased his attacks upon her. They resumed in 1991 – again, she was imperfect. 'I never considered going to the police again,' Narayan told the jury. 'It was a disrespectful thing to do.

Narayan's future disobedience would be covert. Around that time, she secretly converted to Christianity. Her mother, who had taken up the faith, slipped her a copy of the Bible. Narayan kept it hidden, reading aloud from it when she was alone in the house and drawing strength from its words. She told the jury Satish would have been incensed had he found out.

In 2002, Satish introduced his wife to one of his friends. 'She was a very beautiful, very petite lady,' Narayan remembered. 'I was fat and obese.' Although it was the only time Narayan met the woman, her daughter Jessica encountered her on subsequent occasions. Eventually, Narayan said, the woman left for Melbourne. The outwardly perfect, inwardly rotting marriage continued until Easter 2008, when the couple had their biggest argument to date. Narayan told jurors her husband walked out on her and the children. Eventually his family convinced him to return – but things were more explosive than ever.

Narayan said the Visa card arrived in the mail on Friday, 5 December 2008. She immediately recognised the name on the envelope as that of her husband's petite friend. The letter rattled Narayan. 'I felt maybe I should consult a psychic just to get reassurance that my husband loved me, because that would solve everything,' she said. 'The psychic said she could only see good things in the future. She gave me a candle and said "If you ever feel anxious, light this candle and three angels who are guiding you will make you feel happy".'

Spiritually empowered, Narayan returned home. The following evening, she cast off two decades of fear and confronted Satish. Expecting a violent reaction, she was instead greeted with a flat denial and a weak accusation of 'making a mountain out of a molehill'. Narayan did not know how to respond. 'I was panicking, thinking "this is the first time in my life my husband has lied to me",' she told the jury. 'I felt as if some sort of lens had come off because this person I idolised, to whom I had been so faithful, had lied to me.'

She demanded her husband immediately telephone the other woman and clear up the matter. Satish refused, saying his friend was in the US and the time zones were unfavourable. He promised they would call in the morning. 'I couldn't understand why he was unable to understand my feelings and how distressed I was,' she said. 'It just didn't make sense – why was he taking her side?'

Before he went to bed, Satish dropped a bombshell. 'He told me that when he was single, he and that woman had an affair,' she said. 'It was shocking news to me. I thought he was my pure, honourable husband. I said to him, "How would you feel if I had an affair?" and he answered, "I would kill the man if you had an affair".' His reply made her feel more comfortable. 'It reflected on our Hindu religious beliefs and on Lord Rama,' she said.

Having been counselled by a fortune teller and reassured by a Hindu story, Narayan read the Bible. She no longer felt she had to keep her faith a secret. 'I thought I could have the

Bible out in front of me because my husband had just lied to me,' she said. 'I felt like I had the courage to read the Bible right in front of him.' She also watched the couple's wedding video. 'It was a very happy wedding and I wanted to relive those memories because I was not feeling well. I was feeling very distressed and vulnerable. For 22 years my husband had told me "I don't like lying, I never lie". I believed he was not a normal, everyday human being – he was different, above the law. He was like my hero, you see?'

Conflicted and distressed, Narayan went upstairs and asked for her husband's email password. He gave it freely, allowing her to discover the other woman's poem. 'It was like a blow, like somebody had hit me with a hammer,' Narayan said. 'I started blaming myself that I was unable to be, that I had failed to be, a perfect wife. Because of my failure, I was losing my husband. I knew I had to do something to save my husband from getting carried away by this other woman.'

Echoing Ms Powell's opening address, Narayan recounted her 'bizarre idea'. 'It was up to me to save my marriage,' she said. 'Nobody could help me, and I thought I should burn the tip of his penis with the candle that was given to me by the psychic.' Her voice rose. 'It seemed like it was fate that had taken me to the psychic and fate that had given me the candle, because of the significance of fire in Hinduism. I could use that candle to burn the tip of my husband's penis and it would be like a circumcision – just like he had placed that red *sindoor* dot on my forehead at our wedding. This would be a red dot on his penis that signified he belonged to me, and no one else could touch him.' Narayan looked down at her hands. 'He would be mine,' she said softly. 'Solely mine.'

She felt like Rama and Sita, her lifelong heroes, had blessed the plan. 'It sounds strange, but it was like I maybe had all the powers of the goddess and had to look after my husband, my lord,' she said. 'It didn't occur to me that it was going to be dangerous, and I didn't think in any rational manner. I just had this focus on burning the tip of his penis.'

Narayan took the candle and a beaker of fuel upstairs and confronted her husband. She spoke in Hindi, saying she had read the emails. She vowed to reveal his infidelity to their entire family, forever shattering his veneer of perfection. Narayan still loved her husband but was no longer prepared to 'live a lie'. One way or another, their relationship was going to change – and the fiery circumcision, she felt, was their new beginning.

'I had given him a son, had given him children, I had worked hard and I had slaved all my life here in Australia,' she passionately told the jury. 'Right then, it seemed like he did not have the right to abuse me. He did not have the right to beat me up, and I did not deserve the beatings. That's how I found all this strength to tell him how I felt, and that I was going to burn his penis.'

When Sita and Rama were reunited, he turned away from her only to prove her purity. When Satish Narayan was confronted by his wife's true power, he turned away from her out of spite. 'No you won't, you fat dumb bitch,' he said and rolled over. That abusive gesture was to be the last decision of his life.

'I felt everything drop out of me,' Narayan said about that moment. 'The love, it wasn't there in that instant. It was almost as if I didn't know this person. I had taken all this abuse for his love and he had just left me there and turned his back on me. In that instant, I felt as if I didn't have any love left. At that moment, I wanted to hurt him. For the first time that morning, I wanted to hurt him.'

By her own admission, Narayan snapped. She threw both the beaker of fuel and the candle onto Satish's exposed back and he immediately burst into flame. He screamed in agony even as she screamed in shock and despair. Years of conditioning took over and Narayan went to her husband's aid, trying to extinguish the blaze. Their efforts only spread the conflagration. When she saw the curtains were on fire, Narayan rushed herself and the couple's children out of the house. Satish followed, collapsing in the front yard.

Narayan blinked back tears as she finished her evidence. 'He was the love of my life,' she choked. 'I never expected him to die. I felt very devastated.'

The jury retired at 12.25 pm on 12 October 2010, to consider its verdict. It returned two hours later to ask why the Narayan children had not been called to give evidence. Justice Sulan warned jurors 'not to speculate'. They also wanted to see copies of witness statements taken by police. Justice Sulan refused to hand them over, saying the jury should base its decision solely on the evidence presented in open court.

Jurors continued their deliberation the following day. It was clear they had been rattled by the highly emotional proceedings. Less than 90 minutes into their second day, they asked when they 'should consider provocation' as a defence. It seemed to be a good omen for Narayan, but was immediately followed by a bad one. As Justice Sulan answered the inquiry, a large moth flew down from the ceiling, circled the room and landed on Narayan. It was quickly swept away, but she and her children – sitting in the front row of the public gallery – appeared disturbed by the incident.

Having considered the evidence for nine hours over two days, the jury returned its verdict at 2.15 pm on 13 October.

Narayan, again dressed in white, stood facing the bench and away from the gallery. Several of her supporters were overcome with emotion even before jurors took their seats. Narayan's mother wailed loudly, and had to be comforted by other relatives. Narayan did not look toward her. She continued to stare at the bench, clasping her hands tightly in front of her.

By a majority decision, the jury found Rajini Narayan not guilty of murdering her husband. However, they unanimously found her guilty of the lesser, alternative offence of manslaughter. Narayan, they ruled, had not deliberately set out to kill Satish – but she had been recklessly indifferent toward his survival, and that made her a killer.

Narayan's friends and family nonetheless welcomed the verdict as if it were a victory. Some clapped, others cheered and her children cried with relief. Narayan was crying too, but her tears were not happy. If anything, she looked more distraught than she had during her evidence. The enormity of the case, and of her situation, had finally sunk in. She barely registered Justice Sulan's order she be remanded on continuing bail until November.

Under South Australian law, victims of crime may confront their tormentors during sentencing submissions – a hearing to determine the penalty an offender should receive. This normal part of the judicial process was, of course, an entirely abnormal affair in the case of Narayan. On 24 November, Jessica and Daniel Narayan were asked to talk about the effects of their mother's crime. Daniel said he had been raised in 'a rather hostile' environment. 'My father could be hard to live with sometimes and yes, when I was younger he was violent toward me,' he said. 'As I became older it would be verbal abuse, threats and blackmail.' Daniel said his life had 'ironically' improved since the fire, but his mother's had worsened. 'It has impacted her more than us children – she has been grieving the most. She fasts and prays.' He begged the court not to jail her, saying her 'emotional support' was essential to the family's healing.

Jessica Narayan went one step further. 'I was four when I became aware of my father's violent conduct,' she said. 'When I was 12, I wanted Mum to get a divorce. My father was obsessive, controlling and would often blackmail me, saying he would take away my schooling if I didn't agree with his theories or philosophies.' Like her mother, Jessica also suffered physical abuse at her father's hands. 'I was prepared to stand up to him,' she said proudly. 'He would hit my back, my kidneys and leave me with bruised ribs.' Jessica said Narayan now slept on the floor as 'penance' for her crime and, like her brother, asked the court to impose a suspended prison sentence. 'My mother will continue to punish herself for the rest of her life,' she insisted. 'She made a split-second mistake which has changed not only her life, but the lives of all around her.'

Ms Powell took up the baton in her submissions. Unlike most manslaughter cases, she said, Narayan's crime was born not in anger but by 'love draining out of her'. That love, she said, was 'deep and obsessive' and had generated 'depression and sadness, not rage and anger'. Ms Powell said the community's interests were best served by suspending Narayan's sentence, as she posed no risk to the general public and could rehabilitate quickly and easily.

Justice Sulan wanted to know why Narayan had 'changed her story'. It was a valid question – her seeming subterfuge had caused great delays in the case and considerable expense for the justice system. Ms Powell said any deception was unintentional. 'Narayan was unable to admit, even to herself, what had happened in the bedroom,' she said. 'Telling that story, to anyone, brought shame not only upon herself but on her husband. She didn't want to reveal it to anyone because it demonstrated that he was not a perfect god.'

It was a difficult case requiring a painstakingly crafted sentence. Justice Sulan took his time, calling Narayan back to court on 13 April 2011. Once again the courtroom was packed to capacity and divided down the middle. The atmosphere was tense once more, but eerily silent. No one dared to react as Justice Sulan entered, nor as he summed up the facts of the case. Spirits in the pro-Narayan camp rose, however, when His Honour described the killer's thinking as 'muddled'.

'There is no doubt that, when you discovered the affair, your thinking became unrealistic and muddled,' he said. 'For the first time in your life you had confronted your husband and found the courage to be assertive to the person who had mistreated you. His response was to treat you with disdain, dismiss you and turn his back.' Justice Sulan agreed Narayan had snapped out of distress, not harboured any deliberate intent to kill Satish. For those reasons, he said he would suspend Narayan's six-year jail term and her three-year non-parole period. 'Although it is often said that a suspended sentence is not a sentence at all, it is wrong to regard it as letting an offender walk free as if he or she has not been punished,' he said. 'It seems Narayan has suffered a great deal already.'

The sentence delighted Narayan's supporters, visibly crushed Satish's family and inflamed public sentiment. A poll on the *AdelaideNow* news website found 63 per cent of voters considered the sentence too lenient and unjust. Women's advocates, however, praised Justice Sulan's approach.

Dr Elspeth McInnes, from the University of South Australia, said Narayan's case highlighted the dangers faced by so many women. 'Domestic violence can create a belief that there is no way one can survive without resorting to lethal violence themselves,' she told the website. 'It becomes an almost kill or be killed situation. There will be people who say Narayan has "got away with it" but she has lost a husband she loved, her financial support and her standing in the community – and she has suffered two decades of serious domestic abuse.'

The Office of the Director of Public Prosecutions disagreed, and asked the Court of Criminal Appeal to overturn the suspended sentence. At a hearing on 22 June 2011, prosecutor Adam Kimber said Justice Sulan had acted inappropriately and in error. 'Suspension fails to reflect the gravity of this particular manslaughter, and what this court has said about the need for general deterrence for manslaughter,' he said. 'It also fails to provide deterrence for people who are minded to confront their partners in circumstances of relationship breakdown while armed with weapons.' He said Narayan's case was no different than many others, and therefore should not have been treated any differently in sentencing. 'What if she had picked up a knife and gone into that bedroom, with the purpose of slicing his penis and then, in the circumstances that followed, plunged it into his back once? We say there is no meaningful difference between picking up a knife and picking up the items she chose.' Mr Kimber asked the court to 'send a message' to others in abusive relationships. Killing, he said, was never the answer. 'Relationship breakdowns and infidelity are sadly common. This court must do what it can to deter others from entering into volatile situations with weapons.'

The Court of Criminal Appeal took just nine days to deliver its judgment. Chief Justice John Doyle, Justice Margaret Nyland and Justice Michael David agreed their brother judge had arrived at an appropriate sentence. Mr Kimber, they said, had 'inaccurately characterised' Narayan's offending, which they felt was not comparable to other cases of manslaughter. 'This case bears no resemblance to that of an angry woman, armed with a dangerous weapon, going to confront a man whom she believes to be unfaithful with a view to "having it out with him",' Chief Justice Doyle remarked. 'Her motive was not jealousy, it was to save the marriage and keep the family together.'

Rajini Narayan, sitting with her children in the front row of the gallery, did not immediately comprehend the import of the court's ruling. As the judges left the bench, she turned to Ms Powell's junior counsel for clarification. When he gave her a thumbs-up, she put her hands up to her face and mouthed 'Oh, my God'. Her supporters rushed to embrace her. 'It's a new life,' one said. 'It's a new life for you, and you can relax now.'

The truth of that statement remains to be seen. If Rajini Narayan continues to follow the path of Christianity, then she has much penance to pay before entering Heaven. Should she further embrace the tarot and fortune telling, it is likely she will accept her ordeal as fated and move on. But should she cling to Hinduism, Narayan is guaranteed to see Satish again in the next life – and time and again in the lives after that. Lord Rama and Lady Sita's love had a happy ending, but the fire that marks the tale of Rajini and Satish Narayan will cause devastation for lifetimes to come.

Acknowledgements

I'll start by thanking my parents, John and Sue Fewster, and my grandmother, Beth Harradine. Without their lifelong encouragement and support, I wouldn't be writing.

Thanks to Melvin Mansell, editor of *The Advertiser*, for having my back whenever someone comes for my head. Grateful thanks also to my journalistic mentors – Kym Tilbrook, Mark Steene and Nigel Hunt – for making me the reporter I am.

Journalism would be less fun without the 'courts crew', especially Michael Milnes, Graham Hunter and Andrew McGarry. My thanks to you all for the kind words and black humour within our shared theatre of the absurd.

Thanks to my family and friends, particularly Tim Hatcher, David Champs and Maureen Gaudreau, for crystallising the book's themes. My unofficial proofreaders around the world were essential, especially B. Alex Thompson.

Matthew Kelly of Hachette Australia – I'm glad you chased me for two years to write this thing. It's been a wonderful experience. Thanks also to editor Kate Stevens, for refining my raw journalism.

My daughter Laura kept me smiling while I wrote 'Daddy's big book of bad guys'. Said writing would not have been possible without the support and love of my amazing wife, Justine. She kept me focused and enthusiastic, and turned a decade's worth of notebooks into a top-class reference library.

Finally, I want to thank the victims, their families, prosecutors, police officers, lawyers and other court users for trusting me with their stories. It is to them, Laura and Justine that this book is respectfully dedicated.